Sarasvatichandra Part II

Gunasundari's Household

Govardhanram Madhavram Tripathi was born on 20 October 1855 at Nadiad. He published the first part of *Sarasvatichandra* in 1887, the second part in 1892, the third in 1898, and the fourth in 1901. He is also the author of *Snehmudra* (1889), *Navalram Nu Kavijivan* (1891), *The Classical Poets of Gujarat and Their Influence on Society and Morals* (1894), *Lilavati Jivankala* (1905), and *Dayaram No Aksherdeha* (1908). He presided over the first session of the Gujarati Sahitya Parishad in 1905. He died on 4 January 1907 in Mumbai.

Tridip Suhrud works at the Sabarmati Ashram Preservation and Memorial Trust, Ahmedabad.

To the first part he gave all his art. The novel is imbued with aesthetic delight; the characterisation is matchless. The second part depicts Hindu society, his art went deeper in the third part, and he gave all that he wished to give to the world in the fourth part.

M. K. GANDHI

No other work has left such an indelible mark on the life of Gujarat as *Sarasvatichandra* has. In fact ... Govardhanram is the only one before the arrival of Gandhiji who had the greatest success in shaping the cultural life of Gujarat.

UMASHANKAR JOSHI

In the great celebration that is India, Gujarat has two gifts to offer: Mahatma Gandhi, and the jewel among books *Sarasvatichandra*.

MANUBHAI PANCHOLI 'DARSHAK'

Sarasvatichandra Part II

Gunasundari's Household

Govardhanram Madhavram Tripathi

Translated from the original Gujarati
by Tridip Suhrud

Orient BlackSwan

SARASVATICHANDRA PART II

ORIENT BLACKSWAN PRIVATE LIMITED

Registered Office
3-6-752 Himayatnagar, Hyderabad 500 029 (Telangana), India
e-mail: centraloffice@orientblackswan.com

Other Offices
Bengaluru, Bhopal, Chennai, Ernakulam,
Guwahati, Hyderabad, Jaipur, Kolkata,
Lucknow, Mumbai, New Delhi, Noida, Patna, Vijayawada

Originally published in Gujarati as
Gunasundarinu Kutumbjal (Bombay: N. M. Tripathi and Co., 1892).

First published by Orient Blackswan Private Limited 2016

ISBN 978 81 250 6158 8

Typeset by
Le Studio Graphique, Gurgaon 122 001
in Adobe Jenson Pro 11/13

Printed at
B. B. Press
Noida

022187
15122015

Published by
Orient Blackswan Private Limited
1/24 Asaf Ali Road
New Delhi 110 002
e-mail: delhi@orientblackswan.com

Uma & Ashis Nandy
Geetanjali Shree & Sudhir Chandra
Vrinda Dalmiya & Arindam Chakrabarti
Ligia Noronha & Peter Ronald deSouza
Rajshree & Kartikeya Sarabhai
(The Householders)
and
Harmony Siganporia
(Purple Flower)

ramyāṇi vikṣya

Contents

Translator's Acknowledgements*

Taralika—friend and mother—more than anyone else, desired that I attempt this translation. She knew as mothers often do that this text that she knew intimately would teach me humility. Taralika chose to leave us and become one with the immortals. This translation owes much to Taralika and Suhrud. They introduced me to *Sarasvatichandra* when I was ten. They cultivated in me a fondness for Gujarati language and literature, which has informed much of what I have done, and continue to do, and has given me the fitness to attempt this translation.

During the last eight years that this translation has been in the making, I have incurred debts of friendship. The most pleasurable of these is to Harmony Siganporia. Over the last two years, she has tried to educate me in the architecture and cadence of poetry and helped me with the translation of the plethora of verses that form part of this four-part novel. Thank you, Harmony.

Achyut Yagnik and Ashis Nandy taught me to patiently deepen my engagement with the Gujarat of an earlier age, while retaining my anxieties and unease with the literary and political culture of Gujarati in my times.

Sudhir Chandra, whose work on Govardhanram Tripathi, among others, remains a pathfinder for all those who seek to understand the

*Reproduced from Govardhanram Madhavram Tripathi, *Sarasvatichandra*, Part 1: *Buddhidhan's Administration*, trans. Tridip Suhrud (New Delhi: Orient BlackSwan, 2015), ix–x.

social and intellectual history of the nineteenth century, has nourished this translation and the translator. He was the first reader of this translation and his patient care and careful reading has made this a better work. Thank you, Sahib.

For someone like me whose knowledge of Sanskrit is non-existent, Arindam Chakrabarti has been an exerting and encouraging teacher. In Shimla and from Hawaii, he has answered my queries, pointed to texts and traditions of translations of these, tried to teach me Sanskrit grammar and, when all else failed, rendered Sanskrit verses in English for me with flair. The friendship with Vrinda and Arindam has been one of the many gifts of the Indian Institute of Advanced Study.

Hank Heifetz, in a remarkable act of generosity, translated for a complete stranger verses from Magha's *Shishupala Vadha*, which have been included in this and the forthcoming volumes of this translation. Thank you.

My very first conversation with Vidya Rao was about *Sarasvatichandra*. She is the primary reason for the long relationship that Orient BlackSwan and I have developed. Mimi Choudhury has been supportive as always. It has been an absolute delight and joy to work with Moyna Mazumdar; her understanding and fondness for works of translation have evidently informed the many improvements she suggested, making the text read better than it would have otherwise.

Over the years, *Sarasvatichandra* has travelled with me to Shimla. Peter Ronald deSouza gave me sanctuary when I most needed it. His friendship, the long walks in the misty mountains, and conversations which he set up at the IIAS have been a source of joy and solace. Thank you, Peter.

Binita Desai has given a gift of friendship like none else to me and mine. As always, thank you.

Katyayani will hopefully not read *Sarasvatichandra* in translation, especially now that she has threatened to be literate.

For your friendship, Megha, I thank you.

Tridip Suhrud

Translator's Introduction*

I

I wish to produce, or see produced, not this or that event—but a people who shall be higher and stronger than they are, who shall be better able to look and manage for themselves than is the present *helpless* generation of my educated and uneducated countrymen. What kind of a nation that should be and how that spark should be kindled for the organic flame: these were, and are, the problems before my mind. I lay down this as, for the present, the only one fixed objective before me ...[1]

* Earlier versions of this text have been published by the translator as part of an essay titled 'Govardhanram Tripathi and "the Philosophy of Consumption": A Reading of *Sarasvatichandra*', in *Early Novels in India*, edited by Meenakshi Mukherji (New Delhi: Sahitya Akademi, 2002); in Tridip Suhrud, 'Consumption as Dharma', *Writing Life: Three Gujarati Thinkers* (New Delhi: Orient BlackSwan, 2009); and reproduced from Tripathi, *Sarasvatichandra*, Part 1, trans. Tridip Suhrud, xi–li, with a new section added.

[1] K. C. Pandya, R. P. Bakshi and S. J. Pandya (eds), *Govardhanram Madhavram Tripathi's Scrap Book* (Bombay: N. M. Tripathi and Co., 1959), 29–30; emphasis in the original. This first scrap book covers the years 1884–1894 of the author's life. The scrap book for the period 1894–1904, compiled and edited by the same editors, was also published in 1959. The scrap book for the period 1904–06, edited by K. C. Pandya was published earlier in 1957, both volumes by N. M. Tripathi and Co., in Bombay. These volumes are, herein, referred to as *Scrap Book* I, II and III respectively. Although the chronology of publication goes against this arrangement, this has been done for the convenience of citation as well as to maintain the chronology in which they were originally written. Govardhanram Tripathi began writing the scrap books in January

With these words, Govardhanram Madhavram Tripathi (1855–1907) articulated his *swadharma*. Govardhanram was born on 20 October 1855, in a Vadnagara Nagar brahmin vaishnav family at Nadiad.[2] The family had no remarkable tradition of learning. For at least three generations, this family had practised money lending. Govardhanram spent his formative years in Bombay and Nadiad. He acquired primary education in the Buddhivardhak Gujarati Shala in Bombay and Government English School at Nadiad. In 1871, he passed his matriculation examination as a student of Elphinstone School, and joined Elphinstone College for his graduation. Between 1871 and 1875, he studied history, economics, nyaya and nitishastra. He passed his B.A. examination at the second attempt at the age of twenty.

After passing his B.A., Govardhanram made three resolutions which he hoped would govern his entire life. He resolved to acquire a law degree, to start an independent legal practice, and to give up legal practice at the age of forty and, thereafter, dedicate his life to the service of the people through literature.

In 1876, he passed his first LL.B. examination. He was forced by circumstances to accept the post of a personal secretary to Samaldas Parmanddas, the *Dewan* of Bhavnagar state. This gave him the opportunity to observe and participate, in close proximity, the functioning of a native state. He had hoped that his stay at Bhavnagar would be short and only a minor aberration in his plan. He was repeatedly frustrated in his attempts to pass the remaining LL.B. examinations. He failed thrice and eventually passed it in 1883 on his fourth attempt. He immediately left Bhavnagar for Bombay, where at the age of twenty-nine he started independent legal practice. His practice at the Bombay High Court flourished. At the height of his

---

1885 after he had achieved some stability in his profession as a lawyer in Bombay, and stopped maintaining them in November 1906. During this period, he filled seven notebooks, all of which were written in English. He had no intention of publishing them. They were published as a part of the celebrations to mark his birth centenary.

[2] This biographical section is largely based on K. C. Pandya, *Sriyut Govardhanram* (Bombay: N. M. Tripathi and Co., 1910, 1965).

legal career, Govardhanram fulfilled his long cherished dream. At the age of forty-two, he retired from the practice to contemplate the state of his people and society in the quiet solitude of his ancestral house in Nadiad.

II

For Govardhanram Tripathi, the original cause of the universe lies in what he describes as the 'Great Will' or the 'Great Force'. Individual beings are a mere point, a manifestation of the Great Will. 'Our will is a manifestation, at a point, of his will. His will is universal, ours is a point of it.'[3] The vocation of human beings, according to him, is to understand the Great Will and function in harmony with it. 'We are unable to enter into the actual motives of the Great Will, but we can understand and join its music and poetry ... Our final cause—like all final causes—is to understand our proper function in this symphony and join it properly.'[4]

A perfect conscience, according to Govardhanram, recognises that 'I is a fiction',[5] and it is at this moment of recognition of self-identity that the individual being is in perfect harmony and union with the Great Will. In this union and realisation of identity lies salvation. But how is this salvation to be attained? The central question for Govardhanram is: How can an individual reconcile his vocation of final union with the Great Force, and his obligation towards his family, the society and the country? For Govardhanram, this reconciliation can be achieved only through what he describes as a Philosophy of Consumption.[6] 'Total sacrifice of the individual for the good of the whole is consumption ... Complete dissolution and sacrifice of

3 Pandya, Bakshi and Pandya, *Scrap Book* I, 45.

4 Ibid., 123.

5 Ibid., 46.

6 The term 'Philosophy of Consumption' is Govardhanram's coinage. In Gujarati he uses the term *uttsargsiddhi*, or the attainment of higher ideals through sacrifice.

the self for others is consumption. It is through consumption that individual existence and life achieve completion.'[7] 'Consumption' for Govardhanram is an all-encompassing philosophy and praxis. It is by leading a life of consumption that an individual offers his body and soul to the *yajna* [ritual sacrifice] of the Great Force. 'We must consume, both body and soul, ... in the Great and Patent *Yajna* that is blazing around us, we throw as *Havis* (oblation) the patent *Yajna* of body and soul ...'[8]

The philosophy of consumption becomes the sole mediator between the individual and the Great Will and also the individual and society. Through the philosophy of consumption, Govardhanram attempts to offer a critique of the philosophy of Vedanta, which was one of the earliest and most powerful influences on him. Vedanta, Govardhanram believes, leads to asceticism as the mode of attaining salvation. 'Patent is a thing to be avoided, and latent to be sought ... as to the censures passed against the Patent, as to the exclusive acceptance of the Latent as Transcendental Idea.'[9]

In 1877, aged twenty-two, Govardhanram offered a critique of the practice of renunciation as a mode of attaining salvation in an essay entitled 'Practical Asceticism in My Sense of the Word'. Care for the 'self' is at the heart of the practice of renunciation, he observed. Salvation cannot be attained through a self-centred mode. 'The great Bacon has said,' he wrote, 'it is a poor centre of man's action, himself, and it is true. But I go some steps beyond him. I say it is a poisonous centre of man's action—himself.'[10] Asceticism for Govardhanram is an act of rebellion against the Great Will. It is as unjustified as suicide. A real ascetic hands over the care of the 'self' to the Great Will and 'consumes' it for society. 'Asceticism, in its usual sense, is a mistake and a substitution of miscarriage for consumption. Asceticism, in

[7] Ramprasad P. Bakshi, *Govardhanram Nu Manorajya*, 2nd ed. (Bombay: N. M. Tripathi and Co., 1992), 14–15.

[8] Pandya, Bakshi and Pandya, *Scrap Book* I, 148.

[9] Ibid., 100.

[10] Pandya, *Sriyut Govardhanram*, 63.

its real sense, is most beautiful consumption.'[11] Consumption of an individual is conditioned by the capacities of the person. 'Consumption ... is not a promiscuous or unlimited duty. It is actually limited, and potentially unlimited, that it may be enlarged according to capacity.'[12] Notions of morality, ethics and justice are also contingent upon the idea of consumption. Defining vice and virtue, Govardhanram wrote:

> Whatever makes a man feed on the flesh of the world is ordinarily vice. Whatever is his consumption in order to feed the world is a virtue. Whatever is inconsistent with such consumption and the means of attaining it is vice. Whatever is consistent with it is innocent. Whatever furthers it is virtue. Whenever feeding oneself is instrumental to such consumption, it is virtue.[13]

For Govardhanram, poetry and philosophy, ethics and religion must converge in any philosophical system. He is aware that in his philosophy of consumption, he has created an all-encompassing world-view, a mode of life, his swadharma. 'To my mind ... Poetry and Philosophy, Ethics and Religion must eventually converge, and in Ethics, I include the world in all its aspects. Need I say that my vision of Philosophy of Consumption, with all its imperfections, reaches this very point?'[14]

A person who recognises virtue and vice, adopts the former and shuns the latter has a sense of duty. Thus for Govardhanram consumption is not only a virtue but it is *dharma*. This conception of dharma informed his vocation and defined his understanding of personal duty towards the country. While clarifying for himself 'Duties in regard to the country', Govardhanram set before himself the goal of moulding a generation of people who shall be 'higher and stronger' and 'better able to manage for themselves'.

In this articulation of swadharma, Govardhanram denies the relevance and the efficacy of *events*. Events are for him acts uninformed

11 Pandya, Bakshi and Pandya, *Scrap Book* I, 146.

12 Ibid., 125.

13 Ibid., 52.

14 Pandya, Bakshi and Pandya, *Scrap Book* II, 87.

by deep industry and knowledge. It was also not his aspiration to produce an event, which for him was a mere reflection of deeper societal processes. 'To produce a particular event—be it a political constitutional agitation or a social reform effervescence—this is too little for my mind and aspiration.'[15] He also eschewed commenting upon events. 'So obsessive was this concern for clarity that, unlike most of his contemporary creative writers in different Indian languages, Govardhanram tended to avoid journalism.'[16]

Aware as he was of 'the evil consequences which we may inflict on our country by our well-meaning follies', he decided to 'attempt or wish to assist nothing' before proper study; because, 'without study there is no sight and without sight no efficacy of action.'[17] In order to attain the requisite clarity to play out his conflicting, contradictory emotions, desires and ideas, Govardhanram regularly maintained his personal diaries. Readers of his *Scrap Books* cannot but be affected by his constant struggle and deep agony to attain the state of *aptavachana*—in which a person has a certain vision of life and society, and wishes to conduct his life accordingly.

This sense of duty was also conditioned by awareness of his capabilities as 'there is no duty beyond capacities'. He was aware that it was not given to him to be a 'public' person—which he would be forced to be if he wanted to produce an event—he wanted to cultivate the *sakshibhav* [bearing witness to] of a *sthitapragna* [one whose intellect is secure]. 'Glory, Public applause, Eminence, Moneys, Public Leadership, etc., are *Things I do not want at all*.'[18]

His desire to achieve the state of sthitapragna and his disinclination to produce an event should not lead us to conclude that Govardhanram is advocating either *nivritti* [detachment] or a form of

[15] Ibid., 34.

[16] Sudhir Chandra, 'A Nineteenth Century View of the Hindu Joint Family: Notes from Govardhanram Tripathi's *Scrap Book*', Occasional paper, 2, Centre for Social Studies, Surat.

[17] Pandya, Bakshi and Pandya, *Scrap Book* I, 29–30.

[18] Pandya, Bakshi and Pandya, *Scrap Book* II, 176; emphasis in the original.

asceticism. Asceticism for him is an act of rebellion against the Great Will. The state of sthitapragna does not entail a denial of duties. A sthitapragna is not one who is dislocated from the world; on the contrary, he is someone who experiences deeply the world around him, but who does not submit to the rule of the senses. Govardhanram would say that all acts of a sthitapragna are acts of consumption. He describes this state of being as a state of 'Practical Asceticism'.

He was aware that his goal of shaping a generation of people who shall be 'higher and stronger' and who shall be 'able to manage for themselves' and the act of 'kindling the spark of the organic flame'—which will bring about long lasting mediation in the forces shaping the destiny of his nation—was not a task given to mere mortals. At times he is plagued by deep doubts of self-worth: 'I am a pigmy and the pigmiest of pigmies ... I may never be able to attempt so much as a beginning in the right direction for the simple reason that abilities may be extinct ashes ....'[19] He was aware that the life of a country is much longer than that of an individual. Neither the magnitude of the task nor such daunting realisations could deviate him from his chosen path. 'I must fancy', he says, 'that I am an *Ajaramar*, when planning my duty to my country'.[20]

III

It was as a part of his duty towards the country that Govardhanram embarked upon a project which was to consume him for nearly fifteen years. At the age of thirty, in 1885, he started writing his novel *Sarasvatichandra*. When the fourth and final part was published in 1901, fourteen years had elapsed since the publication of the first part. He did not wish to write the novel at all. His initial plan was to write philosophical essays on the human condition; but he found the essay form limiting. This limitation arose from the form, its restricted

[19] Pandya, Bakshi and Pandya, *Scrap Book* I, 151.

[20] Ibid., 27.

reach, and the inability of the general reading classes to appreciate and comprehend discursive prose. Given the limiting circumstances, he came to the conclusion that illustrations of actual and ideal life were the most appropriate mode of communication.

> The conviction has also grown upon him [the author] that reality in flesh and blood under the guise of fiction can supply the ordinary reader with subtler moulds and finer casts for the formation of his inner self than abstract discussions, and that this is especially so with *a people who must be made, and not simply left, to read*.[21]

Govardhanram selected the novel form not for its aesthetic possibilities but for its potential as a medium of 'moulding inner selves' of people. 'Both women and the novel desire to be beautiful', he says, 'but fulfilment of this desire must be a means to achieve higher goals. Striving for mere aesthetic pleasure is not only undesirable, it is futile—indeed it could be harmful—to attain that step and not rise upwards.'[22] He is keenly aware of the functions and possibilities of the novel, which he calls a 'universal luxury', and says this form of literature is unrivalled in its popularity and reach amongst the educated middle classes.

He felt disappointed that the true potential of the novel form was not being utilised by authors, and that instead they used it as a medium to gratify the instincts of the reading classes. Functions of the novel, he says, are 'much higher and sacred'. An author who desires to use it as a means of education must be aware of his audience. Govardhanram takes a critical look at his readership and classifies them into three categories. In the first category are the scholars who read novels to acquire a deeper understanding of the human condition. The second

[21] Govardhanram Madhavram Tripathi, 'English Preface' in *Sarasvatichandra*, Part 1, 18th ed. (Bombay: N. M. Tripathi and Co., 1887, 1977), 8; emphases added. There are two prefaces to the volume, one in Gujarati and the other in English, with substantial variations between the two. See also p. lx of this volume.

[22] Tripathi, 'Prastavana' [Gujarati Preface] in *Sarasvatichandra*, Part 1, 9. See also p. lxii of this volume.

class comprises discerning readers who read the novel to enrich their inner lives. And the third class is the general readership. This class reads novels either because it entertains them or gratifies some of their instincts. This is the class that for Govardhanram 'must be made, and not simply left, to read'. Most novels address themselves to this class and therein lies the reason for their popularity. According to him, the element of fiction or magic does not constitute the central concern of the novel—its function is to 'educate' and 'raise' the reading classes. The novel must show them the path of virtue. The characters and situations depicted in the novel thus assume centrality. Depiction of ideal types cannot inspire readers to aspire for a higher life. Nor can the depiction of evil alienate masses from it. Therefore, Govardhanram says that his novel will depict humane characters who constantly strive to raise their condition.

With the progress of his enterprise, we sense a certain satisfaction of accomplishment. 'The purpose of the writer is to enable the reader to rise to a stage higher than where he was ... *Sarasvatichandra*, thus undertaken at this point, *works* without doubt, and people *feel* the book. This is a mere literary work and will work on society.'[23] Eleven years after the publication of the first volume, Govardhanram notes with satisfaction that 'the progress of the reading classes is equal to the aspirations of the writer to interest them in the principal problems of the day.'[24]

The sense of achievement also brought with it a sense of greater responsibility for Govardhanram, who was plagued by the fear of illness and untimely death. 'I think I owe it as a duty to the world that I should finish before dying.'[25] India, he felt, was undergoing a strange transition in all spheres of community and personal life, and that certain 'forces have cast a gloomy shadow over our eyes'. Henceforth, his

[23] Pandya, Bakshi and Pandya, *Scrap Book* I, 31; emphasis in the original.

[24] Tripathi, 'English Preface' in *Sarasvatichandra*, Part 3, (Bombay: N. M. Tripathi and Co., 1898), 3.

[25] Pandya, Bakshi and Pandya, *Scrap Book* II, 172.

objective was not only to 'raise' readers but also 'to help his countrymen in groping their way out of the darkness into some kind of light'.[26]

Govardhanram captures the predicament of his society: both the advocates of change and those who wish to give 'eternal rigidity to the present' are uncertain as to how this transition will be harmonised. Will the process, which is heterogenous in its inception, result in an inward homogeneity? In this time of transition, only one certainty exists: 'Indian society must yield to the irresistible process of reciprocal assimilation'.[27] Can this society find repose? For Govardhanram, the realm of creative imagination can provide repose in such turbulent times—for the 'only place where we can safely look for a peaceful picture in spite of transient facts is in art and poetry'.[28] Henceforth, he resolved that the purpose of the novel would be to work towards a vision of a harmonised future. The narrative which had hitherto been a blend of the actual and the ideal, enters a different phase as 'the latter acquires a distinct predominance over the former'.

While dealing with the causes of the transition experienced by Indian society, Govardhanram refutes the widespread belief that India was witnessing a fusion of two different civilisations—the modern West and the East. The Indian civilisation has passed through many phases in its evolution and what we are witnessing today, he says, is a fusion of three civilisations—the modern West, the modern East and the resurgent traditions of the ancient Indian civilisation. He is confident that this will one day result in 'reciprocal assimilation and harmony'. It is the possible visions of that day which are the source of anxiety for Indian people. His endeavour would henceforth be to provide one possible path to this assimilation and a vision of the future. In this 'drama of transition', the intellectuals, or those whom he calls the educated Indians, have a crucial function as they are 'directly involved by the actual contact and growing reactions of

[26] Tripathi, 'English Preface' in *Sarasvatichandra*, Part 4, (Bombay: N. M. Tripathi and Co., 1901), 6.

[27] Tripathi, *Sarasvatichandra*, Part 3, 4.

[28] Ibid.

these civilisations.'[29] Their role is one of mediation between these civilisational forces and the masses so as to bring about the inevitable transition. 'It has fallen to the lot of the educated classes to serve as organic sheaths and conductors between multiform sets or organisms forming a repository of these energies.'[30] Although living through ambivalent times, Govardhanram is able to identify the problematic and its possible resolution with a rare sensibility and awareness.

Writing the novel for Govardhanram is a conscious act of tempering the souls of his countrymen. It is through this act that he wishes to fulfil his historical role of an 'organic sheath' between the great civilisational forces and the Indian masses.

IV

Sarasvatichandra is not 'one' unitary text. The novel was not only published in four parts but was also written in four parts over a period of fifteen years. Each part has a distinct thematic content, its own cast of characters and independent beginnings and ends. This is not to deny either the aesthetic or thematic unity of the novel. But readings which privilege one story—the story of Kumud, Sarasvatichandra and Kusum—as the principal theme and consider all others as unnecessary diversions do not allow an appreciation of the complete text.

The increasing influence of the East India Company in the affairs of the 'native states' provides the backdrop for the first part, *Buddhidhan's Administration* (1887). It deals with one individual's sustained efforts to assume complete control of the administration of a native state, Suvarnapur, and to rise above his circumstances. Govardhanram describes Buddhidhan's impoverished beginnings, his constant victimisation by Shathrai, the prime minister of the state, and Buddhidhan's opportunistic alliance and friendship with Bhupsinh—a cousin of the ruling king and a claimant to the throne. Together they

[29] Tripathi, *Sarasvatichandra*, Part 4, 8.

[30] Ibid., 9.

seek support of the British Resident officer of a neighbouring area, and with his intervention, Bhupsinh is declared the legitimate ruler. With patience, wisdom and foresight, Buddhidhan is gradually able to secure the complete trust of the new ruler, and to rid the state's administration of the influence of Shathrai. He also regains the post of prime minister which his family had traditionally held.

Part Two of the novel, *Gunasundari's Household* (1892), deals with the state of a Hindu joint family in the latter half of the nineteenth century. Gunasundari and Vidya Chatura were married as children. Vidya Chatura was educated in Bombay and appointed as a teacher in an English school at Ratnanagari, another native state. He also obtained the post of tutor to the young prince, Maniraj of Ratnanagari. Gunasundari had acquired functional literacy, but as her name suggests, she was endowed with virtues 'natural' to women. Vidya Chatura trained and educated his young wife, enabling them to indulge in the pleasures of the mind and thereby avoiding the fate of many couples married in childhood. But just as they begin to experience a 'conjugality' driven by circumstances, Vidya Chatura's relatives come to live with them as dependents. From being a young, joyous wife, Gunasundari has to perforce become a *grihini* and manage a household of thirteen to fourteen people, all with different needs and personalities.

In this second part, Govardhanram achieves the height of his descriptive powers as a novelist. His minute descriptions of the dynamics of a joint family, his observation of human nature and its strengths and fragilities, his unencumbered prose and his characterisation have made this part most endearing to generations of readers. Govardhanram describes with a touch of humour—otherwise, entirely lacking in his prose—the interpersonal conflicts in the joint family, and pregnant Gunasundari's constant struggle to keep the family united and each member contented. She and her father-in-law, Manchatura, together succeed in both reforming and rehabilitating all constituent units of the joint family, without breaking the 'jointness' of the joint family.

The narrative thus far is a blend of actual and ideal aspects of life. From the third part on, the ideal acquires a distinctive predominance over the actual—a contrast which is immediately recognisable with the first part. Part Three, *Ratnanagari's Statecraft* (1898), deals with the attempts of an enlightened ruler, along with his feudal chiefs and advisors, to create a responsible polity in times of general decay. Ratnanagari had survived the onslaught of British expansion because of the strength and vision of its rulers. It was governed by the concern for the welfare of all sections of society.

From state and society, Govardhanram moves on to dharma. The fourth part, *The Dream-Land of Sarasvatichandra and the Culmination* (1901), presents the ideal community of Sundargiri. This community of ascetics leads their life in perfect harmony with nature and her Creator, in accordance with the principles of dharma, under the benevolent gaze of Vishnudas. Their strivings are those of souls wishing to achieve complete non-duality with the Creator.

The love story—the story of Kumud, Sarasvatichandra and Kusum—links Govardhanram's reflections on state, society and dharma. Kumud, the naturally virtuous daughter of Gunasundari and Vidya Chatura, was engaged at an early age to Sarasvatichandra. Born into great wealth, Sarasvatichandra, as his name suggests, was a scholar and a luminary amongst the intellectuals of Bombay. Ascetic by nature and given to deep reflection on the state of his country, he was greatly enamoured by the natural charm and virtues of Kumud, and they fall in love with each other before marriage. But his insecure, jealous stepmother engineers a misunderstanding between the devoted son and the loving but short-sighted father, which results in Sarasvatichandra leaving home, renouncing not only his family and wealth but also Kumud. Kumud is disconsolate. He decides to live a life of an 'intellectual vagabond', travelling to remote parts of the country to experience the living reality of his countrymen.

As an unknown, rootless traveller with an assumed identity, in desperate search for purpose and peace, Sarasvatichandra reaches Suvarnapur. There he is invited to be the guest of Buddhidhan. Kumud's parents have by then married their uncomplaining daughter to Pramaddhan, the unworthy and debauch son of Buddhidhan. Sarasvatichandra, carrying the burden of his guilt, once again leaves Kumud to her fate, but not before Pramaddhan suspects the tenderness of their relationship. Before he can cause greater misery to Kumud, Sarasvatichandra disappears, and is given up as dead. Through a series of accidents he reaches Sundargiri, where he is celebrated as the heir to Sadhu Vishnudas. Kumud, believed to be drowned in a river, also reaches Sundargiri and lives in the care of *sadhvis* as an ascetic. Widowed Kumud—though she remains unaware of Pramaddhan's death for a long time—and Sarasvatichandra suffer greatly because of their mutual love. Vishnudas asks them to spend five nights together in a cave to contemplate their fate. Under divine intervention, they travel to the 'Land of the Enlightened' in their dreams where they experience a union of souls and emerge from the cave enlightened and pure. The novel ends with the inauguration of Sarasvatichandra's project for the regeneration of the country, and a new phase in the lives of Kumud, Kusum and Sarasvatichandra.

V

For those who came of age in late-nineteenth century India and felt concerned about the state of their society and nation, colonial rule was a fundamental reality. Awareness of subjection coupled with a profound uncertainty about the present and future shaped their response to the British presence in India. Given this ultimate objective—'one which never ought to be lost sight of'—of moulding his people into a great people who would be able to take care of themselves, Govardhanram grappled with the meaning of British rule. In an entry in *Scrap Book* I, dated 13 April 1891, he wrote:

> India is invaded and subdued already. There is no question of Offensive or Defensive here, and Elasticity would be a nice helpmate in Constitutional Warfare. The rulers are a clever set of people—an admixture of selfish aggressors and disinterested, benevolent helpmates. India is worked by "push and pull" among

> these, and naturally the Home Interest generally carries the day. Yet even here we win morsel by morsel, though often it is snatched away—sometimes even from near the lips.[31]

The only unambiguous, unqualified statement here is the fact of India's subjection. Accepting the British presence as given, Govardhanram advises his people to cultivate 'elasticity'. 'Coming after offense and defense have been ruled out, "elasticity" becomes the very epitome of ambiguity. The term here seems to suggest pragmatism.'[32] Relations between the rulers and the ruled are mediated by the idea of warfare. But this is neither an offensive nor a confrontation. The concept of 'constitutional'—given by the colonial rulers—and the need to cultivate elasticity, introduces an element of caution, of pragmatic moderation. Moving on to a depiction of the rulers, Govardhanram again displays ambivalence and a mixed assessment of British presence. Yet he is aware that in the ultimate analysis, 'the home interest carries the day' and that whatever ground is gained by Indians through their elasticity is snatched away.

Govardhanram may have been ambivalent towards British rule, but he displays remarkable consistency in his analysis of the 'native states', and the capacity of his people to effectively counter the colonial aggressor—he has no faith in their ability to take premeditated action and believes they can only indulge in 'well-meaning follies'. He has some faith in the Congress, owing to its 'well-chosen leadership' of A. O. Hume and Sir William Wedderburn.

> But in other matters our leaders are unfit. In view of these things, I would like to leave many things to our rulers rather than to our native leaders, for the former are at least most sensible people. If natives act, I shall not hinder them. If Europeans act I shall have some confidence.[33]

31 Pandya, Bakshi and Pandya, *Scrap Book* I, 51.

32 Sudhir Chandra, *The Oppressive Present: Literature and Social Consciousness in Colonial India* (New Delhi: Oxford University Press, 1992), 23.

33 Pandya, Bakshi and Pandya, *Scrap Book* I, 58.

The high standards he had set himself in private and public conduct may have made him sceptical of the abilities of his own people. This severe denouncement and total lack of confidence in the abilities of Indians informed his vocation of creating a generation which shall be 'better able to look and manage for themselves'. This negative assessment of his countrymen to manage the political and social implications of the colonial encounter pervades all his reflections—whether in the *Scrap Books* or the novel. On the question of British presence, he did not allow any wishful thinking to colour his assessment. In a lengthy entry titled 'India and the foreigner', he wrote:

> India is under foreign control and the foreigner is the kindliest of all foreigners available. To get rid of the foreigner by force or fraud is an idea associated with all incidents that remind us of the rule being foreign. The idea naturally haunts our uneducated instincts; to educated instincts the idea is both foolish and fallacious. It is foolish because it is not practicable, and because any experiment founded upon it would send the country from the frying pan into the fire. It is a fallacious idea, because the distinction between a native and a foreigner is only transient, and the distinction is not a guarantee of a native being a better ruler than the foreigner in such a mass of heterogenous people as my country is.[34]

Govardhanram is not only emphasising his lack of faith in the strategies employed by Indians to get rid of the British but is also questioning the basic premise of 'foreign' and 'native' interests being mutually exclusive. Moreover, his absence of trust in the abilities of natives to manage a heterogenous people with differing aspirations and needs also colours his assessment of the problem. He goes on to articulate the real problem: '[the] problem is not the absolute eviction of the foreigner, but *his accommodation to the native element* ... where India and England *become one on Indian Soil* ...'[35] One can assume that while cautioning against attempts to evict the foreigner completely

[34] Ibid., 149.

[35] Ibid., 150; emphases in the original.

from Indian soil, he is referring not just to the physical presence, but to a civilisational encounter, and his stand is informed by the awareness that Indian culture and society will be transformed by this 'drama of transition'. The source of his anxiety lies in the uncertainty about the future and how these opposing tendencies will be harmonised and what kind of a resolution will emerge. To bring about a resolution where 'India and England become one on Indian Soil', he required to 'create a homogeneous nuclear class'.

This also was the central concern of *Sarasvatichandra*. At the same time, he was not unaware of the opposition between foreign and native interests. He elaborates in the same entry:

> In India the sovereign is enlightened and yet has an interest foreign to the country. Two things have to be done. This interest has to be made to cease to be foreign; and while it is foreign, we want the natives that shall guard against the civic temptations to which the foreigner is exposed by his position, that shall enable the native interests to grow and develop during their minority without any hindrance from the adverse interests of the rulers, that shall in fact watch over the real interests and develop the future welfare of the country. And it is possible to do these both loyally and patriotically.[36]

In the four volumes of *Sarasvatichandra*, Govardhanram attempted to demonstrate this wisdom. The first part of the novel—which is the depiction of reality according to him—portrays the expanding British influence over the native states. It is one of the most severe indictments of native states in the literature of that period. Govardhanram depicts a polity based on personal interests, plagued by widespread erosion of morals and values. The efforts of Buddhidhan and Bhupsinh to overthrow Shathrai's corrupt administration were in the final analysis motivated by personal animosity and gain. 'Buddhidhan had meanwhile turned Bhupsinh and his administration into mere instruments for his

[36] Ibid.

festering rage.'[37] The only thing that differentiates Buddhidhan from Shathrai is the former's high sense of personal morality.

A more condemning attitude towards the native states is perhaps reflected in the *Scrap Books*, where Govardhanram feels no compulsion for moderation. While he was contemplating retirement from legal practice, he had many tempting offers from the native states in Gujarat to join the administration as dewan. Given his financial insecurities, a few years of dewanship would have put many fears at rest. This position would have also provided him an opportunity to work for the good of society. Giving his reasons for refusing these offers, he writes: 'Baroda, Junagadh, Kutch, Bhavnagar, and what not?—all native states in fact stand before my eyes, with their whole nudity of weaknesses, complications and difficulties—from subjects, officers, the princes themselves and even from Agencies ....' The mere thought of being in that environment filled him with a 'vision of pettiest jealousies, meanest natures, foolishest ambitions, ridiculous follies and vanities, and adamantine obstructions.'[38] Perhaps this assessment of the native states has much to do with his unhappy stay at Bhavnagar in the service of the dewan. He also felt that efforts made in the native states for the betterment of society were unlikely to bear fruit. This would amount to narrowing his vision. He adds in the same entry:

> Besides, the greatest result available in this field can only be local influence—while the kind of influence that is wanted is one that could permeate and stimulate the whole constitution of India. This larger effect must be begun and produced in British India where the plant, if sown, can have a freer, larger growth along what Telang called the line of least resistance.[39]

During this period, he returned to this theme with regularity. Perturbed by his thoughts of retirement from active legal practice his family and friends tried to persuade him to take up tempting

[37] Tripathi, *Sarasvatichandra*, Part 1, trans. Tridip Suhrud, (New Delhi: Orient BlackSwan, 2015), 68.

[38] Pandya, Bakshi and Pandya, *Scrap Book* II, 43.

[39] Ibid.

offers. A few days after the entry quoted above, he elaborated upon the 'thorns of inferior society in Political life in Native States'.[40] His chief objection to working in a native state was that he would have to deal with people of inferior intellectual abilities. 'No Prince can be equal to your education, and no fellow servant disposed to have your conscience in the present state of things.' This situation he says is 'not much dissimilar to the marriage of a man of my education and age with an illiterate girl of twelve, whom you must try to please and educate with all the arts of one attempting to make love with such an odd match'.[41]

Govardhanram's other concern is about moral life in the native states. One may be forced to work with people who may not have any sense of duty, and even if they do, it is likely to be 'in a disfigured, mutilated, and even perverted form'. And therefore, 'I shall have to guard warily against the Fallacious Persuasions of the Serpentine Tempter, if ever he takes me near the Tree of Service'.[42] Govardhanram's assessment of the native states is without doubt largely negative and he does not see in them much potential for 'kindling the spark of organic flame'. Nevertheless, large parts of the country were under the administration of native states; he thus felt the imperative to turn his attention to them in the novel. The third part of *Sarasvatichandra*—subtitled *Ratnanagari's Statecraft*—deals with the creation of an 'ideal' native state. From Part Three onwards, the narrative enters a different phase, and normative considerations are given primacy over the depiction of reality.

VI

Given his ambition of creating a generation of people 'higher and stronger than they are' through the philosophy of consumption,

[40] Ibid., 51.

[41] Ibid.

[42] Pandya, Bakshi and Pandya, *Scrap Book* I, 51.

Govardhanram had to engage himself with the institutional structures of social organisation. Despite his self-perceived crucifixion within the family, his *Scrap Books* and the novel reflect a remarkable engagement with the institution of joint family.

Oppressed by the existential realities of living in a joint family, young Govardhanram while studying for his B.A. at Elphinstone College, in an essay entitled 'The State of the Hindu Society in the Bombay Presidency', offered to his countrymen the following advice: 'The moment you get married, start living separately from your parents ....'[43] This unambiguous pronouncement gives a misleading impression of finality. He was to return with embarrassing regularity to the issue of joint family in the *Scrap Books* despite his repeated resolves not to discuss the family.

The joint family was not only an oppressive existential reality for him—with an average of fourteen people living in the house throughout—it was also an important social and cultural institution. As Sudhir Chandra has pointed out, 'both the existential and the normative aspects of the joint family feature in Govardhanram's dialogues with himself'.[44] His *Scrap Books* open with a statement on his wife Lalita's angelic goodness and a severe denouement of other family members, including his parents. So harsh was his criticism that he felt emotionally 'frozen' while referring to these notes.[45] Tired of playing the role of an impartial judge and arbitrator, Govardhanram decided to formulate a 'maxim in domestic management' and vowed to follow it: 'While everybody is to have his or her liberties in my family, the liberties of no one are to go to the extent of clipping the necessary liberties and moral rights of other members, including even minors'.[46]

His search for equanimity by formulating guiding principles does not provide any respite from the 'conjugal jar'. He is forced once again to examine the relative merits and peculiarities of individual members

43 Pandya, *Sriyut Govardhanram*, 49.

44 Chandra, 'A Nineteenth Century View of the Hindu Joint Family', 11.

45 Pandya, Bakshi and Pandya, *Scrap Book* I, 35.

46 Ibid., 37.

of his family. Mother, he says, 'is visited with short-sighted littleness of mind'[47] while father Madhavram's 'patriarchal cares' only result 'in hampering me and the whole family'.[48] Their partiality towards 'Mrs. Brother' (wife of Govardhanram's brother Narhariram) disturbs his wife Lalitagauri, although she has—largely due to Govardhanram's training—'conquered her overwhelmingly uncontrolled temper'.[49]

Govardhanram gives details of familial frictions and the ways in which he tries to resolve them. In an entry titled, 'Family Misunderstandings and the Way to Remove Them', he records his attempts to be an impartial judge between his wife and mother, Shivkashi. He feels an ideal situation would be one where they can resolve their conflicts without his mediation. This would require them both to be 'patient, enduring and forgiving'. But given their lack of literacy, Govardhanram has no faith in their abilities to resolve their conflicts 'intellectually'. 'Swallowing [their anger and pride] and explaining would both be impracticable between such illiterate people'.[50] Instead, he allows both his mother and wife to complain to him in each other's absence. Despite his maxim of allowing each family member their liberty and space, he feels compelled to mediate in their interpersonal relationships as 'illiterate people are sure to tyrannise over each other if left to themselves'.[51]

For Govardhanram, the only way to secure peace and harmony and to steer the joint family away from becoming a joint nuisance lies in the philosophy of consumption and in 'ungrudging and all sided sacrifices'.[52] Accordingly, during discussions on partitioning the family property, he proposed that he shall retain no part of the property; but this was not accepted. Govardhanram was aware that to an observer, his attitude may come across as 'Idiocy and spoilation', but this

47 Ibid., 75.
48 Ibid., 115.
49 Ibid., 110.
50 Ibid., 114.
51 Ibid., 128.
52 Ibid., 120.

deliberate sacrifice fills him with supreme happiness: 'I have begun my consumption *at home*—charity must begin at home. It fulfills my aspiration ... to find myself so consumed into the atmosphere that surrounds me'.[53] With the arrangement of partitioning the family property that was finally arrived at—although they continued to live in a joint family—Govardhanram came much closer to his idea of a nuclear family.

In such an event, the possibility of his sudden death and inability to provide for his wife and children fills his heart with gloom. 'I am a houseless man, and my wife and children are houseless, and my parents think this is good.'[54] Though he is able to overcome such moments of gloom by his faith in the Great Will and his philosophy of consumption, Lalita's subsequent illness and the possibility of her death make him resolve once again not to sit in judgement on family matters. Govardhanram decides to henceforth 'form judgement but be silent' and give full play to the old principle: 'I allow you your liberty and I shall have mine', and to allow his relations to settle their differences themselves and face the consequences of their follies. Henceforth, 'my only objects of care are now my children, neither wife, nor parents, nor brother ...'[55] Lalita's exclusion here from Govardhanram's 'objects of care' is quite puzzling and unexplained. For quite some time before this note was made, he was writing with some pride about her many virtues, and he goes on to write hereafter with great sensitivity about her pain and suffering.

With Lalita's illness, Govardhanram's identification with his nuclear family became more crystallised. He absolves his conscience from any guilt for having passed a judgement against his parents and others in the family: 'My conscience decides in favour of myself'.[56] For the first time in the *Scrap Books* he is willing to commit himself against the joint family: 'My lessons from all this, as a student of sociology, is

[53] Ibid., 119; emphasis in the original.

[54] Ibid., 137.

[55] Ibid., 181.

[56] Ibid., 184–185.

confirmation of my views against a joint family system...'[57] He feels that if the joint family system cannot be done away with completely, an attempt should be made to minimise the jointness of joint families. 'When one son serves in Bombay, the other in Karachi, and the father's home is at Surat. This preserves the nature of the family as a joint insurance and minimises the jointness in other respects.'[58] Lalita's suffering, her illness and his family's insensitivity towards her makes Govardhanram bitter about the nature of patriarchal society. Writing about the status of a daughter-in-law in a joint family, he says, 'It is not the daughter-in-law's maturity but the mother-in-law's death that emancipates the former, probably when she is old, and after all her youthful yearnings and motherly sentiments have been smothered and even violated'.[59]

However, a remark by his cousin-uncle Mansukhram—that his opinions on the joint family were biased by his own existential experience and not really based on an impartial study of that institution—forces Govardhanram to re-evaluate his views.[60] Having oscillated between viewing the joint family as a 'joint nuisance' and as a 'joint insurance', in this enigmatic note of 25 April 1894, he suddenly turns to consider 'the brightest side of the joint family', which he says lies in its being '*Protective*'.[61] Comparing Western and Indian forms of social organisation, he says the former is territorial and 'spends its force in raising up individualism', while the latter is tribal and 'revels in destroying Individualism'.[62] The real strength of tribalism, he says, is that it protects its members 'whom it feeds and clothes and even saves from inclemency of all elements outside the hearth'.[63] He compares the joint family to an insurance society by citing examples from his

57 Ibid., 186.

58 Ibid., 238.

59 Ibid., 262.

60 Ibid., 121.

61 Ibid., 263; emphasis in the original.

62 Ibid.

63 Ibid., 264.

own family. A system 'so holy and so invulnerable', which has provided 'indestructible vitality' and protection to 'society and even the nation' ever since the Aryans came to India, is under attack from territorial nations; therefore, one 'should pause and think a thousand times' before criticising such a superior social organisation which fulfils and furthers the aspirations of socialism, and in fact, 'It is *the* point which would solve many an inspiration of socialism'.[64]

'Joint Family ... provides the fatherless with fathers, the motherless with mothers, sonless with sons and daughterless with daughters, paupers with maintenance, the homeless with homes, the sick with nurses ... socialism never went the length of aspiring to so much.'[65] Given the situation of his own family, Govardhanram asks, 'Could I have left them cold, myself enjoying the warmth of my means? No, not for the world, so long as I was myself—*a Hindu and not a European*'.[66] He is even willing to forget his deep discomfort with his family members and says that all the suffering was not in vain. Having established the superiority of the Hindu (Indian) form of social organisation over the European form, he then cautions those seeking radical reorganisation of society. They can, he advises, 'attempt modifications and reasonable development', even attempt partitioning in a particular family—like his own—but in 'so far as the larger society and the nation of family goes, offer no quackery of medicine to the ignorant masses that are protected by their own old, nature-selected, instinct moulded ways of living, except by slow and well-judged alteration'.[67] Notwithstanding his harsh criticisms of his own family, he appears to largely accept the 'normative authority of the joint family'.[68] But these were in no respect his last words on the subject. Despite his resolve not to 'spoil' his notes by references to the family, during the next twelve years of his life, he did return again and again to the joint family.

[64] Ibid.; emphasis in the original.

[65] Ibid., 266.

[66] Ibid., 265; emphasis in the original.

[67] Ibid., 266.

[68] Chandra, 'A Nineteenth Century View of the Hindu Joint Family', 31.

Govardhanram grappled with the idea of the joint family with equal gravity in his novel. His fundamental ambivalence towards this institution, ranging from total condemnation and rejection to romantic idealisation and acceptance, is played out in *Sarasvatichandra* through two characters—Uddhatlal (as the name suggests, his response is marked by impudence) and Chandrakant, a dear friend of Sarasvatichandra.[69] Uddhatlal adopts the radical, abolitionist stance which Govardhanram had taken earlier, while Chandrakant provides an impassioned defence of the joint family, almost echoing the note of 25 April 1894. During their debate, they at times lapse into English from Gujarati to emphasise their rhetoric. Uddhatlal's trenchant criticism of the joint family is anchored in the argument that tribal forms of social organisation—represented by the joint family—demand sacrifice of individual aspirations. Furthermore, he argues that no fundamental social reconstruction is possible until the root of the problem, the joint family, is abolished.

> Our joint family system has but a blasting influence on the growth of our individuals, on our economical and moral conditions, and even on our national and political growth. It has kept our beings stunted in intelligence and action ... And for any reform, woe be unto every idea of your social or domestic reconstruction or even improvement so long as you have not touched the root of the disease and said: Down with the joint family ...[70]

Chandrakant's reply to such severe criticism is more cautious. He argues that there is an element of truth in Uddhatlal's criticism, but that the picture he paints is an incomplete one. In an almost poetic re-articulation of Govardhanram's views in his note of 25 April 1894, Chandrakant asserts that the European solution to the oppressive tendencies of the family, which result in aggressive individualism, is undesirable. He refers to the aspect of social insurance that joint families provide and, at a national level, emphasises the need to preserve this ancient institution as it arouses feelings of patriotism. He articulates

[69] Tripathi, *Sarasvatichandra*, Part 4, 145–165 (original Gujarati 1901 edition).
[70] Ibid., 153.

the familiar argument that families have socialist aspirations and that the Hindu ideal is superior to the Western one in so far as it aims to further such aspirations. 'The Hindu ideal is eminently socialist in life and practice ... The main feature of our Hindu socialism is that it is *Protective*. It protects the weak, the infants, the women, and the aged from starvation and its consequential crimes ... It protects and protects.'[71]

Chandrakant also shows an awareness that the joint family system in its pure form cannot survive the aggressive onslaught of individualism. And that the responsibility of his generation will be to make the necessary sacrifices to 'secure a combination of the two boons, without their abuses.'[72] This harmony, he argues, cannot be achieved by an aggressive abolitionist stance. The harmonising process may take 'at least one generation' or even more and until then, the present generation will have to live in 'Poverty, patience, forbearance and even suffering.'[73]

To a reader of the novel, this almost unexpected and abrupt articulation of these two distinct positions on the joint family may appear unwarranted; but this exchange becomes more meaningful when read along with the *Scrap Books*. Uddhatlal and Chandrakant's distinct positions, when combined, evidence a direct resemblance to their creator's own complex and ambivalent attitude. Part Two of the novel, *Gunasundarinu Kutumbjal*, is a larger and subtler unfolding of Govardhanram's views as presented in the *Scrap Books*. Gunasundari, the central character of this part, and Vidya Chatura were married as children. Vidya Chatura acquired formal education in Bombay while Gunasundari is 'naturally' virtuous, caring, intelligent and industrious. Vidya Chatura prepares her and educates her so that she can share his intellectual pleasures and appreciate the rich insights and delights of the printed word, of poetry, philosophy, and literature. Govardhanram then describes the circumstances in which more than fourteen

[71] Ibid., 164; emphasis in the original.

[72] Ibid.

[73] Ibid., 165.

members of Vidya Chatura's family come to inhabit their house. He creates a 'typical' joint family comprising Vidya Chatura's parents, Manchatura and Dharmalaxmi, his debauched and unemployed elder brother, his wife, their four children and a daughter-in-law, a sister-in-law widowed in her childhood, a widowed sister and her son, and yet another sister and her daughter whose husband had run away from home as he could not honour his multiple debts.

Their suddenly coming together in Gunasundari and Vidya Chatura's house not only places a tremendous burden on their household economy, it also brings to an abrupt end the joyous celebration of their newfound sensuous and intellectual 'conjugal love'. Henceforth, Gunasundari only aspires to keep the family contented and together. As an embodiment of the philosophy of consumption, she willingly makes all sacrifices and deprives herself of all pleasures and desires. She brings together these different individuals with disparate needs and peculiar characteristics into one cohesive whole. Despite her own consumption, her sacrifices and tireless efforts are neither recognised nor appreciated by the others, preoccupied as they are in furthering their own narrow self-interests.

Govardhanram describes with a touch of humour the complete anarchy which prevails in the household during Gunasundari's confinement after the birth of her first child, Kumud. During this period of ritual confinement, Gunasundari—like her creator Govardhanram—is forced to confront the oppressive reality of the joint family and critically evaluate those surrounding her.

> Oh God, guide me through this ocean! Until the other day, I believed that a joint family was a boon, a source of endless joy. But this is no joy—only conflict and endless blood-boil! Each one has a mind of their own; their true colours are different. Each one has a bad habit as large as a tree; and when their bad habits are curbed, I get all the blame! I have to care for all their desires, but there is no one to care for mine.[74]

[74] See p. 100 of this volume.

Despite this indictment of the joint family, Gunasundari is not willing to absolve herself from her duties. It is the old patriarch, Manchatura, who in his empathy for his daughter-in-law realises that until Gunasundari and Vidya Chatura are relieved of the burden of the joint family, they will not be able to enjoy their youth and the others will never learn to manage for themselves and live independently, and it is Manchatura who eventually relocates all the family members. This is the solution also suggested by Govardhanram in his *Scrap Books*: minimise the jointness of the joint family without destroying the joint insurance and protection that it provides. In *Gunasundarinu Kutumbjal*, otherwise perceived in Gujarati literature to be a celebration of the Hindu joint family, Govardhanram's ambivalence towards the institution is evident.

As Sudhir Chandra has observed, it is perhaps futile to search for Govardhanram's final and definitive position on the issue of the Indian joint family.[75] Even so, it is possible to discern a dominant position. Govardhanram found the reality of his joint family oppressive, and he found members of his family undeserving of his presence and affection; this is quite evident from his chronic lamentations against his family which mark his *Scrap Books*. Although he found it necessary to address the civilisational issue and socialist aspirations while discussing the joint family, his dissatisfaction with his own family and his nuanced position in the novel are suggestive of his deep discomfort with normative aspects of the joint family.

VII

We are concerned not only with the fate of his societal endeavours, but also with the fate of Govardhanram and two other individuals irrevocably bound to him. Their minds and souls were the first that he tried to cultivate in accordance with his ideals and philosophy. These two were Lalita, Govardhanram's second wife, and Lilavati, their daughter.

[75] Chandra, 'A Nineteenth Century View of the Hindu Joint Family', 32.

It is important for us to consider the fates of these three individuals not only because they were played out almost simultaneously to his public endeavour, but also because for Govardhanram there was no marked disjunction between giving his country a vision of an ideal society and of educating and 'raising' his wife and daughter. These two projects were essentially the same—both were integral to his personal dharma towards the country. And as Govardhanram himself put it, 'my country is a term which must be confined in the beginning and made to expand in course of time only'.[76]

Govardhanram shows a keen awareness of the intertwined fates of those inhabiting the inner worlds he created through his fiction, and of his own self and his family. At many places in the *Scrap Books* he draws parallels between his life and the novel, compares his wife to his heroine and asks his daughter to follow in the footsteps of Gunasundari. His life and his fiction seemed to him to mirror each other. Jayanti, another daughter of his, was betrothed at a tender age, a decision which upset him. Two days after the engagement he wrote: 'Curious coincidence! Jayanti betrothed on 25th, and I get the first proof of the second part of my novel on the 26th. The betrothal pinches me, and I compare myself to Vidya Chatura, who accepting in haste a woman's arguments, betrothed Kumud to Pramad, and dropped all talk of Sarasvatichandra'.[77] In a moment of rare passion, Govardhanram says: '*I only want their souls*'.[78] Moreover, the only source of deriving some understanding about the possible fate of his societal endeavour is from the lives of Govardhanram, Lilavati and Lalita, who tried to live a life of consumptive virtue. It is in their biographies that Govardhanram's 'grand project' unfolds itself completely.

Govardhanram's marriage to Harilaxmi was fixed before their birth. A close 'conjugal' relationship developed between the two. But the relationship between adolescent Harilaxmi and Govardhanram's dominating mother Shivkashi was one of constant conflict. Torn

[76] Pandya, Bakshi and Pandya, *Scrap Book* I, 51.

[77] Ibid., 93.

[78] Ibid., 27; emphasis in the original.

between love for his young wife and his sense of duty towards his mother, Govardhanram seriously contemplated running away from his conflict-ridden house to start life anew.[79] His first marriage ended tragically—Harilaxmi died in 1874 while giving birth to their child, who also died soon after. Govardhanram was to express his deep anguish and a sense of permanent loss in two verses—*Hridayruditshatakam* and *Snehmudra*—that he wrote in memory of Harilaxmi and in which he paid her glowing tributes.[80] Reflecting on his first marriage, he wrote in 1893: 'My first marriage was meant to be a cruel hoax which my wife lived and was eventually to leave me a widower'.[81] Though delighted 'at the prospect of a living relieved from future marriage',[82] Govardhanram was married again to Lalitagauri in 1876. Years later, he complained: 'I was then married, under conditions to which I would have never assented, if I had not been kept ignorant of them, to a girl reputedly ill-bred ...'[83] Secure in his faith in the philosophy of 'consumption', he tried to cultivate in his 'ill-bred' wife the high ideals of this philosophy. 'My duty does not end with satisfying her poor ideals, but I am bound to enlarge them. This is my marital duty ...'[84] Govardhanram lists his 'duties' towards his wife as under: 'a) to train her up b) to raise her life c) to make her free d) to provide for her e) to fulfill her aspirations with such luxuries etc., as a husband in love and duty ought to give her'.[85] His primary obligation towards his wife was to 'train' her. By training he did not imply 'educating' her in the conventional sense of imparting literacy, as he time and again laments that he was not able to educate her.[86] Training for Govardhanram primarily meant imparting to her those

[79] Pandya, *Sriyut Govardhanram*, 16–17.

[80] *Hridayruditshatakam*, a long verse in Sanskrit, was written in 1875. *Snehmudra*, an adaption of the former, was published in 1889.

[81] Pandya, Bakshi and Pandya, *Scrap Book* I, 167.

[82] Ibid.

[83] Ibid., 167–68.

[84] Ibid., 64.

[85] Ibid., 61.

[86] Ibid., 62.

virtues and ideals which would enable her to lead her life according to the tenets of his philosophy of consumption.

For Lalita, the first thirteen years of her life with Govardhanram were years of training under his constant guidance and close supervision. Not given to impassioned display of his feelings, he is nevertheless ecstatic in his praise of Lalita's moral strength to continuously lead a life of self-negation and self-inflicted deprivation. There are repeated references of Lalita's moral virtues and a life of self-sacrifice in his *Scrap Books* of this period. He writes:

> last thirteen years have been a life of training for her, and her life is high. Industrious to the fullest extent, virtuous and charitable, active and clever, enthusiastic and untiring in her domestic work and in the work of rendering me happy and all in the family, she has nobly – successfully – and touchingly borne, and willingly undertaken, the heaviest self-sacrifice for all this – the sacrifice of health, of liberty, of all luxuries, of all enjoyments – of her own wants and aspirations, and the most usual of worldly enjoyments, – of her tastes and temper – and of everything possible under the sun ...[87]

Govardhanram cannot hide his feelings of a personal success and achievement in training Lalita.'I have trained wife from the beginning to do voluntary and loving service and sacrifice to my people. She has done it. She has worked like an ass for my people ...'[88] Lalita's sole aspiration of life becomes making Govardhanram and his family happy. For this she earns his unqualified praise. Her latest change of disposition compels Govardhanram 'to adore and make *arti* to her soul—to her goodness, to her virtue—to her understanding—and to her moral power'.[89] Lalita's sacrifice compels Govardhanram—who constantly lived with a feeling of his own moral and intellectual superiority—to put her on a pedestal even higher than himself.

[87] Ibid., 62–63.

[88] Ibid., 184–85.

[89] Ibid., 26.

'Her life is higher than mine.'[90] This was the greatest recognition that Govardhanram could have given to any one; he called her the 'Family's Angel'.[91] Lalita succeeds in acquiring respect even from the quarrelsome Shivkashi. Govardhanram compares Lalita to Gunasundari—the ideal and perfect embodiment of consumption created in *Sarasvatichandra*.[92]

But his 'heaven' does not last long. The familiar discord re-enters their lives. Govardhanram records instances of conflict between Lalita and Shivkashi, and Lalita and his brother's wife. He records, with some satisfaction, his own efforts to be an 'impartial judge' in these conflicts and reflects on 'Family misunderstandings and the way to remove them'.[93] As the conflicts and discord become deeper, he is forced to re-evaluate Lalita's morals and virtues and is ruthless in his condemnation: 'My wife is inadequate to be my heroine, alas, she falls far too short of my Gunasundari'.[94] Lalita's failure to continuously lead a life of consumption forced Govardhanram to grapple with a more fundamental question of how to successfully 'raise' our women. He also reflects on his own failure to do so.

> Are our women to be raised? How? Take a particular woman, and see, how? ... I have tried ... with my mother, my wife ... The result of my labours has been that both mother and wife have turned into discontented imperfect machines—square pegs in round holes—my mother the peg and my wife the hole![95]

Even this clear admission of failure does not introduce any element of doubt regarding his mission of cultivating minds and tempering the souls of his countrymen. Instead, quite characteristically, he sees in this failure a new raison d' etre for his endeavours: '99 out of 100 individuals will give up without thinking of the society,' he says, but

[90] Ibid.

[91] Ibid.

[92] Ibid.

[93] Ibid., 113–15.

[94] Ibid., 200.

[95] Ibid., 236–37.

'my crucifixion in my own family must direct me to rise from this grave and try to relieve my countrymen from the troubles from which I could not relieve myself. *The next generation must always benefit by the adversities of its predecessors*'.[96]

Govardhanram was unwavering in his resolve to cultivate the minds of others, but by 1892 Lalita was not prepared to lead a life of continuous self-negation. Lalita becomes a victim of many physical and mental ailments: 'Mrs. has been suffering from premonitory symptoms of consumption ... she is doomed'.[97] As her physical condition further deteriorated, her mental health also suffered. She became a patient of 'Monomania' and was admitted to a sanatorium at Sion.[98] Lalita's illness forced Govardhanram to examine the cause of her hysteria, which he does with clinical detachment, as is evident from his jottings in *Scrap Book* I:

> *Cure for wife's hysteria:*
> 1. Cause of hysteria: *Prolonged* and *compulsory* abstinence from natural tendencies and sentiments and sickness and agitations of soul and frequent irritations, etc., etc., caused by a sense of enduring injustice and ill-treatment, etc.
> 2. *Result*: Bodily hysteria, and abnormal and incessant irritability and pain of mind, and melancholia and hypochondria, etc.
> 3. *Remedy applied*: A general abstinence on my part from contradicting her and allowing free scope of her *will* and *frenzies* ... and showing sympathy for her real and imaginary miseries ...
> 4. *Shortcomings in the remedy*: I sometimes lose patience and temper, and sometimes fail to study her mind and mood.[99]

Despite care and medical treatment, Lalita's condition progressively worsened and she was faced with imminent death. 'Poor Lalita! Your life is hanging upon a most apparent uncertainty. Most people affected

[96] Ibid.; emphasis added.

[97] Ibid., 162.

[98] Ibid., 166–68.

[99] Ibid., 182; emphasis in the original.

as you are die after lingering pains.'[100] The possibility of Lalita's death compels Govardhanram to articulate his own guilt: 'Poor beloved Lalita, sweet sharer of my cares, brave bearer of the heavy burdens that I have placed on thy frail personality, in this way am I bound to witness thy pangs and smoldering ...'[101] The Great Will willed otherwise, and Lalita survived. But hereafter, Govardhanram gave up his efforts to cultivate Lalita. After her illness, Lalita acquired the self-confidence to rebel against the regimentation imposed by Govardhanram. He indicates that she would frequently taunt him:

> You taught me from childhood to love and serve your people; how do you ask at this stage and age, to be indifferent to their opinions and remarks, and their wounded feelings, simply on the ground that you agree with me in thinking they are mistaken? Why should they mistake? How can I change my nature now? My only way to bliss is to see them love me whatever the sacrifice.[102]

Govardhanram's philosophy had the resources to contain such rebellions. Centred as it was in the ideal of continuous self-negation, without an accompanying awareness of this sacrifice, his philosophy made Govardhanram respond to Lalita's questions in a characteristic manner: 'If she did not feel the sacrifice, she should be right.'[103]

Govardhanram may have been able to respond philosophically to Lalita's taunts but Lalita's life, her 'failure' to be the embodiment of 'consumption', her illness—hysteria which pushed her to the margins of insanity—posed fundamental questions to Govardhanram's philosophy of consumption and his declared mission to cultivate the minds and souls of his countrymen. Neither Govardhanram nor his philosophy had a creative response to this. His only response was silence. After his self-chosen retirement and final shift to Nadiad from Bombay to complete his novel and dedicate himself fully to

[100] Ibid., 166.
[101] Ibid., 163–64.
[102] Ibid., 224.
[103] Ibid.

contemplate the fate of his country and countrymen, there are no references either to Lalita's consumptive lungs, her mental illness, or her being the 'Family's Angel'. When Lalita entered Govardhanram's life, she was around twelve years old. She had received her primary *sanskara* [traditional mores and values]—for Govardhanram, 'ill-breeding'—from her natal home. And as Lalita herself so accurately posed the question: 'Is it possible to divert the branches of the tree at the fag end of their growth without breaking them?'.[104]

VIII

In 1881 Lalita gave birth to their first child—daughter Lilavati. In 1885, Govardhanram started writing *Sarasvatichandra*, at the same time as Lilavati's education began. He assumed complete control of her education and upbringing. In Govardhanram's project neither chance nor *lila* had any play. Each action was to be based on proper study and intense reflection. This 'obsessive concern for clarity' is also reflected in the detailed curriculum that he worked out for Lilavati's education. Govardhanram believed that the sanskara of any individual is the sum total of the accumulated sanskara of her/his *swagotra*, the sanskara imparted at the natal home and the individual's own philosophy of life. Govardhanram did not have any control over Lilavati's accumulated sanskara, but he was determined and duty-bound to impart all those values to her which formed the core of his own philosophy.

Govardhanram believed that keeping girls completely unlettered was both a sin and a curse. His wisdom told him that education without a clear aim could be dangerous, especially for girls. To arrive at a decision regarding Lilavati's education he formulated a guiding principle: 'The decision must be made after considering the in-law's house, mental capacities of the girl and her future prospects'.[105] He

[104] Ibid.

[105] Govardhanram Madhavram Tripathi, *Lilavati Jivankala*, 4th ed. (Bombay: N. M. Tripathi and Co., 1905, 1961), 57–58.

defined, specifically for girls, the role of education: 'In the dark wintry night that this world is, there is no protection, support and light against the piercing blizzards comparable to good knowledge, to guide the helpless girls on the righteous path and give them warmth and solace'.[106]

Lilavati was admitted to a girl's school in Zaverbaug, Bombay, at the age of three. But Govardhanram soon realised the narrow vision of such institutions. After a few months he took his daughter out of the school, and 'keeping in mind her age, sex and body, appropriate facilities were created at home for her play and enjoyment'.[107] Lilavati was never to go to a school after this. This brief stay at a girls' school was to be her only excursion to the world outside—before marriage—without the ever present gaze of her father.

Govardhanram was seized by a sense of urgency about Lilavati's education, which he wanted completed before she was married and sent to live with her husband, as he firmly believed that there were too many obstacles in the path of education once a girl starts living with her husband.

Initially, Lilavati was given basic literacy in Gujarati. Govardhanram was conscious of the fact that his child was destined to live through the 'drama of transition' and hence, that she must be systematically exposed to both traditional Indian wisdom and knowledge systems as well as Western education. A private tutor was hired to teach Lilavati basic Sanskrit and English. She was taught Professor Bhandarkar's *Sanskritmargopadesika* and the English 'First Book'. Once she had acquired basic knowledge of Sanskrit, Govardhanram appointed Shastri Jivram Lallubhai (later Professor of Sanskrit, Elphinstone College, Bombay) to educate her in Sanskrit literature and the *shastras*. Before giving him the responsibility of his daughter's education, Govardhanram reminded Shastri of his obligations and the goals of knowledge.

106 Ibid.

107 Ibid., 61.

> Shastriji, Lilavati is destined to live in a foreign environment. Neither I nor her mother will be able to guide her in good and bad times. Moreover, how are we—worldly beings—to provide her with wisdom? So, if you give her knowledge, give that type of Knowledge which will be a good friend of her intellect and constantly guide her, wherever she may be, on the right path.[108]

They decided to combine the knowledge of literature with that of the shastras because,'Literature is useful in invoking and tempering higher desires and *rasas* of life while, development of the frail intellect requires the support of the *shastras*'.[109] Lilavati was too young to be exposed to *shringara* [an aesthetic of beauty pertaining to love]; hence, together they selected those parts of the texts which did not have shringar as the dominant *rasa* [aesthetic; flavour]. Shastriji taught her Bhartrhari's *Niti Sataka*, Aryashrenishvara's *Chandakaushik* and the fourth part of the *Shakuntal*. While she studied the *Savitri Natak* on her own, at a later stage she was allowed to study other parts of *Shakuntal* herself. Of the shastras, Lilavati was taught *Laghutark Kaumudi*, *Ishavasya* and *Ken Upanishad*, *Bhagvad Gita* and *Panchikaran*. As Lilavati went deeper into the Sanskrit tradition, she became disinterested in English education. Govardhanram allowed her to discontinue her English studies. In order to make sure she did not remain completely ignorant of Western life, she was given Karsandas Mulji's *Travels in England* (in Gujarati). To familiarise her with societal issues, she was made to read a daily, *Gujarati*, and some other journals. Through such complete education, 'the emotional and intellectual core' of Lilavati's life was formed.[110]

Govardhanram was aware that the prevailing social consciousness was inhospitable for a girl who was learned but did not have any housekeeping skills. Therefore, along with the training of her mind she was initiated into the intricacies of household work.

[108] Ibid., 4. For details of Lilavati's education, see 57–58.

[109] Ibid., 65.

[110] Ibid., 66.

> In this training her mother was made her teacher. It is always desirable that a mother should initiate a daughter in this work because this training demands love and delicate tutoring while, at the same time, the teacher should have the right to punish. There is no other person who inspires the same level of confidence in a child as compared to her mother.[111]

From a tender age Lilavati was given the responsibility of cooking for the entire joint family of twelve or thirteen members. Lalita and other women of the house were given strict instructions not to interfere in her work. Lilavati's mornings were spent doing the household work while the rest of the day was devoted to studies. Lilavati's education was comprehensive. No area was left untouched. So total was Govardhanram's involvement with Lilavati that he neglected his two other daughters, Jayanti and Jasu, and also his son Ramaniyaram's education and upbringing. In later years, he would often lament that in his own preoccupation with his literary and professional activities and total involvement with Lilavati, he had neglected his other children. Govardhanram notes that even Lilavati had noticed the wide gulf which separated her from her brother and sisters. She even questioned her father on this, and his meek defense left her unsatisfied.[112]

Lilavati was engaged to marry at the age of three or four. While choosing a husband for her, Govardhanram went against the established norm of his caste of choosing a family from his own native town Nadiad. She was engaged to Himatbhai, third son of Manilal Gangashankar of Petlad. Govardhanram's family was against Lilavati's betrothal to an impoverished and indebted family. But Govardhanram was uncompromising and argued that even his own family was

[111] Ibid., 62.

[112] Ibid., 50. One incident captures this divide. Once while he was going to Bombay from Nadiad, Jayanti requested her father to get for her a book on religious and ritual observances, *Somvar Ni Katha*. After she left the room, Govardhanram expressed his sorrow and his sense of failure to his friend and relative, Chandrashankar Pandya. 'I could not educate this poor girl and therefore she has to ask for books like *Somvar Ni Katha*, otherwise like Lilavati she would have demanded excellent books.' Pandya, *Sriyut Govardhanram*, 207–08.

indebted at the time of his marriage to Lalita, but that her parents had posed complete faith in their ability to overcome the crisis. He argued that they had no right to reject Himatbhai's family on grounds of indebtedness.[113] Lilavati's marriage to Himatbhai took place in 1891 when she was twelve years old. Her marriage at this tender age irked Govardhanram, but he eventually decided to go ahead with it, reasoning that her happiness had to be sought within the existing social structure, and that marriage was necessary to achieve that.[114]

Lilavati's education continued even after she was sent to live with her in-laws. Both Govardhanram and Lalita wrote her frequent letters, in which they counselled her in *grihinidharma*. In one such letter, Lalita wrote:

> You should not differentiate between the natal home and the house of your in-laws ... As long as you differentiate between the two families you shall never be happy. Therefore, it is your duty to consider them as your own and worship them like Gods. You once asked me, who was virtuous? Virtuous is one who considers the in-laws' house as her natal home and who treats all members—whether young or old—with utmost respect.[115]

Father Govardhanram urged her to follow the ideal and noble path of Gunasundari. 'Gunasundari was surrounded by all types of people and she made all of them her own through her *niti* and cleverness. Keep her in mind and follow her example. Notwithstanding the character of others we should always be good and virtuous because ultimately *Dharma* always emerges victorious.'[116] Reminding her of the education and wisdom he had imparted to her, he says: 'Make your mind so strong with the help of your knowledge that the unhappiness of this world does not generate any remorse in you.'[117]

[113] Tripathi, *Lilavati Jivankala*, 16–17.

[114] Pandya, Bakshi and Pandya, *Scrap Book* I, 89.

[115] Tripathi, *Lilavati Jivankala*, 6.

[116] Ibid., 10.

[117] Ibid., 11.

Lilavati made this philosophy of life integral to her existence. She followed each tenet as the truth itself. Govardhanram lists many examples—and not without great satisfaction and some degree of pride—to prove that Lilavati had been worthy of all the knowledge he had given her and that she had completely internalised this knowledge and the principles of 'consumption'. Some rumours regarding her ill health and unhappiness prompted Govardhanram to write a rather concerned letter to her. In reply, Lilavati reminded her father of his swadharma, suggesting that it was his dharma not to be concerned about the wellbeing of a married daughter living with her parents-in-law. She quoted a verse from Govardhanram's own poem *Snehmudra* to remind him that when a bird leaves its nest, it flies on its own. Similarly, a girl leaves her father after marriage and is on her own. She further reminded him of a verse in *Shakuntal* in which Rishi Kanva says that a girl is another's property and the father is relieved by returning her to her husband,[118] prompting Govardhanram to observe: 'My sweet child admonished me in my own words and pointed the way to my happiness'.[119] By reminding her father of his swadharma, Lilavati showed that she had indeed internalised her education. Govardhanram notes many instances to reinforce that Lilavati lived her life in accordance with the two basic tenets of the philosophy of consumption: *yajmandharma* and *manojnadharma*.[120] His success in creating an embodiment of the principles of consumptive virtue through Lilavati was complete.

A writer can bring his literary creations to an ideal end, but life is rarely so kind. Lilavati lived in Junagadh, which suffered a series of

[118] Ibid., 4.

[119] Pandya, Bakshi and Pandya, *Scrap Book* II, 230.

[120] Govardhanram defined virtue as consumption of the self in order to feed the world, while vice entailed feeding upon the flesh of the world. The dharma of the virtuous is to be a *yajman*, while those who feed on others are *atithi*. He imagined his ideal virtuous individual to be a follower of *yajmandharma*. The other quality of the virtuous is to know even the unarticulated feelings and desires of others and conduct their lives accordingly; he calls this *manojnadharma*. He attributed these qualities to the sadhvis of Sundargiri in *Sarasvatichandra*.

epidemics. Her parents repeatedly asked her to come back to Nadiad. But Lilavati refused to leave her in-laws' house until she had nursed every member of the family to health. When Lilavati finally reached Nadiad, it was too late. She had in fact 'consumed' herself through self-inflicted privation; she was diagnosed as suffering from the 'disease of consumption', tuberculosis. She refused to blame anyone or even her fate in the face of imminent death. Reassuring her mother that she had fulfilled her grihinidharma, Lilavati said:

> Mother, in those days of fever epidemic there were only two possible outcomes. If I had pampered and loved myself and not cared to nurse others, someone else would have lost life. But I did not do so, and I do not care what fate awaits me now. Either I could have saved my life or someone else's life, and it is desirable that I lose my life.[121]

Lilavati, the embodiment of consumption, sacrificed her life. Govardhanram wrote: 'Lilavati! By following the righteous path of *Dharma* as suggested by your parents, you sought, like Nachiketa, death. And death shall give you your fulfillment.'[122] Lilavati died at the age of twenty-one, on 8 January 1902. It is perhaps not a coincidence that the two projects which had taken complete hold of Govardhanram's life and being ended almost simultaneously. He completed the fourth and final part of *Sarasvatichandra* and it was published in 1901.

Govardhanram did one final act of duty towards the sacred memory of Lilavati and his country. He wrote her biography, *Lilavati Jivankala*. Even this final act was done not to glorify her memory, but to place before society an ideal life. 'I am not writing this book to glorify you. But I feel that your life, your philosophy and your actions have a message for the society. You are the real author of this work.'[123]

One question must be asked: Who or what was responsible for Lilavati's tragic and untimely death? Father Govardhanram, who

[121] Tripathi, *Lilavati Jivankala*, 28.

[122] Ibid., 29.

[123] Ibid., 3.

assumed complete control of her existence and tried to create a real embodiment of his philosophy at the cost of her life? Or was it his philosophy which demanded a negation of the 'self'? Or should we hold Lilavati's husband and his parents responsible? Or was it perhaps the Great Will? *Lilavati Jivankala* does not provide any answers. We must turn to Govardhanram's *Scrap Books* to understand his real emotions. Initially, Govardhanram is tempted to attribute her pain and suffering to the desire of the Great Will.

> My best, Sweetest, meekest, wisest and most patient child, who has done nothing in this life to deserve this situation, a situation which can only be accounted for by a speculative desire of Providence to kill her, or to test or toughen the 'Philosophy' of which alone her education and wealth consists.[124]

This attribution to the Great Will was only temporary. He feels that neither Lilavati's husband nor her parents-in-law deserved to have such a noble soul like Lilavati in their house. Emotions which are restrained in *Lilavati Jivankala* find free expression in *Scrap Book* II, where there are repeated references to the ill-treatment, agony and prolonged suffering that she was subjected to by her parents-in-law.

> Her services were not only accepted without the slightest effort at limiting her struggle to serve them, but she was taunted for her groans and complaints, which she could not have made except in extremities. Her complaints were belittled, she was allowed to pass latest hours of a coldest winter on a damp ground floor, working to do them superfluous service without being relieved. And when she had fever and shiverings and was in need of warm blankets to cover her, nobody looked to these things. She lay so, listening to talks with hard words about her making too much of her body.[125]

Govardhanram does not see any escape from this situation. If she were to live, she will have to go back to her husband. Only death can save his daughter from this misery, he feels, and he secretly desires her death.

[124] Pandya, Bakshi and Pandya, *Scrap Book* II, 191.

[125] Ibid., 224.

> Not being able to see how the girl can be happy living with such people as those at her husband's, I have never been able to persuade myself to offer a single prayer for her life, and all that I could do in my affection, which cannot bear the idea of her death, has been to request the Great Will to do what is best for her welfare, and for his inscrutable objects, or to make her live, *provided* she is destined to be happy by living.[126]

Blaming others may have given temporary solace to Govardhanram the father, but the thinker in him is not convinced. He knows that the final decision regarding Lilavati's marriage was his, and that he had gone against both the norms of his community and express wishes of his family while taking this decision. He gives a long, agonising justification for his action.[127] Such post-facto wisdom does not however lessen his burden. His search for the truth finally leads him to the realisation: 'I am responsible'.[128] The realisation invokes in him a strong feeling of having sinned: 'I have to thank myself for my having committed this inexplicable sin against my poor child, by choosing for her an unsuitable family'.[129] With her death, this feeling of having sinned becomes magnified and possesses him.

> At 5.30 p.m. yesterday my poor Lilavati died after a stainless, spotless life of suffering. She was a martyr to the cause of our Hindu Social System, to her father's exercise of his power of disposing of her in early marriage ... and to the services she rendered to her mother-in-law and her father-in-law.[130]

Govardhanram's expiation and atonement can now lie only in 'realising my faults and weakness, and my sins against her life and merits'.[131] He also concludes that 'her soul and holiness were superior to *mine* and

[126] Ibid., 213; emphasis in the original.

[127] Ibid., 223.

[128] Ibid., 191.

[129] Ibid., 216.

[130] Ibid., 220.

[131] Ibid., 228.

to that of every other person I see about me'.[132] Only one idea gives him solace: 'I can only feel proud to have had a child like this during my worldly sojourn, rewarded at the idea that I had the privilege of looking after the education and elevation of so aspiring a soul'.[133] His search for atonement leads him to examine the education and 'elevation' of her soul. 'In Lilavati's life, I and her mother always taught her the way to do her duty to her husband and his family, and to seek reward and consolation in the idea of Duty. She was quite equal to her task and her body paid for it.'[134] He continues,

> and with the philosophy and sweetness that her education and innate powers were able to develop in her, her life became one of martyrdom, among other things, to her own very high sense of duty, in which point she outdistanced not only me and mine but all the characters that I have been able to spin out in my books.[135]

In the opening lines of *Sanskarkala-Shodashi*, a long poem on Lilavati, Govardhanram laments: 'I had conceived a Gunasundari in my head. In real life I fathered you, a better version of Gunasundari. You did penance like Gunasundari but unlike her, did not enjoy the fruit thereof. I produced a thesis, you sacrificed your life to prove it right!'[136] Aware that it was his education and his philosophy which was the cause of Lilavati's pain, suffering and ultimately, death, Govardhanram is forced to re-evaluate his project of cultivating minds and elevating souls.

> My daughter Lilavati suffered because of high virtues and would have fared better if she had not got the virtues! Is it right then

132 Ibid.; emphasis in the original.

133 Ibid., 228.

134 Ibid., 224.

135 Govardhanram Tripathi to Janmanshankar Buch, in *Lilavati Jivankala*, 131.

136 Govardhanram Madhavram Tripathi, 'Sanskarkala-Shodashi' in *Lilavati Jivankala*, 4th ed. (Bombay: N. M. Tripathi and Co., 1905, 1961), 133–55. The translated verse is from Sonal Shukla, 'Govardhanram's Women', *Economic and Political Weekly*, WS 65, 31 October 1987.

> to teach these virtues to our daughters? So many people tell my wife that she has killed Lilavati by making her virtuous; the charge comes home more to me. Is a parent right in educating his children in this way at their cost?[137]

He questions the idea of virtue itself. But he is not ready to give up either his project or his faith in the essential goodness and desirability of virtue. For one last time, he reasserts the validity of his principles of consumption: 'This question must be answered in *affirmative* for people like *myself*; my children, like their father and mother, have been educated in virtue, *irrespective of its consequences*.'[138]

The power of his vision did not allow Govardhanram to abandon his project, but with Lilavati's death, his creative self died. He lived his final years lonely and miserable, seeking solace and strength from Lilavati's memory.

> No misery that will reach me now can be higher or more excruciating than that borne by my Lilavati, and I can do no better reverence to her sacred memory than by walking in her gentle and yet, firm, steady, virtuous and heroic footsteps in facing any circumstances that may befall me. [May] Her sweet and lofty virtues be my divine beacon-light in my mundane struggles henceforth! May her example inspire my soul and draw me closer unto hers wherever and whatsoever she now may be![139]

He died on 4 January 1907 after a long illness.

IX

While commenting on the high point that Gujarati poetry had achieved during the seventeenth century through Akho, Premanand and Samal, Govardhanram observed that the vocation of a writer is to expand the human nature by placing before the people 'purer and

137 Pandya, Bakshi and Pandya, *Scrap Book* II, 290–91.

138 Ibid.; emphasis in the original.

139 Pandya, Bakshi and Pandya, *Scrap Book* II, 256.

higher ideals of social life' in a 'beautiful and ennobling' manner. Akho, Premanand and Samal could achieve this only because they were 'above the society in which they live'.[140]

Govardhanram Tripathi's own mission as a writer, of influencing and improving contemporary society, was fulfilled, perhaps beyond his expectations, through *Sarasvatichandra*. 'The educated youth of Gujarat lived in the dreamland of Sarasvatichandra, Kumud and Kusum ... No other book of fiction has made so powerful an impact on its contemporaries as *Sarasvatichandra* ...'[141] For over a hundred years, *Sarasvatichandra* has remained the canonical text of Gujarati literature; perhaps no other work of fiction has been able to match its range of concerns or popularity. 'No other event, before the arrival of Gandhi, had so captured the imagination of the society and had succeeded in moulding the minds of the people on the path of moral, civilised conduct as this epic novel.'[142]

Govardhanram's attempt was to create a new moral universe for the emerging middle class. As mediators of India's colonial encounter, this emerging class experienced deep uncertainties about the old order and felt ambivalent insecurities about new modes of thought, conduct, morality, faith, and culture, creating permanent disjunctions in their public and personal lives. Largely due to industrialisation, the distance between the public and domestic spheres increased, as people came in contact with new ideas and ideologies. This group was in search for new models of thought and conduct which would provide some sense of permanency in times of transition.

Govardhanram provided them with a new ideal through his 'graduate hero'. Sonal Shukla has beautifully captured the essence of this new ideal, which went on to become a dominant thematic category for Gujarat literature.

140 Govardhanram Madhavram Tripathi, *Classical Poets of Gujarat and Their Influence on Society and Morals*, 3rd ed. (Bombay: Forbes Gujarati Sabha, 1894, 1958), 33–34.

141 Mansukhlal Jhaveri, *History of Gujarati Literature* (New Delhi: Sahitya Akademi, 1978), 98.

142 Vishnuprasad R. Trivedi, *Govardhanram: Chintak Ne Sarjak* (Bombay: N. M. Tripathi and Co., 1962), 95.

> He has done extremely well in his studies. He is sensitive and generous but also somewhat haughty and aloof. He has a mission, but no job. He usually belongs to a wealthy family, but does not mind living in poverty, although towards the end he is usually comfortably placed all over again. The novelist and his heroine admire this greatly. Sarasvatichandra is the first modern Gujarati hero of this type.[143]

This acute awareness of having to provide anchors introduced caution in Govardhanram's enterprise. He is willing to question the assumptions and normative principles underlying social and political institutions; he is also willing to reject their moral superiority in some cases. Nevertheless, he does not consider it desirable to posit options which might fundamentally alter the old order and introduce new anxieties. This caution is quite evident in his attitudes towards widow remarriage. This overwhelming desire to provide anchors to society led him to the creation of a new idealised woman—the 'Domestic Angel'.[144] Govardhanram's personal life and the novel reflect a remarkable engagement with women and femininity. For a major part of his life he tried to 'educate' and 'raise' the virtues of his wife, Lalita. So complete and intense was his identification with his daughter Lilavati that he neglected his only male child Ramaniyaram. The novel *Sarasvatichandra* is anchored in the characters of women that he created—Gunasundari, Kumud and Kusum. What could be the reason for his intense encounter with womanhood?

For Govardhanram, tradition was to be 'the bedrock of social reconstruction through much of this transitional phase, when two civilisations confronted each other'.[145] In times of transition, women and womanhood became ideal embodiments of traditional virtues. Govardhanram introduced to Gujarat the Victorian ideal of the 'naturally virtuous woman'. Govardhanram established the moral and cultural superiority of women over men. For many, awareness of the

143 Shukla, 'Govardhanram's Women', WS 63.

144 Ibid., WS 65–67.

145 Chandra, *The Oppressive Present*, 82.

colonial encounter and its social and cultural implications provoked deep insecurities regarding their own traditions and belief systems. In Govardhanram's moral vision, it was through women that harmony and virtue, in both family and society, were sought to be achieved. Women became the sites where the conflict between tradition and modernity was being played out. Govardhanram's philosophy of consumption also placed additional burden on women. Consumption with its emphasis on continuous self-denial, without an accompanying awareness of sacrifice, and valorisation of pain and humiliation as an ideal to be sought to further one's consumption, crushed womanhood.

Govardhanram Tripathi sought to create such an ideal woman in his life, as in his fiction. When his 'domestic angel'—his wife Lalita—became hysterical under his regimentation and ultimately gathered the courage to question his ideals, he made another attempt through his daughter Lilavati. Govardhanram's vision demanded, and received, heavy sacrifices from women. Gunasundari paid through her consumption, Kumud by submitting her desires to a higher ideal of ascetic renunciation, Lalita, through her hysteria, and Lilavati, paid with her life. Little did he realise that it is impossible to create one ideal woman through two lives and one fiction.

Tridip Suhrud

Preface I[†]

Novels have in these days become a universal luxury and in competing for public interest have succeeded to an extent almost unrivalled. The very natural result has been that the bulk of fiction in the West has ceased to aspire beyond an artistic display of such of the sentimental and emotional idiosyncrasies of mankind as happen to tickle the fancy of the ordinary reader. It is however certain—and the higher class of novelists never fail to recognise and claim—that the functions of the novel are more numerous, higher and more sacred than the mere pandering to the taste of the novel reading public.

The writer of these pages admits that the origin of his undertaking was in the first instance neither so ordinary nor so ambitious. Like all who live and look around, he had his memoranda of what may be called the substrata of this our world of human affairs. When he first desired to give an objective existence to all that so sketched out in his mind's book, he intended to give it the form of essays. Second thoughts discovered that the reading class in Gujarat were, for various reasons, difficult to reach through abstruse or discursive matter, and that illustrations of real or ideal life would be the best medium, best in the sense of being attractive and impressive, for communications like those which the writer has to make. Hence, the present contribution.

[†] As earlier stated, there are two prefaces to the first edition of Part 1 of the novel, *Buddhidhan Nu Karbhar* (1887), one in English and the other in Gujarati. This is the original English preface for Part 1, reproduced from Tripathi, *Sarasvatichandra*, Part 1, trans. Tridip Suhrud, liii–liv. Govardhanram Tripathi did not write a separate preface for Part 2, although he did for Parts 3 and 4.

The conviction has also grown upon him that reality in flesh and blood under the guise of fiction can supply the ordinary reader with subtler moulds and finer casts for the formation of his inner self than abstract discussions, and that this is especially so with a people who must be made, and not simply left, to read.

It remains to note that by inducing reality under fiction it is not meant to convey any personal allusion whatever in any part or even a line of the book. The actualities of life or locality are referred to only and strictly so far as they belong to any of the varied conditions of life amongst our people. And even these are on occasions ideal. The ideal and actual are in some places inseparable.

Bombay
April 1887

G. M. T.

Preface II[†]

We live in times where the means of attaining eternal fame in this world are becoming frayed with each passing day. Human sensibility today is not what it was yesterday, and it will be different tomorrow from what it is today. It is difficult to imagine in the present what would be pleasing in the future. In this age of new discoveries every day, classical texts of today are rendered useless tomorrow. Similarly, that in these times of changing sensibilities, novels which by very character are ephemeral would acquire longevity and bind the author to the future through a chain of fame is a belief contrary to experience. Novels in the hands of readers have displaced plays that people watched. This example illustrates the argument. The lust for fame harboured in the writer's heart appears to be futile and lifeless, but its possibility enthuses him in the present. If the value of goods were to rest upon utility, it is a desired outcome. If this utility were to take its seat on the throne vacated by fame, it would possibly expand the scope of the fruits of literary endeavours and give to them a certain enduring significance. But the condition of the Western world and the shadows it casts on us is such that humans are enticed not by innate utility but outward beauty, thereby establishing what is secondary over the primary. But the fact is that beauty, however illusory, allows a thing to be assimilated easily; the beauty of illusion makes the aesthetic

[†] This is a translation of 'Prastavana', the Gujarati preface to the 1887 edition of Part 1 of the novel, reproduced from Tripathi, *Sarasvatichandra*, Part 1, trans. Tridip Suhrud, lv–lx.

sensibility refined, gives it higher aspiration and force; this makes the difference between human life, that acquires newer forms, and animal life sharper. But illusion merges in the essence—illusion seeks that essence—hence, the end of illusion is the beginning of the essential nature of a thing. As illusion disappears, essence must emerge; the egg-shell of illusion must give birth to new life that is essence. This one must not forget. Both women and the novel desire to be beautiful, but fulfilment of this desire must be a means to achieve higher goals. Striving for mere aesthetic pleasure is not only undesirable, it is futile—indeed it could be harmful—to attain that step and not rise upwards.

What then should be the essence of a novel? If one were to know in whose hands the novel would reach, from what perspective they would make use of it, the essence of a novel could be determined.

1. The seekers after truth read novels to study the psychology of the human mind.
2. Those with an assimilative intellect search in a novel aspects such as beauty and leave out the rest.

It is not that writers can relate to these two classes through the means of novels alone. This relationship can be forged through many forms, but one must not forget that these classes also take delight in novels, because among the reading classes they occupy the position of crown jewel. They are small in numbers, but their worship, their God-like control are accepted by all.

3. The number of readers in the third class is countless. They are drawn to reading novels for one or more of the following reasons:
   (a) The sense of anticipation that a story creates. This sensibility is present in all children; among women it is considered characteristic and some do not lose it even with advancing age.
   (b) Minds that have surrendered to stories of passion and women. Such minds become restive at the very sight of a novel and excessive intercourse with such novels eventually makes their minds impotent.

(c) The addiction of reading tales is similar to the addiction of opium or alcohol, it does not go away even after an effort.
(d) The toil of reading classical and obtuse texts. Many among the literate are lazy and after they emerge from the state of being a student, there is no one who counters their unwillingness to labour over a text.
(e) Uncultured sensibility about the classics.
(f) Illiteracy and leisure.

A large segment of both literate and illiterate classes makes up this last class, and this is the reason for the triumph of novels these days. It should be the purpose of a story teller to ponder over such matters and create something that would eventually not harm, in fact benefit, readers of all classes. The manliness of a virile writer is proven not by submitting to the sensibilities of readers but by submission to a nobler aesthetic, and in an endeavour to produce this sensibility in his readers.

The ability to administer wisdom by mixing it in the sense of anticipation of an enticing story, the skill of alluring feeble minds that can be led onto the good path through pictures of ideal lives, the dexterity of administering the potion of virtue to an addict of stories, the ability to produce industriousness among the lazy literati, to fill the enchanting pictures with substance from the classics and infuse the ideal with good aspirations and produce among the illiterate a sensibility for good life and many similar aims of poetry are not unknown to writers of India, and they are considered the epitome of cultivation in Europe as well. Our scriptures say that such stories counsel like a friend, like a woman.

Pandering to the ordinary class of readers might appear to be easy, but satisfying the seekers after truth and the assimilating classes is complex as the ability to cultivate the mind requires greater means and capabilities than the ability to be pleasing to the mind. The scholarly group can sift truth from what appears to be fiction, and to fill their hands with good things requires knowledge akin to the riches of a prosperous man. Some minds that appear to be entwined in this worldly affair have the capacity to enter spaces which remain unseen by others and experience deep poetry. Such consciousness is eager to hear the song of the heart in the midst of commonplace prose. To satisfy them requires the blessings of a pure poetic conscience. Those scholars who study society examine with minute gaze the canopy of a novel in search of history that stands out in the gathering like a groom. They also discern with whom morality, like a bride, would unite. In short, the scholarly class looks for thousands and thousands of details in a novel which inhabit the universe of the human mind. The preceding one is only an example of this quest. If this class can be satisfied even on rare occasions, it would be a matter of great satisfaction.

Such is the pure essence of a novel. It is true that a story should have illusory capacity, but that is secondary. A form bereft of essence is lifeless and its consumption, harmful. The comparison of the extent to which this novel has been able to preserve essence and form should be left to the assessors. And yet, it would add to the story if certain special objectives of the writer are alluded to here.

This novel entwines like a garland of flowers more than one story. The secondary hero draws attention to himself before the hero of the novel makes unambiguous appearance. This breaks the norm prevalent in Europe that the story line must be harmonious and continuous, but it does uphold the divine law of history which introduces many stories in one narrative. It is not the principal objective of this novel to uphold artificial norms. The endeavour is to present a picture of the divine play.

Some books consider it their duty to draw attention only to the impure passions of man. It is true that in God's creation these impure passions have a place; but our life does not find fruition in these passions; scholars have other means available—in the classical texts—to find pictures of these passions and therefore, to the extent possible, the dreary drudgery of etching impure pictures has been kept at a distance in this novel.

If humans, who must rise above, are shown the topmost step of a ladder, it is likely that they would lose courage. But merely showing the base ground also does not accomplish movement upwards. For these reasons the characters of the novel are not supreme, or else readers would see them as merely fictitious and imaginary and not consider emulating their example. At the same time the characters are not so commonplace and everyday that they can neither enthuse anyone nor show the upward path. We have drawn pictures of humans who are subject to our ordinary passions and failings—frailties that need to be pardoned—and yet struggling against them, endeavouring to steady them and rise above their present condition. The attempt is not to find kindred feelings in weak human beings for others who are weak like them. But rather, the path adopted is to suggest possible ways of swimming against the current in the worldly sea. In order to do this it has become necessary to bring in, like black marks, descriptions of impure passions while drawing pictures of unsullied persons as the observation of these impurities allows for a truer measure of the glory of purity.

An attempt has been made to depict the conditions and the evolution of men and women living in light, as also in shadow and in dusk—like a state in-between knowledge, wealth, power, autonomy and purity. So that each reader is able to identify with some character and acquire an exemplar. Human beings are an amalgam of good and bad. There is nothing in the world that is unsullied goodness or pure evil. This complex composition has been shown here and through it, experiential wisdom has been shared.

The time that the story occupies is very close to our times and it is located within the people of Gujarat. This would enable us to hear more clearly the echoes of the past, view the present without obstruction and possibilities of the future to be intertwined, and those aspiring for the uplift of the country would find some suggestions.

Other objectives would become apparent to an assessor, and only then would they be considered fulfilled. So believing, they have not been narrated here.

Vasant
Vikramsamvat 1943
Bombay

G. M. T.

1 On the Outskirts of Manoharpuri

Manoharpuri is about ten miles from Suvarnapur. In ancient times it was a great city and the capital of learned, independent and able kings. Over time, these kings were vanquished by the mleccha. All that remained of this once glorious and flourishing city was a village, and with that its name also came to be corrupted—people called it Manohariyu or Manoriyu. In the present time, it formed part of the territories of the kingdom of Ratnanagari.

The Karbhari of Ratnanagari, Vidya Chatura was born in this same village. Vidya Chatura's maternal family and his wife Gunasundari's parents belonged to this village. The couple had spent their childhood and adolescence here. For this and other reasons, they were both very attached to Manoharpuri. The village had revived through their efforts and was well looked after by the Karbhari, who was learned and endowed with a historical sensibility.

Albeit its manmade glory had been destroyed, the village was still widely known for its natural beauty. Manoharpuri was situated on the borders of Suvarnapur, Ratnanagari and the territories of British India. On its west was the sea, forming a natural boundary. The westerly winds brought cool breezes which eased the impossible heat of summer. On its eastern side, there was a large mango grove, huge banyan trees and sugarcane fields. To its north were the hills of Sundargiri. It was flanked by dense forests on the other two sides. Tall taad trees on the southern side enhanced the beauty of the village. A tributary of river Subhadra meandered through the region from the east to the south. The river nurtured a diversity of flora and fauna in the forest. Leaves and fruits of the teak trees were carried by its sluggish flow until it met with the sea.

It was Shukla Paksha, the fortnight of the waxing moon in the month of Chaitra which signalled the passage of spring and the onset of summer. The mango grove was fragrant with mango blossoms. The road from Suvarnapur, which separated the grove from the taad forest, skirted around the forest to reach Manoharpuri. Dusk, hitherto hidden in the forest, now emerged fearlessly to roll the sun down behind the taad trees. The rays of the setting sun lingered over the tree tops as their long yellowish green leaves fluttered like so many flags.

At this hour, a slow-moving cart could be seen on the dusty but now cool road. Dear reader, this was the selfsame cart in which Sarasvatichandra had set out from Rajeshwar Mahadev. The cart driver was also the same; but neither Sarasvatichandra nor the other passengers were to be seen in the cart. The lone ascetic who was last seen walking alongside the cart now sat inside it. The bullocks who knew nothing of the events that had taken place in the interim were glad to carry a lighter load and pulled with renewed vigour as they neared their resting place. The cart driver and the ascetic joked and laughed with each other as the cart moved along lurching noisily. The ascetic's staff which he had carried in his hand while walking now rested on one side of the cart; one end of it was smeared with blood. The driver appeared calm and composed but the ascetic seemed anxious, his alert eyes constantly darting in all directions.

The three riders who had been following the cart from Suvarnapur were nowhere to be seen. They were part of the contingent that had gone to Suvarnapur to accompany Kumud Sundari on her proposed journey to Bhadreshwar. Concerned by Sarasvatichandra's sudden departure, Kumud Sundari had sent Abdullah, Fatehsinh and Harbhamji to follow him. The beating of drums and the shouting had also ceased.

The mango grove was in British territory. The teak forest was in the territory of Suvarnapur. The road led to Manoharpuri. Roads from three directions met at that spot. A lane oriented east to west met the road that came from the south. As darkness descended to embrace the earth, the cart now lurched to a halt under a banyan tree at this three-way junction as instructed by the ascetic. The cart driver unyoked the bullocks and he and the ascetic conversed softly in the falling dark. The moon peeped out briefly from the clouds and withdrew.

Cart driver: 'Thakore, let me go now. The danger is three-fold here. You are a free man, but I will lose my house and all else besides!'

Ascetic: 'Be quiet! My right leg pains to the bone. That Harbham's blow was hard. I cannot walk. I need to cross the mango grove and reach Virpur. I need you to take me there in your cart.'

Cart driver: 'And which father of yours is going to give you shelter in Virpur? Rana Khachar will arrest us both and hand us over.'

Ascetic: 'Never! You do not know the reach of this Sursinh. These hands have rocked Bhupsinh's throne and given sleepless nights to Buddhidhan. Wait for two days and watch the havoc I wreck.'

Cart driver: 'What will you do in Virpur?'

Sursinh: 'Rana Khachar is our supporter. You have no cause for worry. He might say whatever he likes to the British and write all the reports they want, but he won't allow even a hair on my body to be harmed.'

Cart driver: 'And what do you intend to do with those brahmin and bania passengers?'

Sursinh evaded the query. Just then a bugle was heard in the distance. Sursinh responded with a fox-like call. In a short while, footfalls could be heard. Sursinh went and stood near the hanging roots of the banyan and lit his clay pipe. Soon, some men approached the tree and sat down under it. One of them sat near the hanging roots to keep watch along with the cart driver.

There were no strangers among them. They opened their heart and spoke freely. There was a soft rustle of leaves from above as if someone were hiding in the tree. Sursinh looked up sharply, straining his ears to catch the slightest sound as he lit his pipe again. Just the wind. Reassured, he joined in the conversation. Something shone like a fire fly in the light of his pipe but no one noticed. As the darkness enveloped them, the outlaws became engrossed in their talk. The wind carried their softly spoken words upwards.

2 The Outlaws

In a short time, about fifty to seventy-five persons gathered under the banyan tree. No one spoke at first. Only footfalls and the clink of weapons broke the silence. One man lit a torch and went around to each man present, peering closely at their faces to ascertain their identity. He then sat down close to Sursinh. Four or five men with lit torches stood encircling the group. Four others with loaded guns stood guard around the banyan. All of them had stout bodies. Some were short, some were tall and some broad, but all of them looked brave. They carried an assortment of weapons; some were of olden times while others were of more recent make. Four elderly and two young garasias sat in a circle around Sursinh along with a brahmin.

The elder of the two young men spoke first. 'Bapa, Buddhidhan is caught in our net. His son's wife has set out for Bhadreshwar. If Goddess Amba is with us, she will be in our clutches by early morning. We will capture her right here at this banyan tree. He has snatched away our Dhirpur, but he will not be able to stomach it. It will be like a fly he has swallowed.'

The brahmin came closer and said, 'Thakore, Pratapsinh Bapu is right, but you must listen to what a brahmin has to say. If you take that woman captive, you will make another enemy. You will gain nothing by making an enemy of Ratnanagari. The decision is yours, but mine is the counsel of a cautious brahmin.'

Pratapsinh's younger and more intelligent brother Vaghji said, 'Bapa, Shankar Maharaj is right. It is our norm that we do not harass women and children. People support us because of our adherence to these norms. If we do what Pratapjibhai suggests, we will lose their support'.

Pratapsinh spoke up angrily, 'Vaghji, you are still incapable of thinking right! Rana Khachar harbours greater enmity towards Vidya Chatura than towards Bhupsinh. Therefore, he extends greater support to Samant Mulu than he does to us. If we were to join hands with Samant Mulu, Khachar would support us even more'.

Vaghji looked at his brother, perplexed. Maniraj was the king of Ratnanagari. Samant Mulu was waging a baharvatu against him. Kumud Sundari was Vidya Chatura's daughter; taking her captive would have strengthened the friendship between Sursinh and Samant Mulu. This was obvious, but it was not the real motive behind Pratapsinh's suggestion. He was a lascivious man; he wanted to satisfy his desire for Kumud by capturing her. His father's interest was secondary to his passion. Sursinh understood what Vaghji alluded to. He felt differently.

Sursinh was a bhayat, a cousin of Jadsinh. Shathrai had snatched away Dhirpur from him. Denied justice, Sursinh had taken to baharvatu and become an outlaw. Bhupsinh and Sursinh had once shared an affectionate relationship. Sursinh expected that his garas would be reinstated to him once Bhupsinh became the ruler. But Shathrai was careful not to allow the two cousins to meet. Last year, Sursinh had sent a secret message to Bhupsinh, to which Bhupsinh had replied: 'Be patient. It will be done in due course of time'. Sursinh had refrained from causing any harm to Bhupsinh. Bhupsinh wanted to get rid of Shathrai before taking any action. Sursinh was unaware of this; his patience ran its course and goaded and encouraged by Shathrai, he started robbing people so as to intimidate Bhupsinh and force his hand. Sursinh's plan was to get his men to hold Kumud Sundari captive but conceal his own participation in the plot. His intention was to ensure Kumud Sundari's safe return and thereby regain his garas from a grateful and frightened Buddhidhan in exchange for her. Pratap cared little for his father's wishes. If his desires were to be thwarted, Pratap was capable of spoiling the entire plan. Sursinh wanted to keep both his sons quiet. He ignored their advice and asked an elderly band member, 'Bhimji, so what news have you brought for us? Chandandas, do also update us'.

Bhimji was an elderly garasia. His Rajput blood had cooled with age and wisdom. He had joined ranks with Sursinh out of pure and selfless affection. He was a leader of a special group of outlaws and trusted by all members of the group. He was in charge of the bordering regions of Ratnanagari and Suvarnapur. It was Bhimji who had attacked the carriage by which Chandrakant was travelling. Chandandas, though a bania, was a stout warrior. Through his close contact with Rajputs, he had also acquired some of their qualities. The only difference was that he did not like to use force until he had exhausted all possibilities of conciliation, bribery and dissension to win over an adversary. It was contrary to his nature to pick up a quarrel, unless his interest was violated.

When the cart carrying Sarasvatichandra left the fields behind and reached the part where the mango grove and taad forests began, it was about three in the afternoon. Chandandas was hiding in the forest with his group of outlaws and waiting for Sursinh, who had gone to ascertain the situation in Suvarnapur disguised as an ascetic. Sursinh had met Shathrai in the prison. He had established direct contact with Garbaddas and arranged for an exchange of letters. He knew that Sarasvatichandra was among the select group that had met at the Suvarnapur palace on the evening of the fateful day. He had assumed that capturing Sarasvatichandra would be advantageous for them, and had followed the cart. When the cart reached the forest area, Sursinh walked faster and overtook the cart. On a signal from him, Chandandas came out of hiding and attacked the cart with eight outlaws. One man cut loose the bullocks. The cart driver stood aside shaking with fear and said, 'Bapa! The bania, brahmin passengers are no match for you. Do not kill or hurt unnecessarily. They will give you whatever they have and will do as told. I am just a poor cart driver'. One outlaw picked up the bania and flung him to the ground. The bania started to weep loudly. The young woman was frightened. In her hurry to climb out of the cart as told, she fell down. A few ornaments on her body fell to the ground and two outlaws promptly gathered them. Stunned by her fall and fear, the young woman could neither move nor speak. Her tongue got caught between her teeth and she sobbed helplessly. One man caught the poor woman by her neck and pinned her down; she all but lost consciousness.

The old woman proved to be the most astute. She had some money tied in a small cloth; it was easy to conceal it in her clothes. She left all her belongings in the cart and climbed out. She stood to one side and said, 'Bha, I have come out with nothing but the clothes on my body. All my belongings are inside. Take whatever you want. I am a brahmin, I should be seeking alms from you. But take whatever you like if you ought to do so.'

'Shut up, old wretch!' One outlaw came forward to slap her. But she moved away and meekly said, 'Bha, kill me if you want to. I will die in a year or two anyway. Death can come today if you so wish. You too shall be old one day. Like me, may you live to be a hundred years old, son.' The outlaw was taken aback by this speech. He glared at the old woman sternly, but he let her be. The old woman thought, If I try to flee now, I will be in danger. But if I just stand quietly, what can they do to me? She sat down on a stone by the roadside and watched the spectacle in silence.

Sarasvatichandra, as you will recall dear reader, was fast asleep in the cart. A dhoti covered him from head to toe. His body was still feverish from the heat and dust of the journey, and his mind, with thoughts of Kumud Sundari. The dream-filled sleep had quietened him somewhat when the sudden commotion jolted him awake. He saw the bania couple in trouble and jumped to the young woman's aid. He knew he was powerless against the outlaws, yet he somehow managed to free the woman from the outlaw's grasp. But he was promptly encircled by the men. How could an unarmed, delicate young man confront a gang of outlaws?

Sursinh watched all this from a distance, amused. He laughed and said, 'Chandandas, now stop this drama. Let the women go. Take the men captive. Chandarbhai, I know you well. Go with them.'

Sarasvatichandra was angry but did not know what to make of it all. He stood there, clenching his fists.

'Chandarbhai, we don't want to rob you. I know who you are. I have some work with you. Please go with them.'

Sarasvatichandra stood there unmoving.

Sursinh saw three riders approaching and shouted an alert, 'Chandan, get going now. Drag this young man away and keep an eye on him. If he doesn't listen, use force. He is a wretched brahmin, won't budge without a beating'.

As Sarasvatichandra was being dragged away by Chandandas and his men, the three riders reached the spot. Sursinh challenged them to a fight. Sarasvatichandra struggled to free himself from his captors. Sursinh hit him hard with his staff and knocked him unconscious and bleeding. The outlaws swiftly carried away his inert body with the three riders in hot pursuit. We know that Sursinh was also hurt by a blow on his calf and that he travelled by the cart.

But what happened to Sarasvatichandra? Chandandas had not brought him to the meeting under the banyan tree. Kumud Sundari had sent three riders to follow Sarasvatichandra. They were only three, but they were brave, carried superior weapons and were riding sturdy horses. They pursued the outlaws energetically. The outlaws were certainly more in number; but they were all foot soldiers, they had gone hungry for three days, their weapons were no match for the riders and they were weary of ten long years of futile baharvatu. They had joined Sursinh's band out of false pride. They found carrying two men burdensome, pointless and dangerous while being pursued by powerful riders. Chandandas thought like a bania. He could not imagine that Sursinh could have any other motive but robbery for capturing these travellers. These men are beggars, he thought, let them be. He dumped them on a grassy patch of land and fled. The riders did not realise that Chandandas had abandoned Sarasvatichandra. They followed Chandandas who made good his escape. Dejected, the riders gave up the chase and headed towards Manoharpuri.

A hesitant and frightened Chandandas now related all these events to Sursinh under the banyan tree. Having heard his account, Sursinh said, 'Chandandas, you are brave, but you are a bania after all. You may understand something of political matters, but you think like a trader. You acted within the limits of your capabilities. It is for the king to judge if the person he assigns to a task is capable of fulfilling it. You did what you were capable of. It is not your shortcoming. The mistake was mine that I gave you the task. Truly, for ten long years I have ceased to be a ruler and become an outlaw. How can I think like a ruler? If I had any intelligence and foresight left, what could I have not achieved in company of brave and proud associates like all of you?' Sursinh was dejected. The big chance had slipped out of his hands. He turned to Bhimji. 'Bhimji Bha, do you have anything better to report? Fate helps those who are ascendant and turns against those who are falling. Tell us, no matter how unpleasant the news might be.'

Old Bhimji came forward. He looked straight at Sursinh and spoke: 'Sursinh, your father faced much greater hardships. But he was not weak-hearted like you. He was strong. If you are defeated by so little, what will you achieve? It is your duty to give courage to others. Bapa, aren't you, the son of a Rajput, ashamed of such weak words? Those who ride a horse will fall. Those who never do so will not. Be patient. You may have to endure fifty years in such a state. At least the forest gives us food. What if you had to go into hiding in the barren mountain caves for a few years? Will a bania or a brahmin ever face such hardship? A Rajput is not a Rajput just by wielding a sword. A Rajput can laugh in the face of hardship, the greater the hardship, the greater his resolve. He gains his strength from suffering. A Rajput may worry about himself alone, but a Rajput king worries about the welfare of his subjects, too. Haven't you seen a lion cub growl at dark rain clouds? Sursinh, you are a lion cub. Remember who you are. Remember your father. Your mother. The family you belong to. So long as you do not give up this soft-heartedness of a bania-brahmin and be true to yourself and to your ancestors, I will say nothing. If you are such a weakling, the sun may well rise in the west. Who would see you as a Rajput? If I be with you, I would defile myself. I may be old, but I am a Rajput. I served your father, and I served you as long as you remained a Rajput. Let out a roar and prove that you are still the brave fearless Sursinh I once knew. I have nothing more to say till then.' Bhimji turned his back towards Sursinh and sat down.

Sursinh caught the old man's shoulder and pleaded with him, 'Bhimji Bha!'

'Bapa, I don't wish to be either a father or a mother figure to you. I recognise only Rajputs as kin and no one else. Tell me that Sursinh has not lost his courage.'

Sursinh got up and faced Bhimji. He held Bhimji's hands and said, 'Bhimji Bha, rise! I acted like a bania with a bania. Don't think that I too have become one. Chandandas, if you do not have raging hot blood in you, open your veins and take some of mine. It is true that when the chief of an army loses heart, his army is certain to be destroyed. An army is a fighting body; its chief is the soul. The chief's valour is the hot blood that flows through his army. That blood runs in my veins. I am not going to accept Bhupsinh's promises. The Karbhari can be anyone—Shathrai or Buddhidhan. How does that concern me? My only objective is to reclaim Dhirpur. My group has been wandering in the wilderness for ten long years. My soul tells me that this is about to end. Bhimji Bha, forget everything else and tell us what we should do and where we should use our force. My young blood can fight, but it needs the guidance of the old'.

Bhimji stood up, embraced Sursinh and asked, 'What is to be done?'

The hot Rajput blood cooled somewhat. 'Bha, war is not about jumping into fire. Some people were on their way from Ratnanagari to Suvarnapur. We robbed them. But at times, the fate of the outlaws also forsakes them. They had nothing apart from these bags. The bags contained clothes in the style of sahibs and some papers. We kept the goods and let the people go. We had hoped to be able to buy at least food to last us fifteen days. But these clothes and papers are so useless even a bania won't buy them from us. I feel that we should stop striking in the air. We are not so strong that we can bring the ruler to his knees just by robbing people. We have men, but hungry legs and unarmed hands have no power. We must change our tactics. We should take Shathrai's help. Earlier we robbed his money; now we should accept what he gives. We should be careful about the information he gives us. Bhupsinh may make promises, but once he has the throne, he and us cannot be equal. We should enter the palace with Shathrai's help one night and take what we want. But the time is not ripe for such an adventure.

'I like Pratap Bapu's proposal. There is some merit in Vaghji's caution, but once Buddhidhan is in our grip, we can get him to do what we want, can't we? Even Vidya Chatura will not hesitate in satisfying our demands. We must look after his daughter well once we capture her. If we do that, she may have a good word to say about us once she is released. If that happens, the enmity would come to an end. Vaghji Bha, do you have any objection? If anyone else has different views, voice them now.'

Vaghji did not reply. The others sat in quiet anticipation. Sursinh turned to Bhimji and softly said, 'Shathrai is useless for the present. I found that out yesterday'.

Bhimji responded aloud, 'We must do as decided. We should not waste this opportunity'.

The whole group got up. Sursinh announced, 'We shall meet early in the morning on this side of the Subhadra river. Bhimji, you take position in the ravines. Chandandas, you keep watch over this road; you must signal when you see the party approach. One man should hide in a large leafy tree near the bridge on the river with a drum. All must act on the signal of the drum. Pratap, you hide in the mango grove and come out at the right time. Vaghji, you guard this side of the banyan tree. I will move around in all directions. All men must stay dispersed and come together only when the time is right. It is beyond doubt that Lord Shankar is with us. Our years of hardship are about to end.

'Chandandas, I spent the day in Suvarnapur. Our plan will bear fruit. Kumud Sundari is accompanied by only about ten riders from Ratnanagari. There is a difference though; we are like paupers while they are well-armed. Some of Buddhidhan's men may be with the group as well. We must be cautious. If we do not succeed in our plan tomorrow, we shall never succeed. Then we must give up all hopes of Dhirpur. My brave companions, my brothers, you have stood beside me for years in sorrow and hardship. You have wandered through woods and forests with me. You have for my sake walked on thorns.

You have waged battles in the sinking mud of the river. You have stayed without shade in the blazing heat of summer and without warmth in the bitter cold of winter. You have waded through quicksand and braved torrential rains. You have not been frightened by the roars of lions. You have gone hungry for days and faced starvation even in absence of a famine. You have been shelterless at home and away from home. You have not met your wives nor served your parents. You have spent so many years in such harsh conditions. How can I ever repay you? You have done so much for me. I ask you for this one last thing: capture the enemy so I can give to you your due happiness! Our trials and woes are about to end! Jai Ambe! Jogini Maiya, we cannot do without your blessings. Jogini! Amba! Bhavani! Jai, Jai!'

All shouted in unison, 'Ambe Mata ki jai!' Their voices pierced the night and the darkness trembled. Talking excitedly among themselves, the outlaws dispersed. Only two men stayed back.

The villagers of Manoharpuri had for long seen torch flames come together under the old banyan on some nights and had heard voices. They believed it was the ghosts of soldiers long dead. Hence, no one was suspicious of these gatherings.

Soon, silence reigned under the banyan tree once more. Vaghji and Shankar Maharaj sat in the dark, speaking in low voices. 'Vaghji Bapu, it seems your brother's ploy has worked. Sursinh Bapa has not realised that Pratap lusts after Kumud Sundari.'

'Shankar, I know that. I will not be able to go where the confrontation is to take place, or else I would have taken control of the situation. I must do the task I am assigned. You go. I will go and meet father.' Saying so, Vaghji left.

Alone, Shankar Maharaj talked aloud to himself: Buddhidhanbhai, these people have failed to recognise you. I must go and warn the group accompanying Kumud Sundari. These people do not know your generosity, Buddhidhanbhai. They will now know your wrath. So be it. I know what I must do. Saying so, the athletic brahmin warrior moved like a gazelle through the dark and disappeared.

Someone quietly slid down the tree.

3 The Injured Man

The endeavour to transform the pining lover
into a renouncer has begun.
You can see it all, and yet you cry foolishly!
Having forsaken riches as illusion, what is it
you now seek to grasp?
You can see it all, and yet you cry foolishly!

Chandandas and his men abandoned Sarasvatichandra and the bania on the grassy knoll. Sarasvatichandra was bleeding from his hand and still unconscious. But not a hair on the cunning bania's body was harmed.

The bania was a resident of Ratnanagari. His name was Aarthdas. He belonged to a family of petty grocers but he had made some money from speculation. He was hooked to it and had amassed about forty, fifty thousand rupees. His fortune turned; he lost his all and incurred debts. He tried his luck in Bombay, but failed. He chanced his hand at different things in different places, but to no avail. During his few days of prosperity, he married a dark-complexioned woman called Dhankaur. His family had a low social standing and hence had to pay about eight thousand rupees to Dhankaur's father as the bride price for the marriage. Dhankaur had amassed about eight thousand rupees by sheer duplicity. She had lied, stolen and demanded money from her husband, and did not let him lay a finger on the money. And today, Dhankaur was lost along with all the ornaments on her body. As Sarasvatichandra lay unconscious and bleeding, Aarthdas mourned his misfortune. When he married Dhankaur she was seven or eight years of age, and eleven when she came to live with him. She was sly, lied easily and was greedy. Aarthdas was a good match for her. The man wouldn't part with a pie, while she would want to steal two pies from him. He would scold her, but secretly he felt pleased. The rand is clever, he thought. She is cunning enough even to fool me! Let her steal and hide all she wants. When the creditors come and take it all, what she has amassed will stay. But Dhankaur proved to be so covetous that she wouldn't part with a pie even if her husband were about to die. Aarthdas tried all his tricks, but in vain. He accepted defeat but felt satisfied. The rand is a tough nut to crack, he thought; she is the perfect match for me.

Dhankaur was a consummate miser. She was a terror in the house. She could even make her mother-in-law weep; she would not allow the husband's sister to cross the threshold of her house; she would mock the elder sister-in-law and get the younger one to do all the household chores. She would bark like a rabid bitch at her brother-in-law and then go and weep copious tears before her husband. Thus she ruled over the house. Dhankaur had one quality, however—she was not debauched. Her tendency to lie had created a genuine possibility that she would become debauched. But Aarthdas had given her a free rein in the house. She became so immersed in the household that her other tendencies had no scope of flourishing. Her greed for money overpowered her lust. So, though an annoying nag, Dhankaur was respected and tolerated by everyone in the household because she never budged an inch when she was right. Aarthdas was anxious about her. Who knows where she is now, how she is, but that rand has all the ornaments. Manoharpuri is nearby; there is nothing to worry about. But she is a woman after all; her body and her ornaments are both endangered. The rand will get a good and proper thrashing today. The outlaws must have given her a hard time. But she is a good match for them. Let her face some hardship; the bitch has tied up all her money and won't give me any even to buy poison with. But then all her gold ornaments will be robbed. And however bad she might be, she is still childlike, isn't she? What will they do to her? Alas, I won't ever get another like her! Aarthdas' mind was buzzing with such varied and contrary thoughts. He glanced at Sarasvatichandra lying unconscious on the ground and felt sorry. He decided to revive him. Then he thought, Is he alive or dead? Shouldn't I better go home? What if other outlaws arrive? Why should I invite trouble for myself? Then he remembered that it was while trying to rescue Dhankaur that Sarasvatichandra got wounded. His sense of gratitude proved more powerful than his selfishness. The bania approached the unconscious brahmin, his heart brimming with compassion.

Sarasvatichandra had lost a lot of blood, but for some reason he had stopped bleeding. Aarthdas brought some water from a pond nearby, sprinkled it on Sarasvatichandra's face and revived him. Sarasvatichandra opened his eyes and looked around the unfamiliar place. He seemed timid, frail and sorry. The weakness of injury, fever, fatigue, hunger and being in strange surroundings had given rise to this disoriented state. His father's hurtful words still echoed in his ears; he had found the ill-will towards Kumud Sundari intolerable; he had wept like a child before Chandrakant; he had abandoned immense wealth and luxuries; he was heartbroken when he had to abandon Kumud Sundari. And yet in his moment of renunciation, he had not once regretted his decision or hesitated. His faith in God was so deep that he never asked the question: What will become of Kumud Sundari? His innate sense of renunciation was strengthened by his Indian learning while his Western education had given him the autonomy and the will to take the final step.

Sarasvatichandra, as we know, was born into wealth. This wealth had made his desire for renunciation so acute that to many, he appeared haughty. To his mind, wealthy merchants or gentlemen with a vast following were like subalterns who had earned some familiarity with the British. Even prostitutes possessed both wealth and admirers, he knew; he therefore did not consider his wealth and admirers of great value. He believed that high British officials, governors and even princes were mere playthings in the hands of time. He described newspapers and writers as 'bards of reform' and considered them useful only to that extent. But he refused to consider their views any more important than views expressed by a friend or even by a rank commoner during conversation. He knew very well how the world would judge his adventure; he knew the opinions that the advocates of both the old and new ways of thinking would advance. His dearest friend Chandrakant had also put forth his views; yet Sarasvatichandra had remained steadfast in his decision. We know this. Sarasvatichandra believed that Time was like a great potter who created difficult situations which produced in men a sense of their own insignificance and smallness. This sense of insignificance also corresponds to one's external context. Under different circumstances, individuals fail to realise that they are embodied beings and to recognise their own insignificance as also the salience of others. Sarasvatichandra knew that this was true for him as well. A person who was important in one context was not so in another. There was hierarchy and a sense of high and low everywhere. Born into wealth, he imagined that all the wealthy were suffused with nobility. These ideas had matured with education and age. His learning, his poetic imagination told him that a sense of inadequacy and a sense of nobility could not exist together at one place. 'To possess a sense of relative importance and unimportance of persons, things and events was a sign of inadequacy, and to be conscious of the world and its joys was the only true wealth, the only sign of nobility.' Sarasvatichandra was possessed by this definition. Its power had startled his mind and dragged him into deep dark difficulties. We must still wait for the divine being who shall tell us how our schools and universities show stars to our youth and lead them astray. In such a situation, those who are mere spectators of this drama may find the movement of the actors magical. How is the world, in deep slumber of night, to imagine what the next day will be like? They might even consider the unfolding events and actors as merely imaginary. Until the curtain rises and the drama begins to unfold, for a spectator it is all imaginary. In countries where the curtain has been lifted and the drama has begun, it has seemed strange to onlookers. The same strangeness will be felt in this country as well. Only God can tell what the offspring of this inter-racial marriage of Sanskrit knowledge and Western learning will be like. Sarasvatichandra imagined himself to be a child of just such a marriage. He could do the unexpected, tread paths untrodden because of his nobility. He now described his renunciation as an act of nobility. To be an aesthete but also a renouncer, to put his sacrifice on trial, to visit Suvarnapur to test his hypothesis that Kumud would adjust to the new situation, forget her past and be happy—all these acts were a test of his own character and nobility. It was not his intention to be a cause of Kumud's sorrow; that was accidental. He realised that: I have been the cause of so much sorrow, and that bodily passions are difficult to curb. With this realisation came the understanding that: I am foolish, my nobility lacks something, and human beings are inherently weak. He had experienced strongly conflicting emotions at the time of leaving home, attachment and dislike, anger and sorrow; and yet his act of renunciation was also the result of a deeply felt need. Therefore despite deep sorrow, he had hitherto not felt a sense of inadequacy. He felt inadequate and meek now as he regained consciousness. He was utterly alone; he had no one to turn to except the vast sky above and the expanse of earth below. There were trees all around if they could provide him any succour. Sarasvatichandra remembered Kumud Sundari, and for the first time in his life he truly pined for her. It was his first realisation of the hardships he must confront. His body cried out in pain. Richness of mind seemed to him at that moment like smoke—forever beyond grasp.

Oh sage, I do not want your knowledge
The hungry child craves food, bring that and I will touch your feet

Thirsty, feverish, frail and fatigued, the unhappy man looked at the wounds on his body and felt even more wretched. He stared at Aarthdas who seemed to be saying: You reap what you sow. His vacant mind went into a spin when he realised that there was no one who would take pity on him, for they had no reason to. He realised there was no one who would come to his rescue. He felt abandoned even by God. He remembered the lines of an English poet.

And thorns of life; forgetting the great end
Of poesy, that it should be a friend
To soothe the cares, and lift the thoughts of man.[1]

Once he had wealth to match Kuber, luxuries to match Indra, respect among men of learning, prestige in a city like Bombay, the companionship of a true friend like Chandrakant, and the divine fragrance of Kumud that combined with the power of renunciation and a sublime song of love. But all that was in the past. What was he now? There was no one in the world from whom he could even beg; he was a beggar among beggars. He did not even possess the ash that a mendicant smears on his body to protect himself from heat and cold. Even fools did not respect him and his social standing was so low that he was abandoned in the forest like a dead fox. In place of a friend he had the bania for a companion, and in place of Kumud, a heartless, dark forest. In place of the serenity of renunciation, he had an orphaned mind and a body in pain. Love had given way to heart-wrenching repentance. Sarasvatichandra felt such emotions surge like waves in his unsteady mind. 'Keats! Keats! How true you were! Even you had such experiences?' He spoke these words out aloud and startled the bania.

Aarthdas went up to Sarasvatichandra and helped him to sit up. He examined Sarasvatichandra's wounds and pressed something like cotton to the wounds. Then he asked, 'Do these outlaws know you? That man disguised as an ascetic had spoken your name'. Aarthdas recalled that the outlaws had called the injured man Chandarbhai. 'Chandabhai!' he addressed him, 'Such is the grace of Thakorji that your wounds are as good as healed. Here, take this'.

Sarasvatichandra felt revived at the mere mention of healed wounds. He sat up straight, pondering this further corruption of his name. He asked the bania, 'Bhai, what is this?'

'It is called gha bajariyu, a grass that heals wounds. It grows in this grass and it got stuck to your wounds and stopped the bleeding.'

'Oh, is that its quality?'

[1] Author's note: 'Sleep and Poetry,' John Keats.

'Yes, it heals wounds; your wounds are as good as healed. Are you in pain now?'

'No, in fact there is none.' Sarasvatichandra was overcome with gratitude. He looked up to the sky with misty eyes and murmured to himself,

> *Lord, you ease our trials and tribulations,*
> *Never taking to heart our foolish ways*
> *As I lay unconscious in the forest,*
> *You took on the form of this healing grass.*

This prayer came to him by itself. He felt a new energy and excitement surge through him, as if God Himself had come to reside in his sad eyes, subdued heart and excited mind. Hitherto he had found all the prayers contained in books, in societies and temples dry and empty of meaning. His suffering had given him his first glimpses of divinity. Sarasvatichandra looked at the bania with grateful eyes, his heart filled with reverence, and the awareness that the bania had acquainted him with his own worthlessness. In a state like that of Dattatreya, he came to believe that the bania had guided him to the path of God; he was the guru who had helped him see God face to face. 'Bhai, what is your name?' he asked.

The bania was the kind who would give away nothing for free. This proved to be a tough question for him. He thought, That ascetic in disguise knew his name. What if this man is also one of those outlaws? Aarthdas is not so stupid as to reveal his name. He laughed to himself, evaded the question and asked a string of counter-questions, 'Chandabhai, you will now feel better; it will just take a little longer. But how did you fall in with these people? What is your business? Which native village do you come from? Where are you going?'

'You know well where I have come from and you have seen how I came to be in this state.'

'But what is your business?'

'Business? Eat, drink and travel.'

'Oh, is that so?' The bania became even more suspicious, even fearful. 'And where do you intend to go from here?'

'Wherever my fate takes me, bhai. I will gladly come with you if you allow me to; both of us are hungry.'

Aarthdas said to himself: This man is certainly an outlaw. He wants to come to my house. But then why did he jump to her rescue and invite injury? Who knows! He could be an informer of the outlaws and that could explain his behaviour. A fish of selfish waters, the bania could neither imagine nor comprehend selflessness in any form.

Sarasvatichandra enquired once again, 'Bhai, will you take me home with you? I will prove useful to you. I am a stranger in these parts, but you must be well acquainted with all roads'.

Aarthdas muttered to himself, Hah! Take you home and invite death? I am Aarthdas. You can't fool me. I am more than a match for you. But he said, 'Of course, why not? But on the condition that my wife must be returned to me'.

Perplexed, Sarasvatichandra replied, 'But bhai, how can I do that! Let us go to your house and I will certainly help you look for her'.

So crafty! Aarthdas thought and said aloud, 'All right, Chandabhai. How long can we stay here anyway? Let us go towards the village,' telling himself, I will take you straight to the Ratnanagari police. After that they can deal with you.

They got up and began to walk towards Ratnanagari. On the way, Aarthdas started his drama. He suddenly sat down on the road and started wailing, 'Oh mother! What will happen to you now?'

Sarasvatichandra was utterly baffled, but tried to comfort the man nevertheless. 'What is it, bhai? What happened to your mother?'

'Oh, they have taken away my wife. The poor woman must be in a wretched state ... Oh mother! Oh my poor wife!'

'Be patient, bhai. Let us go to the village. I am sure we will find a way out.'

'But she has the ornaments! That is all the wealth I have! I don't even have a pie to buy poison with. How will I pay the rent? What will I eat? I will have to sell the utensils and everything else. With what will I pay the grocer? How will I pay the state to mount a search for my wife? Oh Chandabhai, I must give up my life right here!'

Sarasvatichandra tried everything he could, but Aarthdas refused to budge. He went on moaning and wailing, 'I will hang myself right here. If God had made me a brahmin, I could have lived on alms. My stomach churns. I can't get up. I can't speak. Oh Chandabhai, a ... bab ... ab ...' The bania pretended as if his tongue had got stuck. He lay down in the dust, rolling his eyes and dribbling from his mouth.

Sarasvatichandra thought: What can I do to relieve this man's misery? Even my hunger has vanished in his wretchedness. He is not sorry for the loss of his wife. He is bemoaning the loss of his wealth. I had enough riches to end all his miseries, but that I have given up. Little did I realise that wealth could be so useful in ways. God has not given him learning; he was also not born into wealth. My nobility has turned to dust. His only remedy is money. From where shall I get money? If I had not given up my wealth, such a day would never have come. He looked at Aarthdas again and thought, But if I had not given up my wealth, how would I have known that people have miseries such as those of Aarthdas?

Sarasvatichandra's mind cleared and he could think with a calmer head. He remembered the ring tied to his janoi, and his face lit up. Ah, the remedy is at hand! He took out the jewel-studded ring and looked at it. O ring, you were meant to grace Kumud Sundari's finger. I had you made for the delight of her heart. You would have dazzled on her finger like a little sun. But all that is futile now. You and I are banished from Kumud's life. The sun is about to set; its light will be sullied. Now you will bring joy to another's house. That is your destiny. Is there any comparison between Kumud and this bania? No. But I, too, do not deserve you. You were the last gift of my father's wealth, the last reminder of my beloved Kumud. But the wretched hand that caused her heart to break does not deserve you. My sacred janoi is impure, my body defiled. O ring, the charred ash of my cremated love, I give you away having soiled you with my tears. Go and light up a poor man's home! Sarasvatichandra sat down beside Aarthdas and slipped the ring onto his finger. And at that instant, the hungry, exhausted, miserable youth pining for his lost beloved suddenly fainted.

Aarthdas had taken Sarasvatichandra for an outlaw. He had staged this drama of poverty and wretchedness to get rid of him. Instead, the drama took an unexpected turn. He peered closely at the jewel encrusted ring. The bania understood nothing. The ring fitted him well. Sarasvatichandra had fainted. His thief-like cunning saw an opportunity. He got up and ran without once looking back.

4 Gunasundari

The outlaws' selection of the junction where the three roads met was not without reason. It was difficult to capture them as they moved between the boundaries of three states. If they were pursued by the police of one state, they could easily enter another. The road itself had many turns and forks which allowed them to disperse quickly. Moreover, the sea, the hills, the mango grove, the taad forest, the grasslands and the river facilitated quick movement and offered easy and diverse hiding places. Manoharpuri was a small village and its inhabitants were simple-minded. The outlaws did not harass them. The day the outlaws created trouble on the outskirts of Manoharpuri, the village was also bustling with activity. The arrival of newcomers gave some business to the village folks.

The same evening on which the outlaws captured and injured Sarasvatichandra, who gave his ring to Aarthdas, who slipped away like a thief, we know that Chandrakant who had set out from Ratnanagari for Suvarnapur was also robbed by the outlaws. On the way Chandrakant had received a message from Vidya Chatura, warning him that the outlaws of Suvarnapur were expected to strike and asking him not to proceed further until the additional soldiers he had dispatched for Chandrakant's protection reached him. The soldiers from Ratnanagari had also warned him. But impatient to meet Sarasvatichandra, Chandrakant decided to brave the danger. He was robbed, but his life was saved by the soldiers. Forced to halt at Manoharpuri that evening, Chandrakant became a guest of Gunasundari's once again.

Gunasundari had reached Manoharpuri earlier that afternoon. Gunasundari, as we know, was on her way to the temple at Bhadreshwar. There was no danger from outlaws on that side. She had decided to halt at Manoharpuri with her family and retinue. They were all waiting for Kumud Sundari's arrival.

That evening, there were about forty armed riders in Manoharpuri. They included the soldiers accompanying Gunasundari, Chandrakant, and the soldiers stationed at the local post. The three riders sent by Kumud Sundari for Sarasvatichandra's protection had failed in their mission; dejected, they had turned towards Manoharpuri. On the way they heard rumours that the outlaws were to meet that night under the banyan tree. Harbhamji decided to spy on them and concealed himself in the tree, while his two associates went on to Manoharpuri.

Vidya Chatura and his family shared bonds of deep affection with the villagers, who in turn responded with equal warmth. Women of the village would freely approach Gunasundari and share with her their joys and sorrows, their dreams and aspirations and claim her time for many such matters. Occasionally, she, too, would share small details of her family life with them, much to their surprise. Hearing of Gunasundari's arrival in Manoharpuri, the women rushed towards her rest house like a monsoon river in spate. Religious brahmin women, generous garasia women, bania women adept at running the household with severe economy, industrious Kanbi women, and even the poorest of the poor outcaste women gathered at the back door of the house, talking excitedly among themselves, all eager to meet her. Enthused by the presence of their minister's wife in their midst, the villagers did all they could to accord due hospitality to her.

The peasants were engrossed in conversation with the forty-odd soldiers. They accepted payment from them, as was customary, but provided superior fodder for the horses in return. Some patted the horses, asked after their history and pedigree; some engaged the soldiers in talk about their families; others enquired about news of Vidya Chatura's staff. As the evening sky turned crimson with the dust raised by cows returning from pasture, the peasants broke into song. Gunasundari witnessed these tranquil and joyous scenes from the raised platform of her rest house and welcomed the women who had gathered in large numbers to meet her.[1]

The village had a population of about three or four thousand. Most of them were peasants, hardworking and brave. The thanedars and other local administrators dealt with them honestly and justly. The landlords and peasants of Manoharpuri were seen as worthy of emulation by the neighbouring villages. Manoharpuri had a small but well-run school; a few of its students had even gone up to Bombay for further studies. Vidya Chatura followed a strict code: no one in his family should accept anything from the villagers for free. His family's conduct served as an example for his subordinate officials. The villagers, through their long association with state officials, had cultivated a sense of pride and a superior morality. The agricultural produce of the village was traded by land as well as by sea. This had attracted a few bania merchants to the village. In earlier times, bania money lenders from the surrounding villages had made it their business to lend money to the residents of Manoharpuri and they would visit the village occasionally to collect their repayments. Over time, encouraged by Vidya Chatura and advised and educated by his officials, the peasants learnt from the example of the higher castes how to reduce wasteful expenditure. They also became more industrious and learnt how to economise in both production-related as well as social expenditure like marriage, birth and death rituals. The only tax levied was on the land and this, too, was insignificant. Vidya Chatura encouraged the peasants to lend money to each other. By doing so, they learnt the value of money. As they managed their own money and expenses better and learnt how to accumulate wealth, from debtors the peasants gradually became creditors. This change had several important consequences. Agriculture became an independent and energetic activity. The whole village was motivated to try new experiments and apply intelligence to farming. With the improved living conditions and all-round contentment, the children of the farmers found new pride in the traditional occupation handed

[1] Author's note: The threads of this part of the story are picked up in Chapter Six.

down to them by their forefathers. They used their education to make improvements in existing age-old agricultural practices. They were grateful to their prime minister for the low taxes they had to pay and considered themselves more fortunate than villages under British administration. In times of famine and other hardships, the people of Manoharpuri were self-sufficient and hence not a burden on the state exchequer or on the British administered areas. Vidya Chatura was satisfied with all these developments. In India, inspired by a sense of religious obligation, people have dug wells, step wells and ponds, built village squares or chotras and diverse other such structures. The prime minister in his wisdom considered it his duty to encourage this sense of religious obligation. It was not surprising therefore that the people of Manoharpuri felt such deep affection for him.

Vidya Chatura wanted nothing for himself. He urged people to pay their taxes honestly and gladly. He also impressed upon them that in times of need the state may be forced to impose higher taxes as taxes were not subject to the people's will. Vidya Chatura strongly believed that discontentment, bitterness and resentment of the people was far worse than the annexation of the state itself; their goodwill and prosperity was for him far superior to the British Agent's pleasure or any titles awarded by the British government. He thus endeavoured to cultivate a similar philosophy of governance in the ruler of Ratnanagari, Maniraj. If the state treasury amasses more revenue than the state expends, it amounts to depriving people of their wealth. Rulers tend to misuse this excess revenue while state officials waste it on satisfying their lusts and whimsies, childish aspirations or vain attempts to secure personal glory; they spend it on women, luxuries, sports, expensive crafts, foreign travel, and on foreigners. Such surplus revenue inebriates the ruler's mind and becomes the envy of neighbouring rulers. Instead, if this surplus wealth is with the people, the state can levy higher taxes in times of crisis and need. And, if the taxes are lowered once the crisis is past, why should the people not have faith in their rulers? Surplus wealth is far safer with the people and hence they should be treated as a 'bank'. Such was the counsel given by Vidya Chatura to Maniraj, and the king in his wisdom would generously heed his prime minister.

Being under Vidya Chatura's direct care and supervision, the village of Manoharpuri was an example to be emulated. Other state officials closely followed developments in Manoharpuri as an indication of the desires of the king and his prime minister. Consequently, many villages had prospered.

Vidya Chatura had closely studied the governance of British administered provinces and native states. Based on his observations he had formulated a principle that if the administrators of native states have the wisdom, intelligence, conscience and will, they can work for the welfare of the people and uplift the state to a level which subjects under English rulers cannot even dream of; for the British, however well-meaning, are ultimately guided by self-interest alone. Those who have carefully observed and compared the conditions of villages under native states and under British India cannot but conclude that even where the rulers are immoral, selfish and tyrannical, villages under native states still tend to be more prosperous. Vidya Chatura wanted to set an example and demonstrate the heights that people could attain if the rulers were not tyrannical. Gunasundari often heard such talk from her husband. These ideas left a deep impact on her mind. She sought to fulfil his wishes by working for the people of Manoharpuri. This gave him greater joy than even the birth of a son would—he could rest content that the education he had given his wife had borne fruit. And his joy enthused Gunasundari even more. Where two hearts experience the same emotions, the same pleasures and provide mutually nurturing joy, a marriage is said to be consummated in its true sense. Gunasundari was delighted by their marriage.

Just as friends who share personal details feel their friendship grow and strengthen, just as a clerk who knows his employer's trade and business secrets considers himself his confidant, just as a prime minister acts autonomously when he knows his king reposes total confidence in him, just as subjects feel devoted to a righteous and wise king, just as a pure conscience coupled with virtue generates supreme bliss, in the same way Gunasundari knew and understood the thoughts and aspirations of Vidya Chatura. She considered herself his confidante. Secure in his love she acted autonomously; she was devoted to her husband and her love, as distinct from bodily desire, grew and illumined their relationship. Unlettered but intelligent women tend to be expert at household work and social relationships. Gunasundari saw Manoharpuri much as an extension of her household and visited it often to work for the welfare of its poor and illiterate. Children, in imitation of elders, play with their toys as if they are real people and derive great joy from such play. Gunasundari was akin to a child in matters of statecraft. Vidya Chatura observed her experiments in Manoharpuri with great delight; he would express his joy by a squeeze of her hand, a furtive kiss of her fingers and in moments of solitude, an embrace. These moments of togetherness came back to Gunasundari in Manoharpuri. Like a peacock's feathers ruffled gently by the wind, her heart beat faster at these warm and pleasant memories.

Gunasundari was about thirty-five years of age. She had given birth to two daughters who were now grown up. Only careful observers could tell her real age from her face. She had a well-proportioned body, neither slender nor fat. Her complexion was neither golden nor silver. Her features were well formed. Her hair was smooth, black and shiny, and when not tied up in a bun, it reached down to her knees. She had a broad forehead. Though not very large, her eyes were bright, playful and sharp. Her voice was not as refined as Kumud's but it had the delicacy of a woman's voice. She could sing as well as Kumud. Both of them were of similar height. Gunasundari was always smiling. There were many who wished to see her face first thing in the morning and believed that their day would pass well if they did so. Like her husband, Gunasundari was hardworking and conscientious. She preferred to do her own work without meddling in the affairs of others. The forbearance and virtues possessed by Kumud Sundari were her inheritance from her mother. So were her childlike eagerness and enthusiasm. Gunasundari loved her family, was always forgiving and bore no malice towards anyone. She had cultivated these qualities through her association with older women from her paternal as well as her in-laws' family. All those who came in contact with Gunasundari and Vidya Chatura were familiar with these qualities of hers. The people of Manoharpuri believed that Gunasundari had a special place in her heart for them, but no one would ever abuse her kindness as no one could bear to see her unhappy or hurt. This was not a quality that her husband possessed; his position required him to judge the conduct of others and also wield punitive power when necessary.

Gunasundari's natal home was in this village. Vidya Chatura, who was five or seven years older to her, had spent his early years at his maternal household. The house of his maternal grandparents was adjacent to that of Gunasundari's parents. Even before Gunasundari was born, her mother had a great fondness for little Vidya Chatura. She would play with him, tell him stories, comb his hair, give him food and pamper him. The young boy was playful, sharp and talkative. When a daughter was born to her, she fixed her child's marriage with the boy without waiting to consult an astrologer. When Gunasundari was old enough to talk, her mother would play with both the children, make them speak lines and enact roles for her own amusement; too young to understand or know any shame, they would happily oblige. But soon afterwards Vidya Chatura's maternal uncle, who had no children of his own, called him to Ratnanagari for further studies. Vidya Chatura went on to Bombay to complete his education. When he returned to Ratnanagari after his studies, he was twenty-three years old. Gunasundari was about sixteen or seventeen and had been visiting her in-laws' house for the past three years or so. She would regularly write to her husband while he was in Bombay. In her letters she often composed verses or duha, sakha and garba, much to their mutual pleasure, and she joyfully shared his responses with her friends. Vidya Chatura, who read and studied English and Sanskrit poetry of love and desire, was delighted with these letters of his young betrothed. Their long separation only served to strengthen their love. Marriage in infancy proved for him to be a matter of great joy. So much that Vidya Chatura often wondered later in life if his staunch opposition to child marriage had any basis at all. Our universities have placed books filled with love and longing in the hands of our young men. One result of this is the cultivation of an artificial sense of chivalry towards women. Often, the child bride becomes the recipient of such chivalry. Many women, themselves unlettered, but married to educated men have felt their conjugal happiness take root in a similar way. Gunasundari did, too. Those who have read the first part of the book know how she learnt to read and understand poetry in company of her husband. The couple lived apart during the years that Vidya Chatura spent studying. Gunasundari thus began her conjugal life at an age when both her body and mind had matured and developed, and she was well poised to enter a new phase of life.

Soon after he completed his education, Vidya Chatura obtained a teacher's position in a school in Ratnanagari. His job was undemanding. They did not have a child for another two-three years. This was the best and most blissful period for the young couple. They experienced the heights of passion and love, an intimacy which was at once intellectual, aesthetic and sensual. During these years, the young wife and husband would often sit together after dinner with books. They would read books together, discuss burning political and social issues of the day. The wife would ask pithy and pointed questions, the husband would respond in detail as if engaged in solemn debate. Sometimes the adolescent wife would raise doubts based on her newfound education which would force him to rethink, even change principles he had firmly established for himself. And their intellectual camaraderie would find its fulfilment when he would close the doors of their room and take her to the window overlooking a garden, kiss her lips over and over again and sing,

Sleep's embrace is as delicate as yours:
The world rests, enticed by its touch
The moon smiles upon this peaceful scene
Open your eyes slowly: Look, my beloved!
The bright moon moves, clinging to the sky
Wait a while: Listen—
Hear what the moon whispers to the stars

The pleasures of these moments, and many like these, were repeated over many days. Gunasundari heard this poem many times and she not only understood it but her heart and being felt suffused by its meaning. Initially, she was unable to appreciate simple romantic verses like, 'Touching foreheads we remained/Conversing in soft whispers', but she soon acquired the sensibility. The experience of understanding a poem, its meaning, the arrangement of words and the ability to take pleasure in it is one kind of aesthetic experience. Some poetic rhythms capture the mind which sways to their cadence just as a serpent sways to a flute. One is immersed in an experience at once intensely erotic and sublime, like the gopis who were captivated by the melody of Krishna's flute. One who is bound by love experiences a sense of unity and oneness; the poem of Jaydev and Padmavati is a fine example of this. One who is immersed in devotion forgets the world around him. The lives of many saints bear testimony to this. A soul who experiences the supreme bliss of Brahman knows the world to be a dark place and craves only for the one permanent and pure light—such is also the experience of immersing oneself in beautiful poetry. Vidya Chatura held forth in such a manner to Gunasundari that her thirst for aesthetic experience grew stronger with each passing day. That day, the song oft repeated by her husband assumed a life of its own. Perhaps this was due to the familiarity gained by repetition; or because her eyes had been opened by education; or because of the aesthetic lamp lit in her mind and heart by the great poets; or because she was at an age when erotic experiences are deeply felt; or in anticipation of being in bed with her husband; perhaps because of one or all of these reasons, by divine grace as her eyes turned inwards, they saw what they had never seen before—Gunasundari gazed unblinking upon her husband, lovelorn. As he beheld his own perfect tiny image in her shining eyes, Vidya Chatura felt: Today, in the form of a poem, I have entered your heart. Like your eyes, your unwavering heart and your entire being captures my image. He looked at his wife with temperate joy. For both of them this was the first experience of intellectual love. Like a woman experiencing the joys of first pregnancy, Gunasundari spent that day in bliss. She who wrote songs to her husband composed a poem for him, as if she too, like Valmiki, were blessed by God. Once again that night, Vidya Chatura thirsting for that experience recited the same verse. They felt their hearts unite once again, but the experience of oneness was much deeper than before. She responded unabashedly to her husband. Her eyes intent upon his face, she placed her fair and delicate hands on his shoulders like the rays of the new moon that reach out to rain-filled clouds, and was flooded by desire at his touch. She softly began to sing the poem she had composed for him.

Bright stars of the night sky
My heart sings the song of my love
As the moon spreads its light in the sky
So your heart spreads its joy within me
In the blessed silence of the night
Look how Solitude delights in the moon's company
As they are one, my love, be one with me
In the moon's embrace, Silence itself shines forth
Look how well they are suited
As they are one, my love, be one with me

Vidya Chatura was immersed in her song as long as it lasted. As she finished, he felt as if he had a revelation and he saw Gunasundari anew—like the first flowering of erotic desire in an untouched girl. As the young woman abandoned her shyness and opened her heart, he saw her latent poetic abilities emerge. Vidya Chatura was astonished, enthused and delighted at this discovery. He felt that Gunasundari's poem was more delicate than his and had a natural energy that his own verse lacked. His heart filled with joy and pride as he took both her hands in his and kissed them. Experiences of pure joy are rare and fleeting. As the enchanting night passed, this priceless moment proved to be the first and the last such experience for Vidya Chatura.

Vidya Chatura's maternal uncle Jarashankar called him the very next day. Jarashankar was the private secretary to the then ruler of Ratnanagari, Mallaraj, who was the father of the present ruler Maniraj. The British Agent Buskin Sahib, whom you may recall we have met in the first part of this story, insisted that young prince Maniraj should be taught English. A trustworthy teacher was required. Jarashankar recommended Vidya Chatura, who was made the prince's tutor. Vidya Chatura was under the impression that he was simply required to be a conventional teacher who taught from a book. But he was wrong, for this proved to be only a secondary task.

Mallaraj was a staunch kshatriya in disposition and physique. He was considered to be the finest example of pure royal lineage among all the native rulers. He had witnessed the early wars with the British at a young age and treacherous diplomacy and enemies both within and outside the state. He liked to first ascertain his final goal and then searched for the means appropriate to accomplish that goal. Statecraft for him was a game of chess, and he played his games accordingly. For him, that was the beginning and end of statecraft. Mallaraj was not acquainted with English learning and hence did not value it. For him, English education was a means to an end. He had no objection if Maniraj were to acquire this means.

Mallaraj gave elaborate instructions to Vidya Chatura that he might teach Maniraj English, but that he should under no circumstance forget his principal duty. 'I give you my prince, but not so that you turn his mind and make him English. He is at an impressionable age—nurture and guide him carefully. I do not want to turn him into a brahmin like you or even a vaishya. Teach him to understand the ways of the brahmin, the vaishya, the mleccha, the English and all others; teach him to fathom their tricks, teach him his duties towards all. But take this as a warning: if I see him acquiring any traits of the English or the brahmin or anyone else, even you, I will take it as a sign of your negligence. Your duty is to imbue him with the qualities of a pure Rajput, a kshatriya. That young prince will be my support in old age. He is the hope of this state, the future of my lineage, the glory of my family; and you, although his teacher, are my servant. He is destined to be a king and not a subject; hence you must make him fit for all his duties. My kshatriya warriors will work with you to develop his body and to enhance his valour. Do not hesitate to ask for any facilities you might need to teach him statecraft. Make Maniraj *a king*. It is our ancient custom that a Rajput learns his own dharma from a brahmin teacher. I give Maniraj to your care. Jarashankar will tell you what else you need to do in your free time. Remember, Vidya Chatura, you are not to be a school teacher here. Let me list for you the duties of a woman. She raises children, serves elders, takes work from servants, looks after the household and household goods, protects and enhances the family's prestige and is virtuous. At night a woman must rule over the husband in amorous games. Even an ordinary woman does all this. She must also gracefully bear the brunt of people's words, silently bear insults and torture in the house, disregard her own suffering and always be generous and forgiving. All women are required to do so. If she fails in her duties, she is neither a woman nor a man. In the art of sex she is called shankhini; such a woman is required to be equally adept in social intercourse. Now tell me, if a woman is required to perform so many duties, how many duties would a man, her master, need to perform! A man who cannot do what a woman does is incompetent and unfit to serve my state. Only one who can perform the duties of a woman as also those of a man is fit to serve my state, and you must acquire that fitness. Secondly, I do not say that you should not be greedy, but your greed should not damage another's house. My priest often quotes a Sanskrit verse which says that a cow should be milked only after the calf has drunk his due; likewise, a king's treasury should be filled only after his subjects are content. I say to you that think of your interest only after the interest of the king and his subjects are secure, or else be clear that we shall have nothing to do with each other. Vidya Chatura, I know that you are honest, but honesty is not only about not being corrupt. Experience will teach you that honesty has many other aspects. Such honesty will appear easy to practice; but once you acquire authority you will understand the saying that wealth tempts even the sages. Do not let your pride lead you astray because I have put young Maniraj in your charge. Remember that he is a jewel, but that jewel is placed on the head of a serpent, and you have to deal with the serpent. If the serpent is pleased, it will open the treasure chest for you; but if displeased, death lurks in his bite. Always remember that Mallaraj is like that serpent.'

These words became etched on the heart and mind of the man appointed to be the prince's tutor. To Vidya Chatura, each word seemed to encompass the wisdom of books. He realised that a man unsheathing his sword from the scabbard must also protect his own fingers. This took possession of his rational mind in such a way that from that day onwards his love of poetry, music, his amorous play with Gunasundari all became a distant dream. He became so intent on observing and teaching statecraft to Maniraj that he only caught fleeting glimpses of the goings on in his own household, much as one glimpses a falling star.

Around the same time, Gunasundari came to be embroiled in the complex web of family relationships and responsibilities. The training she had received from her husband proved useful in untangling this web. Vidya Chatura considered Mallaraj's advice priceless; he had it written down in a notebook. Gunasundari read these notes and learnt from them how to deal with the situation she suddenly found herself in. Even the erudite learn from the experiences of the intelligent; in fact, one who is learned gains much more than an average person. A library is a key to the thoughts of many scholars. Vidya Chatura believed that learned is one who understands the key to knowledge; others merely possess bookish knowledge. He considered the experiences of the intelligent as valuable as the wisdom contained in books. The excessive kshatriya wisdom of Mallaraj's first instructions to him as a tutor left a lasting impression on Vidya Chatura. He considered the king's pride in his rule and his kingdom worthy of devotion. And just as a bee collects honey from a flower considered beautiful by all, Vidya Chatura took vital lessons from Mallaraj, which came to form the seed of his morality. While he found them most instructive in statecraft, Gunasundari used these same lessons in the domain of the household.

As we know, Vidya Chatura was raised in his maternal household as his maternal uncle Jarashankar had no children of his own. At the time of Vidya Chatura's birth, his father Manchatura was about thirty-five years old and a clerk in the office of a mamlatdar or revenue officer in a British administered area. Though not highly educated, Manchatura was considered intelligent. Those who believed that the intelligent are more prone to youthful excesses would give Manchatura's example—he could not restrain his debauchery even in old age, contracted a grave and incurable disease, had to resign his post and was forced to go and live with Vidya Chatura. Vidya Chatura had four elder siblings: two brothers and two sisters. Manchatura's eldest son had died young; his widow Sundargauri lived with her parents. When Sundargauri's parents died, her brother and sister-in-law had no use for her. One day they beat her and drove her out of the house. Hungry, thirsty, Sundargauri spent the entire night on the doorstep, shedding copious tears. Gunasundari came to know of this, and she went and brought home her elder sister-in-law who had nowhere else to go. Ganchatura, Gunasundari's other brother-in-law, was ten to twelve years older than Vidya Chatura. Spoilt by the father, Ganchatura had adopted all his bad habits and taken to a life of pleasure from a young age; repeated attempts to educate him had failed. After much pleading with the mamlatdar, his father had obtained the position of a talati, a village revenue official, for him. Ganchatura had several addictions and expensive habits. He saved nothing. There were also rumours about his relations with the wife of the village headman, who thus had cause to harbour animosity towards him. One day, Ganchatura took four-five annas from a farmer as bribe. The headman made a 'report' of this to the mamlatdar and got him suspended. Ganchatura was forced to return to Ratnanagari with his wife Chandika and four children, and became Gunasundari's guest.

Vidya Chatura's elder sister Dukhba was married to Sahasrai who had incurred several debts in business. Sahasrai began to speculate in the hope of paying off his debts; instead he incurred even heavier debts which were beyond his capacity to repay. Harassed and ashamed, he left town and went into hiding, sending his wife Dukhba to her brother's house. They had a daughter of marriageable age, Kumari. Dukhba was unhappy and anxious about the bleak prospects of Kumari's marriage. Unable to share her concerns with her brother and sister-in-law, Dukhba withered with a sorrow that gnawed at her every day. Vidya Chatura's other sister Chanchalba was widowed around the same time. She had the qualities of her name; she was quick with household work but proud and had a habit of lying. Therefore, she found no place at her in-laws' and was tolerated only as there were no other women to look after household chores. Once her young sister-in-law grew up and learnt to manage the house, her brother-in-law had no need for Chanchalba. She faced daily insults. Finally, when she could no longer bear the insults, at Gunasundari's urging she went to live at her brother's house. Chanchalba had a fifteen-year old son, Yashprasad; his wife Salasba had begun menstruating; but once Chanchalba moved in with her brother, Salasba went to stay with her parents.

The year in which Vidya Chatura was appointed tutor to Maniraj, Manchatura, Sundargauri, Ganchatura, Chandika, Dukhba and Chanchalba along with their respective children came to live with Vidya Chatura and Gunasundari. All of a sudden, Gunasundari was expected to bear their burden. She had to nurse their individual sorrows, adjust to their diverse dispositions and also endure their bad habits and idiosyncracies. Her youthful passions which had just begun to flower were crushed under the weight of this burden, and Gunasundari was required to search deep within herself for the forbearance and wisdom of old age. Their house was small and Vidya Chatura's income was far less compared to the expenditure involved. But the expectations and demands from his relatives were high as he was seen to be occupying a high position. Hence their desires and aspirations remained forever unfulfilled, they were forever discontented and disgruntled, and they blamed Vidya Chatura and Gunasundari for it.

When this immense change was thrust upon her, Gunasundari was barely twenty. She was not yet worldly wise. She could not even begin to imagine how this burden would crush her being or what infinite restraint and patience would be demanded of her. She had spent her childhood and youth with her husband. She hungered for family ties. She truly believed that her life would be fulfilled if she could extend her love for her husband to his entire family. She imagined everyone to be as pure-hearted and generous as she was. Raised by kindly older women, Gunasundari had imbibed their affectionate nature, kindness and virtues, and with these qualities she hoped to carry the yoke of family responsibilities. She had experienced only the pleasant and positive aspects of social life and hoped that the web of family would help her further her own goodness. She was thus filled with many hopes and aspirations, but experience taught her the unbearable drudgery and pain that family responsibilities could be.

As their house overflowed, Gunasundari was initially pleased and felt at ease. There were some difficulties; the house was small and felt cramped, but the joy of having everyone around her, the hustle and bustle of a large family compensated for it. At least for a time. The women and children were accommodated in the verandah or parsal, which led into rooms; they also slept there. Above the parsal there was a room accessed by a staircase; this was given to Ganchatura and his wife as their bedroom. The room adjacent to theirs was used to store valuables. It now had a human lock; grains were stored in this room which had to be accessed from the room occupied by Ganchatura and his wife. They were disturbed only when grains had to be taken out from there. There was an inner courtyard or khadki facing the parsal. On one side of it were the kitchen and water storage. On the other side were two rooms; Manchatura was given the exclusive use of one while the other was given Vidya Chatura's mother, Dharmalaxmi. There was a room above the courtyard and a terrace. Before his family moved in, Vidya Chatura and Gunasundari used a room above the parsal as their bedroom while the room above the courtyard, accessed by another staircase, was used by Vidya Chatura as his office. They now moved their bedroom to the office and shifted his office downstairs. A curtain was hung between the chowk and the rooms of the khadki; this made a separate enclosure for the women. There was a smaller quad which could be approached from the parsal; a kitchen door opened into this quad and meals were served in this area. There was a small storeroom adjacent to the quad, a narrow passageway, and also a water storage room. Vidya Chatura often spoke of the wisdom of the ancestors and marvelled at their ability to create innovative spaces in homes with judicious use of money and space. He was extremely pleased that his wife could provide a space for each one of his large family in his small house. Gunasundari had done justice to the vision of those who had built the house. He called her to their new room and embraced her. As she received this gift of love, she said, 'Pitaji keeps indifferent health. He needs solitude and would find the young ones bothersome. If he were given a room on the first floor, he would have to shout for someone every time he needed something. Therefore, I made a ground floor room available. I had to give up what used to be my sitting area, but this is most convenient for him. Motabhai would have found all the noise bothersome; he likes to be by himself and sing. The new arrangement would be agreeable to him. There are so many people around now that I will not be able to visit you as often as I used to in your office, but we have the whole night to ourselves, don't we?' Vidya Chatura was happy and proud of Gunasundari's willingness to sacrifice her own convenience and pleasure to accommodate and provide for his family. He smilingly embraced her once again and said, 'You did well, my Gunial'. She would remember these words for years to come. She did not forget the embrace either. For many days thereafter, in her rare moments of solitude, she brought his embrace alive in her memory and enveloped herself in its warmth. Vidya Chatura usually called her Gunial, but that day his utterance had a very different import for her.

Running a large household is akin to administering a state. The responsibilities of a woman are as complex as that of a minister in a state. Foresight, abnegation of self-interest, forbearance, conscientiousness, generosity, managerial abilities, capacity for service to others and many other such qualities are required of a woman in charge of her household. A woman's responsibilities cannot be fulfilled by hired servants. For this and other reasons Vidya Chatura did not like the Western practice of degrading household work and pushing women into the outside world under that pretext. Gunasundari expressed similar views to him one day. A Parsi newspaper had published an essay about bringing women out of their homes. She read the essay and while returning the newspaper to her husband, she commented, 'My beloved Chatura, do you think what they write has any merit? Do we not do enough? Our bodies raise and nurture the race. To push such a body into the world of men is to desire that the tongue should behave like the teeth. You men are like teeth; we women are like the tongue. You do what is given to you to do, and we shall do what we ought to do. You go out and earn; we shall manage the household. Who but women could render your work meaningful? If you live to earn a livelihood and we also do likewise, who shall care for your children, your family, your household, your mind, your pleasures and your religion? Has God made the world such that even women should strive after money? You should assist us to learn better the task that is before us. If you have more money, accord us a higher status in what we do. Poor, unmarried men are their own servants and cooks; so are women married to poor men. People who say that women have been degraded because they are required to cook speak without thought because under certain conditions both women and men are required to do it. Which God has made cooking inferior to hard labour that earns ten miserly rupees, or to the duties of a doctor who must boil medicines and wash people's oozing wounds for a few hundred rupees? We will use our intelligence in cooking. If you have greater means and can keep someone to cook your meals, we shall convert your houses into palaces, raise your sons to befit you. We shall cultivate learning for which you may not have the time. We shall nurture your aesthetic desires, your poetic inclinations, your learning, your valour, your patriotism according to our fate and ability. The tongue shall perform delicate tasks, while the teeth shall bite into hard things. You cannot do what is required of us. Only when we do what is required of us well can you manage your worldly affairs. If you cannot deal with your affairs well, we too are at a loss for it. This is what I think.'

Vidya Chatura smiled and said, 'You argue well, Gunial. Among us, women call themselves servants of their husbands. A servant accords to the master the higher status. But I have received English education; hence you and I have equal rights.'

Gunasundari said, 'Who says we do not enjoy equal rights? Food and drink we need as much as you do. But by claiming equal rights you will not be able to bear a child, and we cannot give up what is given to us. No one becomes higher or lower just because one is called master and the other a servant. The master cares for the servant just as the servant toils for the master. On the surface it appears that the master is higher and the servant lower, but both need each other. The hands are in the upper part of the body while the feet are lower, but for that reason God does not consider hands more valuable than feet. Can we do without either? The same is true for men and women. You and I have equal rights, but God made me a few inches shorter than you. Can I be taller than you or become a man instead of a woman? Yes, you would certainly be at fault if you place unnecessary impediments in our way, treat us callously or consider us bovine instead of human! But what is all this talk? Some say men should do what they have been doing but women should not look after the house; they should dress up and chat all day, be idle and tell the husband that I need delicious food, good clothes and a cook. Some say, so what if your parents are old, shall I give up my youth for them? It is like saying that what belongs to you belongs to both of us, but what is mine is exclusively mine. If we adopt such ways, we would spoil our households and our daughters who would then bring grief to our sons-in-laws—that would be nice, isn't it? If you become a dewan, I would keep your house as befitting a dewan's status, give joy to your family, and when you return home tired from the problems of the state and world, I would bring delight to your heart. The joy of your home would be as high as the position you occupy in the world outside. This is my work and also the source of my pride and glory.'

Vidya Chatura said,'All right, do that when I become a dewan. For the present, demonstrate your cleverness in this cramped household of ours. How are you doing with your reading?' He had expected a weak response. But Gunasundari retorted, 'Reading? Isn't all this education? A book printed on paper, and a book of the world—one can learn much from either. I will go back to reading gradually once the household settles down. Right now the household is a source of great delight for me. Do you know that I get up at four a.m. when the cock crows for the first time? Then I go down and light the lamps which bring light to your still dark house. The servants go to sleep at around midnight. The second thing that I do is to commit the sin of waking them up. What else can I do? I wake them up quietly so as not to disturb the sleep of others. Sometimes they wake up, but there are times when they just can't get up. I take pity on them and allow them to sleep. Once they wake up, they heat up the water. Meanwhile I clean my teeth, perform other daily functions, bathe, comb my hair, apply the bindi and get ready. After this I put together everything that mother-in-law needs for her daily worship. I can assign this work to someone else, but she is finicky about these things and can also be harsh, which can cause friction between her and the one who does her work; therefore I prefer to do it myself. Meanwhile, everyone wakes up and performs their daily ablutions. During this time I organise the meals. Dukhba is preoccupied with her own woes and tends to neglect the task at hand. She cannot rush around or do things in a hurry, so she prefers to cook. Kumari assists her in cooking as she needs to be trained in it. If I try and teach her, Kumari does not always approve, but she does not mind it much even if Dukhba scolds her. There are many children in the house these days. Sundarbhabhi likes to bathe and dress them, which she does without being asked to. Chanchalbehn spends the morning preparing tea and medicines for Pitaji. I run all the other errands in the house, organise provisions and keep an eye on the servants. I am compassionate towards them but do not make a show of it because then they tend to get spoilt. The whole day passes in such activities. There is great joy in the house.'

Vidya Chatura asked, 'But Gunial, how does this prove your cleverness?' Gunasundari's face betrayed concern and she replied, 'About that, God only knows. But I am seven months pregnant and I cannot do as much as I need to. Once I am delivered of the baby, I will be able to do nothing and I am worried about that. Let us see what happens.'

Just then someone called for her from downstairs and she was required to attend to that. Gunasundari's concerns were not misplaced. Each member of the family had a different character and peculiarities. She ensured there was no cause of conflict and intelligently accommodated herself to all of them. She was agile and did most of the work herself. But Gunasundari was convinced that at the time of her confinement after childbirth, she would no longer be the link that held the household together; people would go their separate ways like beads unattached to a string. She anticipated differences about work, expected wastage of provisions and disputes in the household. Even after her confinement was over, she would have to look after the newborn child and would neither have the energy or the scope to resolve these conflicts. This, too, was a cause of worry for her. She now had a good measure of each one's disposition, their qualities and faults. She had taken precautions to ensure that no conflict broke out in the family. She knew that precaution was easier than resolution of conflict. In her sweet and kind voice, she would give instructions in guise of requests, make gentle suggestions and assign responsibilities for which the person was best suited. Her conduct never suggested superiority or condescension. She set an example by working tirelessly and with enthusiasm all day long. She possessed the art of patient counselling. She loved the family greatly. She was generous, self-sacrificing and clever. Thus, young Gunasundari navigated the family's ship through stormy waters with ease. The joy and sense of oneness in the family was at its height. We recognise goodness only in absence of it just as we value happiness greatly in times of sorrow. Similarly, Gunasundari's absence was felt by all when she gave birth and was in confinement. Gunasundari possessed untiring industriousness, youthful enthusiasm and an affectionate, generous temperament usually associated with elders. Vidya Chatura was indeed fortunate to have her as his wife. The time to test her true worth was approaching. He desisted from praising her, but felt happy and satisfied as her hitherto unknown qualities came to light and flowered in service of his large family. He thanked God for his fortune and kept in mind the instructions of Mallaraj in his service of the state. As time passed he found these instructions to be even more valid. His own experience had taught him patience while dealing with all sorts of people; he had learnt to turn them useful. He had become both forgiving and generous. Vidya Chatura saw many similarities between his experiences and Gunasundari's.

The presence of the extended family proved quite useful at the time of Gunasundari's simant. But even on that day, she had to ensure everyone's happiness and oversee all the other arrangements as well. Ganchatura proved quite useful in organising the feast for the caste and in purchase of provisions for the feast. Jarashankar and other relatives also did their bit, but it was Gunasundari's care that prevented total anarchy and mismanagement. Everyone was eager to do their bit, but Gunasundari had to assign them the tasks and ensure that they were done on time. The reason was obvious: no one had the sense to think that this is my house, too, and it is I who must ensure that the ceremony passes without a glitch. The women were glad to fetch the provisions from the house, but Gunasundari had to ascertain who needed what and also point out where exactly they were kept in the house. Moreover, there was also a lot of wastage, some of which could have been prevented while one had to overlook the rest. No one else had this fine judgement. There were many instances of friction and conflict, but Gunasundari managed to prevent a flare-up and also ensure minimum wastage. The caste norms were stringent and so were the rituals. Gunasundari's mother-in-law Dharmalaxmi was an expert in social exchanges within the caste. She was also old and infirm. She rarely came out of the house and consequently could not keep a watch over the transactions. She operated from within the house with the help of intermediaries. Gunasundari accorded her mother-in-law all respect due to her and always sought her opinion. Despite that, Dharmalaxmi made enquiries as to whether her advice was followed or not, whether the daughter-in-law acted independently; she wanted to know if people spoke ill of her or praised her. She used Chanchal to obtain such information. Chanchal added her bit to make the tales juicier. Dharmalaxmi was wise and understood her daughter-in-law's worth, but in her mind she still held Gunasundari at fault. Sometimes her face betrayed her displeasure in ways apparent to Chanchal. At times she counselled Gunasundari and at other times she singed her with her words. Gunasundari felt hurt but kept a large mind. She would constantly remind herself that the mother-in-law was after all an elder and made an effort to put the unpleasantness behind her. The simant should have been the responsibility of the elders in the family, but in this case it became the responsibility of the woman whose simant was to be celebrated. At a time when her body needed rest and her mind sought joy, Gunasundari worked from early morning to midnight without pause. And instead of praise she received only criticism. Dukhba was given the responsibility of welcoming the guests and dressing the children in new clothes and ornaments. She behaved as if it was Gunasundari who had brought ruination to Sahasrai and grudged her for holding this auspicious ritual when her husband was away. She moaned unhappily every time she saw Gunasundari and wept and spoke ill of her to anyone willing to listen. These stories were carried to Gunasundari with exaggeration; true to her patient and calm disposition, she responded to each with temperance and did not take these stories to heart. Chanchalba was to look after Manchatura and Dharmalaxmi; any other work had to be secondary to this responsibility. She was a help to Gunasundari and lightened her burden. But she blamed Gunasundari for any neglect on part of Dukhba in caring for her children. Chanchal carried her complaints to Dharmalaxmi. Sooner or later Gunasundari received reprimand for these lapses. Gunasundari never talked back. She did not transfer the blame on to Dukhba; instead she arranged the affairs even better. Chandika was given the task of inviting the guests. She liked to dress up and go out visiting but she lacked courtesy; she also gossiped with other women and brought their quarrels home. These tales were inevitably carried to Gunasundari, who was blamed for Chandika's lack of courtesy. Chandika routinely taunted Gunasundari. Gunasundari would allow her elder sister-in-law to have her say, reasoning with herself: Chandikabhabhi is angry and incapable of appreciating my side of the story; she will understand once she cools down. Gunasundari would praise Chandika for her good work, send her off on an errand and go back to her own work.

Sundargauri was given the responsibility of keeping a watch over the ornaments and was also made responsible for the provisions. Gunasundari trusted her completely. A destitute widow, Sundargauri was overwhelmed by this trust and hence immensely grateful to Gunasundari. The other women in the family were jealous of this relationship and felt pleased every time Sundargauri made a mistake. Gunasundari knew this and was prompt to protect this widow who had no other support. But she was discreet, for she also knew that if her support for Sundar were made apparent, Sundar would be subjected to even greater hardships. Sundargauri's brother and sister-in-law were also invited to the celebration. Aware that Sundar enjoyed Gunasundari's support, they felt slighted and openly showed their displeasure. During the feast, Sundargauri was required to come out of the house for some work. Her brother saw his opportunity. He caught her by the hand, dragged her and abused her. 'Rand, you have brought discredit to our family! Have we ever denied you food that you had to seek shelter in your brother-in-law's house?' Poor Sundargauri wept helplessly. On hearing the commotion, Gunasundari came out with servants and freed Sundargauri from her brother's clutches. She issued strict instructions that under no circumstances was Sundargauri to be sent on any errand outside the house. In return, Sundargauri's brother and sister-in-law showered abuses on Gunasundari. Gunasundari went inside the house and the weary abusers gave up. But people kept whispering, 'Why should Sundargauri be given so much prestige? The rand brings bad luck. Why do we need to keep her in the house? Would we lack for anything if she were not here?' Chanchal made faces, Chandika made odd noises. Gunasundari saw and heard all this and more. Her heart was filled with pain. She had so much to do, but she sat with Sundargauri right in the middle of the chowk, holding her hands. Sundargauri was fair and extremely beautiful. Her golden hued cheeks grew flushed as she wept, her bosom heaving with her sobs. Just as ambers covered by ash flare up at the slightest touch of fire, attired in a widow's simple clothes her whole body trembled with pain and anger. As Sundargauri cupped her face in her palms and wept, Gunasundari sat beside her and held her close; Gunasundari's eyes also filled with tears as she tried to console the distraught woman. Other family members came and stood around them, joining Gunasundari in consoling Sundargauri, even those who had berated her. Sundargauri did not want to appear weak and feeble. She composed herself, wiped her tears, got up and went back to work. There were many such dramas during the simant celebrations. This was also the time that the English Sahib was visiting the state. Vidya Chatura thus had no time for domestic matters. The tasks that he could have shouldered also became Gunasundari's responsibility. The simant celebration received praise from all quarters; among men Ganchatura and among women Dharmalaxmi received all the credit. No mention was made of Gunasundari's contribution. Still, Gunasundari was content that the event was a success and that the praise due to her had gone to her brother-in-law and mother-in-law.

Two months passed. Gunasundari found no relief from work till the day she was delivered of her child. The house was hers. No one found it strange that she should work in her own house. Gradually, it became difficult for her to work. She could no longer assuage hurt feelings or avoid conflict. Others began to shirk responsibility; mismanagement increased. People devoted their free time to family squabbles. Even Dukhba changed colour. Gunasundari, out of consideration for her, had assigned the task of cooking to her. Dukhba complained, 'I am the family's cook. I eat a handful of grain and cook all day long'. Dharmalaxmi supported Dukhba. The matter eventually reached Gunasundari's ears. She did not feel offended. Instead, she entered the kitchen. She was in the ninth month of her pregnancy. Therefore, at least for the sake of form, the others initially tried to stop her, but only half-heartedly. Gunasundari was eventually cooking for the entire household of seventeen-eighteen individuals when she was about nine and half months pregnant. There was no help, no relief. She had to get up many times. One day just after she had filled a heavy pitcher with water and carried it to the kitchen, her labour pains started. Gunasundari rushed to the room of confinement and lay down on the cot that was kept ready. For once she felt sorry for herself and cried. Sundargauri followed her. Chandika saw the two of them go towards the room of confinement but made no enquiries. Chanchal was busy chatting with Chandika. Dharmalaxmi was engrossed in her rituals. Dukhba was in the khadki feeling sorry for herself as usual. The only other person who felt for Gunasundari was Manchatura. Old and ailing, he saw the family drama play itself out. He often scolded his daughters and showed his displeasure to his wife. Manchatura was lying in bed when he saw Gunasundari rushing to the room prepared for her confinement. Forgetting his illness, he immediately got up from bed and came out of his room leaning on a stick, screaming, 'Dukhba! Chanchal! Are all of you dead? Let your mother and her worship go to dust! Is there anyone who cares for this poor woman about to deliver a child?' On his call everyone turned towards the delivery room like a tide. Dharmalaxmi's weary body moved with a youngster's agility as she snapped out of her rituals. Chanchal rushed down. Dukhba walked slowly. Manchatura berated her, 'Oh! As if you are the only one to carry the burden of sorrows. Are your legs broken? Run, or else I will give you such a shove that you will move faster!' Dukhba moved as if crushed by some great tyrannical force. Chandika was the last to come down, making faces of contempt. Manchatura saw her and muttered to himself: God knows from where we got her! Her husband earns nothing, and she behaves as if the slightest movement will erode her body!

Everyone converged in the room. Gunasundari was almost unconscious. Sundargauri sat next to her, holding her. The women encircled them. Chanchal called out to her elder brother and sent him to fetch the midwife. He woke up inebriated with opium and song and walked off in a daze. Manchatura heaved a deep sigh of disappointment. Dharmalaxmi was old, ritualistic and superstitious; she was stern of speech but affectionate and capable of rising above her prejudices at such moments. She was experienced in matters of birth. She sat down beside the writhing Gunasundari, issued instructions to Chanchal and had the necessary things fetched. Gunasundari's labour pains became intense. She went cold. With great effort she took out a key and handed it to Sundargauri saying, 'Give it to him' and she lost consciousness. Sundargauri burst into tears. Chandika was incredulous that even in such critical moments Gunasundari should repose such trust in Sundargauri. Everyone else was anxious. Even the otherwise useless Dukhba turned useful for once. She got up, went to her father's room and said, 'Who will call Bhai? I fear that Bhabhi may not survive'. Sundargauri, who had never before encountered such a situation, helplessly looked at her mother-in-law and sisters-in-law. Chanchal, who was more experienced, quickly lit a fire, brought healing herbs and warmed Gunasundari's cold body with hot poultices. Sundargauri assisted her.

Manchatura had trouble walking; despite this he raised himself with the support of a stick. He contemplated if he should go and fetch Vidya Chatura. If he were to go there would be no other male member in the house. But he made up his mind and stepped out. He asked Dukhba to watch the door. As he stepped out he saw the midwife approach. In the distance he could see Vidya Chatura approaching accompanied by Ganchatura. He was satisfied that Ganchatura had used his intelligence. Dukhba took the midwife to Gunasundari. As soon as the two brothers had walked in, Sundargauri came out of the labour room, handed the key to Vidya Chatura and, giving him the frightening news, hurried back. Vidya Chatura immediately sent his brother to call a doctor. This was his first experience of deep shock. He went cold and felt as if he were breathing hot air, his tongue became dry, his mind was in a whirl and tears welled up in his eyes. Hindu social custom forbade him from going to his beloved to comfort her, to be by her side. It would be a transgression. He looked at the key in his hand and wondered why she had sent it to him. He could only guess her intentions. He went up to their room and opened Gunasundari's trunk with the key. There was a letter kept on top. He picked it up and read it through.

My beloved Chatura,

I will bathe again to go into the kitchen, but my body is giving up on me. I feel that by this evening I may no longer be alive. For the last two months there has been so much work in the house that I have not spent even fifteen minutes with you. At night you come to bed tired and wanting to sleep. I could not make myself disturb you with my idle chatter and I would let you rest. As a result, much has remained unsaid. How much can I write in a letter? And today, I don't have the strength to write.

Oh beloved, what will befall you once I am gone? Why did you love me so that now you must suffer my absence? I am so unfortunate that even in death I will become the cause of your sorrow. I believe that the child will die with me. But if it were to live, I am not worried about it. I have full faith in your love. Once I am gone, our child will remind you of me. Is it possible that you will not care for your child? It is possible that the love I received will be directed towards someone else. Even so, my beloved, you are wise, impartial and thoughtful. You have so many precious qualities apart from your love. May God keep you virtuous. I have full faith that you will care for your child, and with that knowledge I will accept the snares of the God of Death. If I have a worry, it is about Sundar. Her brother has snatched away her ornaments. She has no place where she can even go and weep. Take care of her. Our family has good people, but you must take special care of her because she has no one else. Give all my ornaments to her, only then will my soul find peace. And my last memory, my child, if it survives, should be given to Sundar to raise. Please do this much for me, dearest beloved!

And what will become of you? Why did you love me so that now you must suffer? Won't you do something for me? I have already spoken to Yashoda. Her daughter is ten years old; she will prove to be even better than me as a wife. Will you not accept her once I am gone? I am worried for you, dearest. You must do what I ask of you. Those who are unmarried suffer less, but a fish that has lived in the waters of love cannot live without it. Forget me. All the pleasures and joys that we have shared flash before my eyes as I write. My marriage to you filled my life, my being. God, pray grant me my beloved as a husband in the next life as well. But for now, you must forget all that. Take it that none of this ever happened. My beloved, are we then to part? God's will be done.

My dearest, you must forget our love and drown your sorrows.
Forget that we once wandered this illusory world together.
Your virtue-less Gunial.

Vidya Chatura ran his hand over his forehead and looked up from the letter. These words written by his wife in the face of death left a deep impact on his heart. If he could, he would have cried. His mind grappled with the past, the present and the future as depicted in the letter. He felt somewhat calmer then. There cannot be a man harsher than me, he thought. Two months have passed. We live in the same house; yet we could not talk to each other. It is natural for her to feel this way. I was caught in my work and she in hers. I had no time. She, too, had no time. I allowed her to be caught up in work and other worries—all this is a result of that. I also pushed her to the limit. I should never have allowed things to come to such a pass. What a brave woman! She is still so young, and yet she freed me from all responsibility towards the family. But her mind seems to have weakened. There is no danger to her life as she fears. No, no! If she were to die, that would be my misfortune. If she were my brother, she could have been the Karbhari, she is such an able woman. She is my fortune. God, whatever You do will be for the good. I must be firm. I must not waver. Today is the day of my trial. What a noble and generous heart! How much she cares for my family and me! Gunial! My dearest Gunial! What can I possibly do for you? I cannot do even a fraction of what you do for me. I am grateful. Oh God!

Just then Doctor Asharansharan Babu's carriage drew up outside. Vidya Chatura snapped out of his reverie at the sound of the approaching carriage. He got up and said aloud: 'The first thing I will do is not care for customs. I will accompany the doctor to my Gunial. I will stand beside her and assist the doctor. It is my duty to break custom and give up shame. I will do so. Customs are not dearer to me than my Gunial'. Vidya Chatura accompanied the doctor into the room where Gunasundari lay unconscious. The women stared at him as he walked past them. Vidya Chatura said without hesitation or shame, 'Sundarbhabhi, please tell Doctor Sahib everything in detail'. Vidya Chatura was the breadwinner of the family. Who could chastise him? Who could have said: This is a woman's domain and such transgressions are not permissible? If Ganchatura had so transgressed, the skies would have fallen on him. But everyone adjusted themselves to Vidya Chatura and made a show of concern for Gunasundari. Sundargauri, who was sitting with Gunasundari's head in her lap, had just begun her narration to the doctor when Gunasundari stirred and seemed to regain consciousness. Her heavy-lidded eyes slowly opened and she saw her husband standing next to her bed. As she gazed at him unblinking, these words uttered softly seemed torn from the very depths of her being.

Bereft of compassion, O Yama
Your fearful eyes blind me
Today, you must wait: let me look
Upon my love to my heart's content
Even at the hour of death, you

Are implacable, O Yama, fixed like inlaid gold
Let me gaze upon him a while yet—
I see him, and still the heart yearns
Though the light in my eyes dims
He remains engraved upon my iris
Wait, O Yama, wait! I cannot leave with you just yet!
Demon, how can I abandon my beloved for you?
He is the jewel of my heart—not worthless like you
Let me cry, let me cry just once in his embrace
My beloved, you must forget our love
Yama pays my entreaties no heed
Dying, I chant your name and weep
Yet I smile and pray that in another birth
I will find my Chatura again

Gunasundari caught Sundargauri's hand and said, 'Sundarbhabhi, do not consider me shameless. Do I not have the right to say even a few words of affection to my beloved from the deathbed?' And exhausted, she slumped back in bed. Vidya Chatura could no longer curb his emotions. He told the doctor, 'I will be back,' and almost ran up the stairs to his room. He kneeled down on the bed and wept without restraint. He got up, washed his face but the tears still flowed unabated. He composed himself and washed his face again. But he could not bring himself to go down. His pride in his equanimity had vanished. Finally, he looked down from the window and told Kumari, 'Please tell Doctor Sahib that I am upstairs and that he should come up when his work is over'. The doctor was long in coming. As he waited anxiously, Vidya Chatura's mind was full of strange thoughts. Once Mallaraj's dearest friend was killed in battle. In order to attack the enemy, Mallaraj had to walk over his friend's dead body. That is true equanimity. How can I even compare my feebleness with his forbearance? A kshatriya is a kshatriya, and a brahmin just a brahmin! Even Jarashankar Mama says that social responsibility and the feebleness of love do not go together. That should be the motto of doing one's duty. The dharma of performing one's duty lies in overcoming all personal sorrow to face one's obligations. Gunial, you have proved far superior to me! You have done penance by performing your duty to perfection—till the very last. What supreme sense of duty! You kept things from me so as not to cause me pain. Such industry and so much love! Will I be true to your love if I show forbearance in the face of this adversity? Let the kshatriya do his duty; but even if I am considered effeminate, my Gunial, I will weep for you. You remembered me even in the face of death! 'Yet I smile and pray that in another birth, I will find my Chatura again.' God is compassionate. You shall live, Gunial. God is merciful, both on you and your Chatura. Fortitude, which had eluded Vidya Chatura even on consideration of his duty, came to him at last on the realisation that God was merciful. He rose. His eyes lit up, his heart filled with new life and hope. He thought: How can I, a man, cry? As he slowly began to climb down the steps, he was suffused with joy and pride. A smile played on his lips. My Gunial, it is you who have made me aware of God's mercy. Even if I were to put aside your love, your virtues alone would enable me to conduct myself in this and the next world. Unknown to yourself, you have taught me how to administer the state. You have also shown me the path to God. Mallaraj had said that the administrator requires the qualities of a woman. If that be true, Gunial, I shall be made the Karbhari someday. There can be no love without partiality. Moved by a profound gratitude and love, the husband regained his composure and came down to meet the doctor.

Some respect vaidyas and hakims and disparage doctors. Others do the reverse; they praise only the doctors. Jarashankar and Mallaraj were of the same age. Jarashankar also had the right to jest with the king. He would say, 'People are not at fault. It is the doctors and vaidyas who decry each other; so people learn to do the same. When healers fight amongst themselves, people get their services cheaply, so it is in their interest to fuel these quarrels.' Mallaraj was partial to neither doctors nor vaidyas. For him, whoever could heal effectively was good. He gave the example of Emperor Akbar who had collected men from all faiths in his court. Similarly, Mallaraj had made place for the doctor, vaidya, hakim and barber. He encouraged all of them and would say that if they competed among themselves, it would benefit the people of his state. However, in two or three native states, doctors had taken advantage of their English education to gain proximity to the British

Agency, and used this proximity to further their influence in the state and meddled in the Karbhar. This had greatly angered Mallaraj and prompted an outburst. 'Merely because he knows English, a doctor becomes a Karbhari. If tomorrow a barber learns English, should he also lay claim on the Karbhar? With such doctors and barbers, the state will turn upside down! I have no use for people who neglect their own work and meddle in other people's work. These dakshini doctors are given to doing such things. And all doctors are dakshinis! We shall do without a doctor.'

Vidya Chatura, quite naturally, was partial to doctors. He was in fact instrumental in the appointment of a Bengali doctor in the state, and he did this so skilfully that Mallaraj had no objection. There were several reasons for this. The Bengali doctor was learned and able; he had come on a relatively low salary; he had travelled far in search of livelihood and hence his only interest was in doing his job well. Moreover his relatives were less likely to visit him often here; he also had little chance of gaining favour of the government in Bombay; and though he appeared tough as a tiger, he was in fact meek as a cow. For all these and similar reasons, Mallaraj had agreed to his appointment, and the credit for it went to Vidya Chatura. The doctor knew he had obtained the job on Vidya Chatura's recommendation. He also considered Vidya Chatura a man of refinement and kept cordial relations with him. The wise doctor now gauged the reason behind Vidya Chatura's sudden departure from the labour room and allowed the husband to take control of his emotions alone.

The men sat around the doctor. In a while Dukhba walked up to them and gave them the news that Gunasundari had given birth to a girl. While it was not considered to be a matter for great celebration, it was also not devoid of the contentment typical of Indians at a child's birth. The new child was duly welcomed. 'Good, Goddess Laxmi has come to our house.' Manchatura enquired about the new mother. Her good health and wellbeing was something to cheer about. The doctor gave necessary instructions for care of the new mother and child and got up to leave. Vidya Chatura walked with him to the door where the two conversed softly for a while. He went up to his room after that.

Gunasundari was naturally confined to her bed. Each one of the others did their assigned work. Things worked well for three or four days, after which the wheels of the household began to move sluggishly and erratically. The absence of the one person who looked after the household was now felt. Her true worth was recognised. Initially, everyone felt that their own needs were not met well. Manchatura felt a slackening in his care as the person responsible for his care was now also required to do other tasks in the house. Not just that, the woman who assigned everyone their tasks and ensured their perfect execution was confined to her bed. Her intelligence, patience, gentleness and affection were sorely missed. The old man was now neglected. There were daily disputes in the house. Gunasundari was also neglected. Dharmalaxmi could not move about easily. She tried to do her bit for Gunasundari, but for her, worship was most important and came first. A task that has to be jointly performed tends to be neglected as no one claims responsibility for it. As a result no one cared to make special food for the new mother; even the infant girl was neglected.

One day, no one had prepared Manchatura's medicines until noon. It was almost lunchtime and there was no sign of food either. The irate old man got up and silently walked around the house, observing everyone. He first went up to Vidya Chatura's room. Vidya Chatura had come home tired and hungry from work and fallen asleep. Bed bugs walked in a line on his bed; the bed sheet was dirty and litter was heaped in a corner of the room. Manchatura cursed everyone and went down. He walked into the kitchen. Dukhba was freshly bathed and ready to cook, but the vegetables were still uncut. Manchatura found her staring undecidedly at the vegetables. His anger shot up. He walked towards the parsal. He could hear Ganchatura singing in his room. Chandika lolled on the swing while Chanchal stood talking to her with a broom in her hand. They were so engrossed in their chatter that neither noticed Manchatura. He walked towards Gunasundari's room of confinement. Sundargauri was trying to prepare medicines for Gunasundari and also care for the infant in her cradle. Gunasundari was pressing her stomach to relieve her hunger pangs and issuing instructions to Sundar as to what should be done.

Manchatura felt sorry for her. He came out and saw the children rushing around and pushing each other on the terrace. The door of the house was left wide open. A street dog had walked in. A servant had gone out to the well to draw water, but Manchatura saw him chatting with someone. He drove away the dog, closed the door and went towards Dharmalaxmi's room. She was absorbed in her worship. The wick and the ghee in her lamp were burnt out and the light had died. She was searching for a wick, ghee and a matchbox to light the lamp. Her back was towards Manchatura who was at the door. Unbathed, he stealthily went up to the shrine, picked up all the idols and walked out unnoticed, unheard. He was so angry he thought of throwing the idols into the water tank. On second thoughts, he kept all of them in the water pitcher, quietly walked back to his room and lay down to watch the drama unfold.

Manchatura and Dharmalaxmi were quite unlike each other. But their conjugal life was not without substance. Manchatura was intelligent. He not only had the ability to become adept at any task he faced, he also wished to complete the task as soon as possible; he was ill at ease with incomplete tasks. He did not hesitate to remove any obstacle from his path—be it in his own character, the disposition of others, divine or manmade, of religion or morality, of his own self-interest or the good of others. The only thing he understood was that obstacles should be overcome and the goal attained. From his young days, Manchatura had become skilled at dealing with peculiarities of human nature. He could cajole, entice and, if necessary, tyrannise others and make them useful and valuable to him and adjust to his needs. If that person happened to be someone from his own family, he dealt with them in a high-handed way. If he found that his own disposition was coming in the way of his goal and that he was required to do something that was repugnant to him, he did not hesitate. Just as the elephant trainer uses a prod to guide the elephant, Manchatura prodded his conscience to do what was repugnant to him. He would convince himself that it was obligatory for him to do so and took pride in its fulfilment. He was not a non-believer, nor was he on the immoral path. He followed both religion and morality so long as they did not hinder the pursuit of his goals. He remained steadfast in his pursuit. The strength of his character enabled him to overcome all obstacles.

Dharmalaxmi was born and raised in an atmosphere of deep religiosity and had an abiding faith in religion. She had imbibed all the traditional norms of social and religious conduct. She spent her entire day in observing these norms. She was required to exercise the same level of expertise and effort in resolving issues of social conduct as required by theologians to resolve questions of religious conduct. Women from her caste and the entire village brought to her problems and disputes of social conduct. Dharmalaxmi would cite precedents from olden times, authorities of texts and norms, and she would provide an acceptable resolution. This pleased Manchatura no end. He liked to pose new and difficult problems to test her intelligence. She was considered an expert in 'women's science' and her prestige was a matter of pride for him. It was natural that a woman like Dharmalaxmi was superstitious beyond reasonable limits, that she would create hindrances even in the smallest of matters and stand like a stone wall when faced with larger issues. Manchatura was amused by her preoccupations so long as they did not hinder his activities. But he was prompt to remove any obstacles that she put in his way. He would mock her, at times order her out of his way, try to reason with her, and at other times create such situations that she would not want to displease her husband. Manchatura was also given to losing his temper in a way that could turn a wedding celebration into a funeral. He would thus try all possible means to shake off any obstacles that she might place in his path. He saw the household in utter disarray during Gunasundari's confinement and realised that the wheels would not move smoothly so long as Dharmalaxmi did not take charge. Engrossed in her rituals she was oblivious to this. He felt that she needed to be jolted by some drastic measure. And so he took all her idols and kept them in the water pitcher. He appeared unconcerned but he was in fact quite anxious to see if his shot would find its mark. He bit his lower lip and twirled his moustaches and waited to see what would happen.

Dharmalaxmi found the matchbox and lit the lamp. As she placed the lamp in the shrine she realised that her gods had disappeared. Her devout heart fluttered—she was stunned. She looked for her gods all over. Dharmalaxmi could not understand this miracle. She came out of the room which housed her shrine and looked around. There was no one out there. She thought: Did someone come in and steal my gods when my attention was elsewhere? She opened the main door and found the dog that Manchatura had driven away patiently waiting outside. The servant was still chatting away. Dharmalaxmi asked the servant, 'Did you see anyone come inside?' He shook his head and said, 'No, Mataji'. She scolded him and called him back to his chores. She shouted in irritation, 'Chanchal! Chanchal! Where have my gods disappeared?' Chanchal rushed in with a broom in her hand. Chandika, Sundargauri, Dukhba and the children followed her and they all crowded into the courtyard. There was much confusion and they all made a lot of noise. Ganchatura stopped singing and came down. Vidya Chatura woke up with a start and also came down. Everyone was simultaneously asking questions and suggesting possible explanations for the sudden disappearance of Dharmalaxmi's gods. Instructions were shouted and a search was mounted. Dukhba suggested that the children could have taken them for their play. Chanchal and Ganchatura opined that mice might have dragged them away. Vidya Chatura suggested, 'They might have fallen off the platform, just look around the shrine'. Finally, Manchatura came out rubbing his eyes and asked in anger, 'What is all this ruckus about? No one is concerned about food. It is almost one o'clock and no one says come, the lunch is served. It is as if there are no women in this house!' Vidya Chatura replied, 'Pitaji, Matashri cannot find her gods. That is the problem. They have suddenly disappeared from the shrine and cannot be found'.

Manchatura retorted, 'The gods will be found if they wish to be found. But is anyone bothered about feeding all of us, the living gods? Gods will be displeased with those who don't care for the living. When displeased, the gods can disappear even from locked temples, let alone home shrines. Dukhba, go and give us the food. She will have to fast until her gods are found.'

Dharmalaxmi's distress only deepened with these bitter barbs. His words were not only harsh and sharp, he also insulted her gods. Her eyes filled with tears. She clamped her hands over her ears and said, 'Oh why do you utter such things fit for a non-believer? The merit of organising the worship of gods in Kaliyug is greater than performing rituals in Satyug. You and I have suffered so much in this birth. Do you want suffering to be our lot even in the next birth? We share each other's merits and sins. You do not worship nor do you allow me to do mine in peace. Woe be to your hunger and your grey hair! Your hunger has made you abuse the gods. You do not remember the gods even in your old age. If I earn some merit by worshipping, our children will see better days. Have some consideration. Dukhba! Chanchal! Chandika! It is because of you three wretches that I had to listen to such terrible words today! If the younger daughter-in-law were managing the house, I would never have seen such a day. Couldn't all of you look after the house even for a month or two? Chanchal, I now know where my gods are. You know your father's temper. Go, feed him and the others. I do not want to eat until my gods are restored'. Dharmalaxmi sat before the empty shrine and wept copiously. She pleaded and supplicated before the shrine, 'Maharaja, You are all merciful. Please forgive us. Please disregard his words and deeds. Let my merit be his and let his sins be mine, but please forgive us'.

Manchatura raged and shouted at everyone. He glared at Dukhba, pursed his lips at Chanchal, gnashed his teeth at Chandika and made faces at Ganchatura. He raised his hand at the servant as if to slap him. Manchatura did not wish to appear partial to Vidya Chatura and so he stood with his back to him. But he ignored Sundargauri. He pointed out to everyone their irresponsible and callous behaviour and showered abuses on them. Finally he sent Sundargauri to look after Gunasundari. Raising his stick at them, he drove Chandika and his two daughters out of the house and latched the door. Then he ordered Ganchatura, 'Go and cook food for all of us. These wretches deserve what they get!'

Vidya Chatura had stayed away from the family since childhood. Witnessing his father's wrath for the first time, he stood petrified not knowing what to do. Neighbours gathered outside the house and some of them banged on the door. Dharmalaxmi saw that the scene had gone out of control and that Manchatura would not relent. She wiped her tears and came out of her room. Just as a priest knows the character of her divine, Dharmalaxmi knew Manchatura. She knew that he was more concerned about everyday life and living than questions of dharma and right conduct. She saw that he was like a stormy sea at present. It would be easier to submit to him rather than try to go against the current. With this realisation, her mind cleared. She also recognised that Manchatura's anger was not without basis. She could see that the house was in total disarray. She realised that to remedy it was well within her grasp. Dharmalaxmi felt it was also her duty to care for the family. With this thought, she felt at peace in her heart. Her visage grew grave. If she were to look after the family's welfare, it would give a lot of people joy. If the good of so many was within her reach, why should that duty not be considered superior to her rituals? She felt that the Creator who loves all beings and who imbues creation with bliss must also hold duty towards the household as a supreme obligation. These thoughts acquired the conviction of faith for her. With her faith renewed, Dharmalaxmi forgot about her idols and decided to take the reins of the household in her hands. She resolved to put behind her the chaos of the house, Manchatura's bitter words, the ignominy of the family drama being played out in full public view, and the distress that it had caused to everyone. She emerged from this quagmire feeling purified for having immersed herself deeper in her love for the family. Just like a river broadens its course as it approaches the sea, Dharmalaxmi became more expansive as she approached Manchatura. He recognised the change in her and knew that his ploy had worked.

Dharmalaxmi's basic constitution was religious. Women tend to develop some qualities more than men; their bodies and intellect also mature sooner than men. Dharmalaxmi was a good example of this. Her father was blindly religious. She had absorbed religious instructions from a very tender age; so her religious belief had formed and hardened quite early. Even at the age of ten Dharmalaxmi was considered to be the most religious among all the girls in her neighbourhood. She was also intelligent, but given the overtly religious atmosphere of her house, she could have grown into a blindly superstitious person. She was married to Manchatura who was frequently transferred and changed jobs. It was difficult for her to strictly adhere to all religious observances. Moreover, Manchatura was temperamental and she was required to constantly adjust and accommodate herself to his moods. This balancing act was like walking on a sword's edge. If she had not possessed a sharp intellect, Dharmalaxmi could never have lived in harmony with her husband. Even outsiders knew this. 'Only Dharmalaxmi can deal with Manchatura's temper. Anyone else would not have lasted even a minute with him', they would say. She was religious but not blindly superstitious. She lived with a Rishi Durvasa-like husband till old age, loved and received the love of a man of fiery temperament, and still remained steadfast to her religiosity. This was made possible by her pure affection, earth-like forbearance, Vishnu-like peace, her sharp intellect and superior virtues. Vidya Chatura had hitherto remained ignorant of these qualities. As they became manifest, he felt proud that he was born to such a mother.

Manchatura had turned red with rage. His eyes were blood-shot, his brows furrowed. As he stood there still trembling, in this fearful aspect he looked like Lord Narasimha himself. Greatly anguished by the insult of her gods, Dharmalaxmi could not bring herself to smile. But she concealed her pain from her husband. As she approached him with a grave mien, her heart beat faster. Her cheeks appeared more sunken in her toothless mouth, a film of tears appeared in her bright intelligent eyes; her fair forehead was crinkled as her pristine white hair glistened with sweat, the kumkum in the parting of her hair was damp. She quietly said, 'I have realised your intent. But you know me well, when I get absorbed in worship I forget household chores. I admit it is my fault. But so much anger is not good. You have driven those three out of the house. People have gathered to watch the scene. It brings us nothing but ill repute'.

Dharmalaxmi walked up to the door and asked the three women to come inside. Manchatura drove out the onlookers and closed the door. Then he turned to his wife and said, 'Go and pick up your idols from the water pitcher. Today I threw them into the pitcher. But if I have to ever go hungry again, you will find them at the bottom of the well!' It took better part of an hour for his anger to subside completely. Dharmalaxmi removed the idols from the pitcher; no one thought of doing this for her. Clutching her gods to her bosom, she tearfully put them back in the shrine. Then she turned her attention to the house. But until the day she died, Dharmalaxmi could never forget that her gods had been consigned to an impure place. This remained her lifelong regret.

It seemed that the household would get back on track under Dharmalaxmi's watchful eyes, but her concern by itself was not sufficient to set the house right. She assigned work to everyone but she did not have the energy to go around checking to ensure that each task was done. The situation was reminiscent of the saying: good counsel stays with one only till the house gate. Soon, the younger women began to see her as crotchety and nagging and their affection for her diminished. They also began to flout her instructions. Initially they abused her in private, but over time they also insulted the old woman openly and spoke ill of her. Dharmalaxmi was also fed up. She took her complaints to Manchatura and often went to Gunasundari and cried. Gunasundari seized his opportunity to obtain her mother-in-law's affection. She also realised that she would have to achieve what her mother-in-law had failed to. She eagerly awaited the day when she would be allowed to take up household chores again. But little did Gunasundari know that she would be asked to perform tasks that she had neither previous knowledge nor experience of.

In Hindu society, joys and sorrows come in myriad different forms. For those who have not experienced or observed them closely, it is difficult to imagine them or explain. Gunasundari had come to believe that she had experienced all that one possibly could within the realm of the household. But knowledge and experience are limitless, and a young mind cannot fathom that apparent experience conceals deeper import and meanings. As one gains in education and age, new forms of experience and knowledge reveal themselves, just as having climbed to the top of a mountain, one glimpses higher peaks beyond. Experiences come like sea weaves. As one bears witness to new experiences, there are moments in which the mind, unknown even to itself, merges with the infinite, the divine. Having experienced the infinite, one becomes capable of discerning new hitherto untrodden paths and taking the first tentative steps. Gunasundari observed the household from her confinement. She also contemplated many things above and beyond this domesticity. She would often talk to herself thus: This was a novel experience, but what lies in store for tomorrow? Even in mundane everyday matters, a questing mind can find ideas to sustain itself, and thoughts and words like divine utterances can come together from unexpected quarters to nurture and enrich the mind. As she lay in her dark room of confinement, Gunasundari realised for the first time that in many ways, in many things, she was as inexperienced as her infant daughter, and she felt a new bond with her.

The day after Manchatura's show of temper Gunasundari's friend Yashoda came to visit her. When they were alone, Yashoda told her about the rumours circulating in town. 'It is being said that yesterday Vidya Chatura drove his sisters and sister-in-law out of the house. The old mother prevailed and got them back, but the mother and son had a bitter fight during which Vidya Chatura picked up the idols from her shrine and threw them away.' Gunasundari was astonished and deeply hurt that her innocent husband had been blamed. She quietly narrated the previous day's events to Yashoda. But in her mind, despite herself, she momentarily despised the entire family's conduct. When she was left alone she lay down, pulled the covers over herself and cried for hours in despair. This gave her a fever, which too went unnoticed and unattended.

Two-three days later a new problem arose. All the groceries were stored in a room on the first floor. Sundargauri was required to go up and fetch grocery whenever required. This poor widow had no other support but for Gunasundari. All the women were either jealous of her or bitter while the men appeared to be indifferent. Only Gunasundari's affection sustained her. That day all the women were eating their meal. The men had dispersed to their rooms. Sundargauri finished her meal quickly and went up to the grocery room to fetch some condiments to prepare Gunasundari's medication. It was noon. Standing in the bright sun, the young widow's fair complexion acquired a rosy hue. As she bent over to pick the condiments from a pot, her saree fluttered in the wind. The black saree covered her fair form as a dark cloud the sun. Her supple back was visible, arched like a rainbow. A lock of her hair had come to rest on her breasts. The heels of her soft bare feet were visible from below her saree. The dazzle of her body could have blinded any onlooker. Sundargauri was engrossed in her work and oblivious of such matters. Little did she know that eyes blinded by her beauty were watching her intently.

Males consume and females are objects of their consumption. This is a trait shared by human beings and animals alike. Among animals, the female is pursued by the male like a hunter pursues his prey. The difference is that the hunter kills while the female is possessed and kept. The male preserves the female as one protects a goose laying golden eggs. This sense of protection and nurturance tends to be more refined among the higher species; human society exemplifies this. A daughter unknown and unloved to begin with becomes the most intimate of associates and one who is loved like no other. The tradition of marriage is an outcome of this sense of preservation and possession. As long as the human in us dominates our animal instincts, this sense of protection survives. But when the beast in us triumphs, men pursue women as prey. Such men become incapable of any consideration of right and wrong, for we lose this capacity for discernment when we lose our humanity. Nevertheless, there are exceptions; it is possible for this to unfold more subtly. Ravana captured Sita as if he were the hunter and she, the prey. And yet, he could never violate her. He abducted her in his bestiality, but his higher sensibility taught him:

> I do not approve of the union, even if successfully brought about,
> of two lovers, one of whom is ardent and the other heart-whole,

> it is better that an equally enamoured pair should ever pine away hopeless of mutual happiness.[2]

All men are capable of being human and this enables them to be protective of orphaned and weak women. If all men were to acquire 'chivalry', the conduct of both men and women would become purer, and women would be freed from fear.

When Sundargauri stood up and turned around, to her surprise she found Ganchatura standing right next to her. Ganchatura was satiated with food and seemed drowsy. Roused from his slumber by the rustle of her feet, he had come out and seen Sundargauri standing alone, looking ever so beautiful. The beast in him asserted itself as soon as he saw her. He lost his capacity for judgement. He did not consider morality or his relationship with her; he did not consider that the house was full of people. Ganchatura had the audacity to come and stand close to Sundargauri, but not the courage to advance further. He stood there petrified, his limbs refusing to move. Only the flicker of his eyes betrayed his base desire. Sundargauri turned pale at the sight of him. She was gripped by fear. She dropped what she had collected and ran down the stairs. She missed the last step and fell down, but was not hurt. She rushed into Gunasundari's room, trembling as if his odious presence still shadowed her. Tears flowed from her eyes. Gunasundari had gone out of the room to eat. Sundargauri calmed herself with great effort but she was frightened. One has to constantly guard against the animal instincts. If they overpower us there is a danger we may lose our humanity for good, for the human beast is far worse than the animal one. The fear of this beast now pierced her heart like an arrow. Try as she might, Sundargauri could not rid herself of it. Her mind was in a flurry. She thought: Whom can I tell? How? How can I utter those words? Will I have the courage? Will anyone believe me? Why did this thought even occur to him? What will he do now? What will happen to me? What am I to do? How will I live in this house? Where else can I go? These and similar questions began

[2] Translator's note: C. H. Tawney, trans. *Malavikagnimitram* of Kalidasa, Canto 3, Verse 15, 2nd ed. (Calcutta: Thacker, Spink and Co., 1891), 49.

to torment Sundargauri. Her response to each such question was a deep sigh and tears. Over the next few days, she found no solace even in household chores. Usually the last resort of the friendless is sleep, but even that eluded her. She withered, her face appeared sunken and withdrawn, joy and laughter became alien to her. Tears welled up in her eyes every time she spoke to Gunasundari. Only one observant would have noticed how often she sighed while speaking. It never occurred to Sundargauri that someone might notice these changes in her. Ganchatura noticed, but felt helpless in face of his lust.

Gunasundari's affectionate heart did not take long to see these changes but she did not understand the reasons for it. Why would anyone else in the house bother? Gunasundari asked Sundargauri repeatedly and pleaded with her. But Sundar's response was the same every time, 'No, it is nothing. Your suspicion is baseless. I am just not feeling well since the past few days. There is nothing else to it'. Gunasundari did not believe her. Ultimately Gunasundari asked Sundargauri to touch and swear by her newborn daughter. She also threatened to go on a fast. Sundargauri forced herself to smile and said,'Why would you do such a thing? But for you, who else can I talk to? Can we women keep a secret all our lives? I will do what you want me to, but you must also swear by me and promise to do what I ask of you'. Gunasundari agreed. Sundar said,'All right then, I will tell you. But you must not ask me anything about it until I tell you myself. Both of us are bound by a mutual pledge'.

'Why can't you tell me right now?' asked Gunasundari.

'There must be a reason', replied Sundargauri.

'As long as I am alive no harm will come to you.'

'I know that. Is there anyone else I trust or consider my own?'

'All right then, will you tell me this evening or tonight?'

'I will tell you when I feel up to it. Ask me after two or three days.' The two went on arguing like this for a while, but Sundargauri was determined to say nothing; her heart would not allow a word to escape her lips.

Gunasundari's period of confinement finally came to an end. She had a ritual bath and could freely move about the house. She was not yet considered ritually pure and hence she could not touch anything in the house. But as she moved around and observed the goings on, the family drama became apparent to her.

5 Gunasundari (Continued)

You are forever changing, O' world.[1]

Gunasundari was still ritually impure and not allowed to touch anything in the house. In some other families it was permissible to touch dry utensils and clothes. But Dharmalaxmi made no such allowances. Hence, Gunasundari used this time in other pursuits.

She tried to fathom the minds of her family members. She spent time in Manchatura's room, talking to him about his childhood and life thereafter. She tried to understand what shortcomings the old patriarch saw in the house, what his wants and desires were. Gunasundari tried to assuage his anger towards other members of the family and assured him that she and her husband would fulfil all the wants that they were capable of fulfilling. She also gauged if he harboured any discontent or resentment towards her and Vidya Chatura and what he thought of them. She anticipated his anxieties and vexations and she took preventive measures. All this she did quite cleverly and unobtrusively. Gunasundari's intelligence, her patience and affection had its desired effect. Over time, Manchatura came to trust her. His anger subsided; he appeared to be largely content. His volatile anger was one of the reasons for his illness. Gunasundari soothed his mind and body. Not only Manchatura but gradually other members of the family, too, came under her spell one by one. Gunasundari would sit with Dharmalaxmi when she performed her rituals, spend

[1] Author's note: *Kusum Mala*, Narsinhrao Bholanath Divetia, 1887.

time with Dukhba in the kitchen patiently listening to her woes, talk to Chanchal in the afternoons and converse with Chandika as well. She would gather the children around her and tell them stories, sing for them, read out to them, listen to their troubles, counsel them and enjoy their company. Gunasundari was an elder among the elderly and a child among children. In this way, like Manchatura, everyone else in the family opened up to her. They shared with her their frustrations, they saw her as their confidante, grew affectionate towards her and genuinely sought to make her happy. They even took care not to hurt her feelings. Before too long, Gunasundari became the thread holding all the dissimilar beads together. This apparently happy and tranquil dream was not without its shadow, however, nor was it everlasting.

One afternoon when Gunasundari was alone, she sat reminiscing about the history of her own family. Happy and sad memories of her childhood flooded her mind. As an adolescent, unable to understand her husband's aspirations, Gunasundari had felt distanced from him. This had distressed her; but it was her husband who had come to her aid and eased her distress. Vidya Chatura was a school teacher. She had little to do in the house. There were no other family members then. She had every opportunity to enjoy her husband's company and affection. The two had not a care in the world. They were in the bloom of youth and as the world of senses opened up before them, they took as much delight in the pleasures of the body as in cultivating higher aesthetic sensibilities and sharing the myriad subtle pleasures of the mind. Abruptly crushed under the burden of a large joint family, these pleasures were now a distant dream. Gunasundari was of a sudden gripped by an overwhelming sense of despondency that her desires were to forever remain unfulfilled. This hopelessness took possession of her mind much as a cruel creditor lays seize to a debtor's house. For five long months, she had not had one conversation with Vidya Chatura despite living in the same house. Tears welled up in her eyes and coursed down her cheeks. Kumud Sundari was lying in her lap. A few tears fell on her. Gunasundari wiped them and said, 'Oh my child, how blissful you are! Will you too have to face all that I do one day?' She lifted little Kumud up in her arms. Kumud smiled—it was her first smile. Overwhelmed with emotion, Gunasundari pressed her to her bosom. It was almost as if she had a premonition, that in future, despite their deep and abiding love for each other, Sarasvatichandra and Kumud were destined to live their lives as strangers. Gunasundari pressed her daughter closer to her heart and sobbed out aloud. Just then she heard the soft movement of someone's feet. Someone had heard her crying. But who? She quickly wiped her tears and composed herself.

That day, the family had been invited for a meal at Jarashankar's house. Gunasundari, still not free of the impurities of childbirth, had remained at home. She was alone and had not latched the door from inside. Vidya Chatura was busy and was to go for the meal a little later. He had finished his work and come home. He opened and shut the door so softly that Gunasundari did not hear him enter. Finding no one else in the house, Vidya Chatura turned towards the parsal. He thought he had heard Gunasundari weeping. It was as if his heart had silently understood Gunasundari's longing, her despondency and drawn him to her. When he entered her room, she had just wiped her tears. Gunasundari looked up and saw Vidya Chatura standing at her door. It was after many months that the two were alone. She had no patience even to gaze at his face. She forgot that she was not yet permitted to touch him. She put little Kumud down on the bed and she ran to him and embraced him. Like a ray of moonlight that envelops a cloud in its embrace, her arms entwined themselves around his neck. She lifted herself off the ground and hung from his neck like Lord Vishnu's garland which reaches down to his feet. Vidya Chatura lifted her up in his arms and carried her to the swing. He seated her on the swing, which had become a pleasure boat, and sat down next to her. He picked up their daughter, lay her in his lap and asked Gunasundari with a smile, 'What is the reason for such irrepressible joy?' In response, Gunasundari kept a hand on his shoulder and with the other, she drew his hand and touched it to her face. She looked at him unblinking for moments, smiling. Then her eyes were drawn to some papers he was carrying. She could see something written in his hand on the back of an opened envelope. She took it from him and read it.

True love no time nor distance can destroy;
And independent of all present joy,
It grows in absence, as renewed delight,
Some dear memorials, some loved lines excite.[2]

She said, 'My answer to your question is this: how did you think of this verse?'

He said, 'These lines from the *Meghdoot* came to me all of a sudden while I was sitting in office, and I wrote them down.'

'But why did *this* very verse come to you?'

'Now you are cross-examining me like a lawyer, Gunial,' he said, smiling.

'Of course! Those who do not give straight answers need to be cross-examined.'

'All right. Ask whatever you wish.'

'Why did this verse come to you in the middle of office work? And even if it did, why did you have to write it down on an envelope that could have gone to some other hand? Have you lost your heart so completely? Come on, give me an answer. See, even this little girl is looking at you expectantly. She is a witness.' Gunasundari's eyes seemed to be laughing triumphantly at him. She playfully kept her hand on his shoulder again, as if the glorious morning sun had kept a rainbow against a mountain.

'All right, Gunial. You win.'

'No, that is not sufficient. You are caught now, answer you must. I, too, have learnt something of your craft, you see.'

Vidya Chatura laughed. She continued, 'You could, for instance, say that the feelings that took possession of me when I looked at you also possessed you when you thought of me.'

'All right, yes, that is what it was. Anything else?'

'So your condition was the same as mine. If you ever ask me again about my feelings for you, you will be caught just like today.'

[2] H. H. Wilson trans. *The Cloud Messenger*, Kalidasa (London: Richard Watts, 1843), 98.

The husband and wife thus talked pleasantly for some time, moving joyfully from one thing to another. But their youthful emotions soon gave way to household concerns and they both turned grave. Vidya Chatura asked Gunasundari in detail about each member of the family. From her descriptions and responses, he also gauged how she felt towards each one of them. This allowed him to fathom the core of her emotional life. One by one, the layers of distance and silence that had grown over their hearts began to peel off, and he saw the startling purity of her heart. Just as the eyes feast on the beauty of the body, Vidya Chatura with his mind's eye feasted on the unsullied beauty of Gunasundari's heart. He saw in her heart a vast and unblemished love for him. He saw as much love and concern for the family as his father had, forgiveness like that of his mother, more industriousness than Chanchal, more delicacy than Sundargauri, a far greater capacity than himself to bear the entire family's burden gracefully, and the childlike joy and innocence of the newborn. The beauty of her heart enticed him. Just as a lover tries to undo the knots of his beloved's garments, he gently tried to loosen the knots of her heart and lay it bare. Bashful all at once, she tried to stop him, and then he could no longer contain himself. In a moment of desire he drew her to him and embraced her tightly, and these words escaped his lips:

The bold presumption of her lover's hands
To cast aside the loosened vest, withstands;
And, feeble to resist, bewildered turns
Where the rich lamp with lofty radiance burns;
And vainly whelms it with a fragrant cloud
Of scented dust, in hope the light to shroud.[3]

'Gunial, this is our Alakapuri. We could not speak to each other for five months. But haven't we made up for all those lost months today? Speaking for myself, I am satiated, replete. Who else could have showered such nectar of love and joy on my family but for you? Men may try, but they can never look after the house as a woman does. You have cared for my old parents and my immature selfish siblings

[3] H. H. Wilson, trans. *The Cloud Messenger*, 68.

with such generosity of spirit. I am truly fortunate to have you, Gunial. But there is nothing at all that I can do for you. What have I ever done for you? The days when we took delight in sublime conversations and lofty thoughts are over. You are reduced to doing the work of a cook and a servant from dawn to night. Is this my gift to your many virtues? Am I lacking in means? Am I wanting in generosity?' A deep sigh escaped Vidya Chatura. His hands no longer held Gunasundari's, they clutched the chain of the swing. His face was lined by anxiety and concern.

Gunasundari took Kumud from his lap and said, 'No. The mistake is mine. I shared with you the goings on in the house and I had to hear your praise. You praise me but not yourself, which means that you consider me separate from yourself. Let us close this matter now'. With her adroit response, she attained two objectives: she cut short his praise of her, and she made him laugh.

'All right, Madam Sahib. I realise my error. I will not praise you. Now do go on with your narration.'

Gunasundari continued with her narration which rolled on like an incessantly moving Persian wheel. Finally she came to the point. 'I have spoken to everyone in the house. Firstly, you are doing so well but the elder brother has no work. This does not behove you. Pitaji is unhappy about this. Secondly, everyone but Dukhba is happy in the house, which does not look good. If you extend some help to Sahasrai, his days of running around in hiding will end and he will be able to come home and start some work; he is like a brother to you after all. Kumari is betrothed but there is no money to arrange her marriage. Dukhba is withering away everyday in this worry and she is unable to share it with anyone. Our child will have all the good things but Chanchalbehn's children have no ornaments. This does not behove us. Even Mataji feels this is not right. She also wants a silver shrine for her gods; it is her heart's desire. For the present, these are the wants. The rest I will tell you later.'

'There is more?! Tell me now itself.' Vidya Chatura was stunned. He did not earn much. Moreover, he had to bear the brunt of expenses for the entire large household. The expenditure had greatly increased.

Gunasundari's simant ceremony and feast cost a lot of money. All their savings were spent on it.

Gunasundari realised what she had done. She said, 'Those who have to bear the burden realise the weight of it. I did not realise your situation to begin with. You praise me but remain silent about the burden you bear. Why don't you praise yourself? It is true that our hardships are apparent to all; but the burden you bear remains hidden. You tell me that you are unable to do anything for me. But what have I done for you? For the last five months I have not seen you have one free moment for yourself. I can share my worries, but you have no place to go and no one with whom you can unburden yourself. After so many months you came to talk with me. But the sinner that I am, I could not even bring myself to speak of things that would give you joy ...' While she was still speaking, the door suddenly flew open and Sundargauri rushed in, panting. Vidya Chatura wore the pagdi on his head with a disappointed look and got up to leave for his meal. Gunasundari watched him leave, full of remorse. As he receded from view, she closed the door feeling close to tears. She turned around and saw Sundargauri trembling with fear and ready to burst out crying.

'Sundarbhabhi, what's wrong? Why are you trembling like this?' Before Sundargauri could respond, the door burst open again and Ganchatura entered in some haste and caught the shoulder of the woman standing with her back to the door. He had expected to find Sundargauri, but he found he was holding Gunasundari's shoulder instead. Realising his mistake, he immediately removed his hand. 'Oh, it's you!' he said, ashamed, 'I assumed it was your sister-in-law.' Gunasundari, initially startled, was now enraged at his attempt to conceal a sin with a lie, and was about to retort, 'Which sister-in-law?' But before she could say anything, Ganchatura had rushed up the stairs and gone into his room. Gunasundari realised that nothing would be gained from whipping up the matter further. She composed herself and turned towards Sundargauri who stood shivering in a corner of the room, and gently said, 'This must be the reason for your tears the other day as also the cause of your trembling today. Now I understand everything.'

Sundargauri could no longer contain herself. Her lips quivered from fear and shame as tears streamed down her eyes. She could not speak. She leaned against a wall, petrified. Her sari slipped from her head. She covered her face with her hands as leaves cover a flower. Even before Gunasundari could make a move to comfort her, Chandika rushed into the room in some rage. It seemed that something untoward had happened at the meal. She pounced on the terrified and weeping Sundargauri and pushed her further against the wall. 'Rand! You revealed your true character today!' she screamed at her. Gunasundari came to Sundargauri's aid, pleading, 'Bhabhi, what is this! Let her be!' She somehow freed her from Chandika's clutches. Chandika left the room in a huff, showering abuses on her as she went up to her room. She stood before her husband and beat her breasts and wailed as if she was in mourning. Gunasundari was stunned by Chandika's rage and wondered: Did Sundar have a part to play in this? She corrected herself, No, there seems to be some misunderstanding. But before she could ask Sundar anything, the other women and children walked into the house. Gunasundari pretended as if nothing had happened. She asked about the meal. She waited for someone else to bring up the matter. Not wanting to draw attention to herself, Sundargauri got busy with household work. Gunasundari realised that no answers were forthcoming from anyone. Dharmalaxmi seemed angry; she sat with a surly face. Dukhba appeared nervous and, unable to find anything to do, she went and lay down on the swing. Chanchal busied herself with some work but kept muttering under her breath. Gunasundari watched the scene. For some reason everyone seemed to have lost their tempers that day. This was new for Gunasundari. Are they angry with me? Has someone been spreading false stories about me? Or are they angry with my husband? Oh God! I constantly watch their moods, I try my utmost to keep them happy, and still I am subjected to such things. Is this also a part of the burden of the household? Did I really do something wrong? Thousand such questions swamped her mind. Gunasundari looked at everyone's face one by one but found no answers. She went to help Dharmalaxmi who snapped at her, 'No, no, leave it. Let everything be as it is. I do not need any help nor do I want anything from you'. Gunasundari pretended she had not heard the rebuke and carried on with her work. Suddenly, Chanchal rushed towards her, visibly angry, took away the work from her and started doing it herself. Gunasundari went and sat next to Dukhba on the swing. Dukhba instantly got up as if Gunasundari's touch would defile her and sat further away on the threshold of the parsal. Gunasundari tried to talk to her, 'Motibehn, what has happened?' Dukhba did not answer her straight. 'Let it be. Why do you bother? You do what you have to.' Spurned from all sides, tears welled up in Gunasundari's eyes. She did not wish to respond to anyone in anger or hurt. She needed to be alone. Though the period of her ritual impurity was not yet over, Gunasundari took Kumud and went up to her room. Sundargauri saw her go up the stairs. Seeing Gunasundari upset, she forgot her own distress and thought: You need to please and plead with everyone, but no one needs to please you! How is this fair?

Before she stepped into the room which she and Vidya Chatura used as their bed room, Gunasundari saw the state it was in. The room was dirty and in utter disarray. She was unable to care for it and no one had attended to it. She wondered how Vidya Chatura was able to sleep here. She could not bring herself to enter. A sudden desolation possessed Gunasundari. Forgetting her insult, hurt and anger, she stood on the last step of the staircase and gazed forlornly at their bed. She was nudged out of her thoughts by Sundargauri's touch. They walked into the room. Gunasundari lay Kumud down on the bed and sat down beside her. Sundargauri held Gunasundari's hand to comfort her. Wrapt in their own thoughts and silences, neither woman moved or spoke for some time. Finally, Gunasundari spoke.

> *In this unsurpassable ocean of the world, I am sinking*
> *O my beloved and compassionate master, tell me who is my true refuge?*
> *The master replied: The great boat of the feet of Vishvesha, the Lord of the Universe, is the refuge.*[4]

[4] Author's note: *Adi Shankar Prashnottari.*

As soon as she had uttered this verse, as if the master's benedictions had reached her, her attention was drawn to Vidya Chatura's books. She picked up a notebook of his personal jottings. She opened a page—it was the page on which he had written down Maharaja Mallaraj's counsel. 'Sundarbhabhi, come, take a look at this! The day your brother-in-law joined the Maharaja's service, Mallaraj had counselled him. This is what he had said. Do take a look. How many duties of women has he enumerated! Men have even more obligations. Even we would benefit from this counsel.'

Sundargauri read it and returned the notebook. She said, 'Bhabhi, all this is fine. We, too, are human. The others can feel bad if they want, but you should not feel hurt! Your husband earns and provides for all of us. You do all the housework and you also deal with everyone's tantrums, complaints and taunts! No one cares at all for what you do or think. Not just that, they accuse you unjustly of all manner of things and you have no hope of getting a fair hearing. Is this the way of doing things? Is this at all fair? Even Mallaraj would not advise you to bear with so much!'

Gunasundari was silent for a while, her eyes on the ground. Then she said, 'Sundarbhabhi, it is not how you take it to be. God places thousands of hardships upon us. It cannot be without a reason. A person is formed by suffering'.

'Let your God go to sleep! What are you talking about? I have not experienced any joy, even a moment's happiness ever. And I am certain that I won't, not in this life at least. A widow's lot is ignominy and suffering and relentless suffering until death relieves her of her misery. Bhabhi, where is my share of happiness? Don't I deserve any? It is said that my present suffering is due to my deeds in my past life. That may be so, but all talk of redeeming our sins for the next birth is false. Hope brings nothing but dejection, misery and more suffering.'

'What you say is not entirely false, Sundarbhabhi. But if one believes in the validity of one's past life, then why not in the next birth? It is an incessant cycle of eighty-four lakh births. A person does penance for the next life. The suffering we bear is a form of penance.'

'How can it be called a penance? People who undergo hard penance do so voluntarily. But the suffering that befalls us is not what we asked for. It comes on us, and we bear it as God's will. We have no choice.'

'But there are two ways in which we can deal with this suffering. One can complain and blame God. Or, one can believe that whatever God does is for the good. One way is to bear the suffering simply because it has befallen us. But the other way is to gladly submit to it and become willing servants of the divine will and consider this submission as our penance. Everyone in the family is displeased and angry with me right now. But soon, if not today then tomorrow, their anger will surely subside. We know this. But despite this knowledge if the two of us were to feel angry with them because they are angry, this is not fruitful. This momentary pain is insignificant compared to the lifelong suffering that is your lot. When the elders are angry with us, we should say: Let them be. If we, too, behave like petulant children, why should we then be called adults? To my mind, this is the only way to true happiness and inner peace.'

'True. Somehow, we have to teach the mind to compromise.'

'No, Sundarbhabhi, that is not quite what I meant. If by such submission, we can find a way for everyone to be happy, only then we should do so. If we see it only as suffering or joy, what is to befall our lot will befall our lot anyway. And if this be so, it is wise to consider even suffering as happiness.'

Sundargauri looked intently at Gunasundari. She felt her anguish somewhat assuaged, her misery somewhat more endurable. She took the book from Gunasundari's hand, read something in it and said with a smile, 'It is true. Your wisdom, your knowledge of life must come from my brother-in-law. What you have received from him has also proved beneficial to me. But not everyone is as fortunate as you. You must have worshipped the gods with true devotion, with all five fingers of the hand as they say, to have been blessed with a husband like my brother-in-law. And yet, despite everything that I endure as a widow, I am still better off than living with a husband like your Jethji. Listen to them, you can hear their farce being played out even from here.'

'Let their drama be. But tell me whatever happened at Jarashankar Mama's place? You must know?' Gunasundari asked. So Sundargauri narrated to her the events of that morning. While talking to Manchatura, Jarashankar had enquired about the family's wellbeing. Manchatura had for long observed the daily goings on in the family. He had also heard a few things from Gunasundari. He was exasperated and fed up beyond patience with everyone in the family. He brought out his anger on Dharmalaxmi. Manchatura had thought that Jarashankar would say a few words of censure to his sister, which would help restore some order in the family and improve matters. In this belief he enlisted all her shortcomings and berated and shouted at his wife in her old age in front of her own daughters, her daughters-in-law and her brother. Naturally, this was too much for Dharmalaxmi to bear. She was most grievously hurt. She felt Jarashankar would believe everything Manchatura said about her. Moreover, Manchatura had harsh words for everyone except for Gunasundari. This convinced Dharmalaxmi that it was Gunasundari who had carried all the tales to Manchatura. For instance, Manchatura knew that Dharmalaxmi wanted a silver shrine; he also knew what each of the others wanted and desired. Dharmalaxmi felt rage and revulsion for Gunasundari. When the women were alone, Dharmalaxmi complained bitterly to her daughters. 'It is true—we eat what our son provides, which is the same as the daughter-in-law providing for us. We are helpless in our old age, so we are pushed around by a daughter-in-law. So be it. What else can she do? She has to bear the brunt of it. Why should and why would she have any affection or consideration for us?' The daughters, too, added their bit, commiserating their mother's hurt and helplessness and expressed their anger and righteous indignation at Gunasundari. Dharmalaxmi had tears in her eyes. Chanchal wiped them and said, 'Ma, why are you so upset? The ways of the world are such that we have to sing praises of those who are ascendant'. Dukhba wept copiously and wailed, 'All this is because of me!' They had sat talking in the parsal of Jarashankar's house. Sundargauri was also there, mixing mustard in the pickles. She recounted the entire episode to Gunasundari with a grave face.

Having heard her, Gunasundari said, 'They are not to be blamed. The situation was such that their hurt is natural. I am not at fault, but that they should hold me guilty is not surprising at all. Pitaji has so much affection and compassion for me that he is forever finding faults with the others. What can I do so that he loves me a little less? Now I understand why I was being spurned by everyone. But Sundarbhabhi, you are promise-bound to tell me what happened with you'.

Fair Sundargauri at once turned pale. Her lips froze. She stared at Gunasundari with eyes full of dread and a silent plea. Finally, she said, 'Can it be that you do not ask me about it? If you forget about it, I shall be ever grateful to you'.

'I do not want your gratitude. Tell me without any sense of shame or anxiety. Tell me like you would your own sister. Do I not share things with you?'

Sundargauri was about to relieve her heart of its burden, but she stopped herself again. 'No. Let it be. I will tell you some other day.'

'No, we will not have this time together again. And I will find no peace until I hear about it. I swear upon this daughter of yours, if she is dear to you, tell me right now what happened,' and saying so, Gunasundari picked up little Kumud and put her in Sundargauri's lap.

It was the widow who first realised the repercussions of this act. 'Bhabhi, you are still not pure. Do you know that you have defiled me, this bed and the entire house!' In her excitement, Gunasundari had completely forgotten about her state. In Vidya Chatura's presence it was the outburst of joy that had caused her forgetfulness. And now it was the intense anguish, her own and Sundargauri's, that had caused her to forget. Even Gunasundari was startled at her breach.

'What can we do now, Sundarbhabhi? You go and take a bath, but can one bathe the bed? But you are digressing.'

Sundargauri replied, 'I am helpless. I cannot bring myself to speak about it. Even to you. But until you know about it, I will also not be at ease. You know what it is in any case. So why do you ask me? I am required to go up to the store room every day to fetch grocery and other things. I do not know what has possessed him, but every time I go up, he comes and harasses me. So far I have managed to escape.

God has kept my virtue intact. But those who fetch water daily may slip and fall into the well one day.'

Gunasundari said, 'From tomorrow onwards, you shall not go there. In any case I am to take my ritual bath tomorrow, after which I will myself go up and fetch things from the store room. But tell me what happened today? Why was Chandikabhabhi so angry with you?'

Sundargauri replied, 'Please let us not even mention it. I am a widow, while she has a husband. I am a woman, and her husband is a man. That a wretch like me should be considered lowly is no surprise. What they say and do is right, and I must always be wrong. Why do you even ask me? If I could take my own life, why would I see such a day? I could jump into a well and drown or hang myself. But can I escape what is my destiny? I believe that if I take my life to escape this misery, the same suffering would befall me for the next seven births. If it were not so, would I have become a burden on my brother and now, on you? Yet, with all my sins I must have done something good, and so God resides in your heart and you take pity on me. Otherwise why should you do so much for me? What am I to you? But times are such that my own kin are not my own, and those like you take me for family. Bhabhi, I am incapable of taking my own life. Every time I go to the well, I pray I would slip and fall into it, but I don't. And there is no one who would even give me a push. Why do you want to know what happened?' Sundargauri could not go on she was trembling so much. Unable to speak any further, she put her head down in Gunasundari's lap and sobbed, 'Oh Bhabhi, you are truly like a mother to me! You gave me life!' She was inconsolable. Racked by incessant sobbing and heaving, Sundargauri's delicate body was exhausted; gradually she stiffened even as she kept trembling intermittently, and then finally she lay in Gunasundari's lap still as a dead body. Gunasundari, too, had been weeping with her, clasping her to her bosom. She, too, was unable to speak and kept rubbing and caressing Sundar's back, trying to comfort the widow. She suddenly realised that Sundargauri had stopped moving. She tried to lift her head, and failing in her attempt, Gunasundari cried out, 'Sundarbhabhi! Sundarbehn! Please get up! I shall die if you feel so forsaken. I swear, this daughter of mine will die if you do not get up. Sundarbehn! Sundarbehn, please look up! Behn, take control of yourself. Don't tell me anything if you can't. I will not ask you anything more.'

Sundargauri looked up and embraced Gunasundari even more tightly. 'Bhabhi, you are more than a sister! More than a mother to me! Even my brother threw me out, but you gave me shelter. Who else but a mother would do that? Even a mother won't care as much for a daughter's pain as you have. If I don't tell you, whom shall I tell?' She wept aloud. Her cries could be heard downstairs. But everyone was still seething and self-absorbed with their individual woes and paid no attention to her weeping. Manchatura had just returned home. His anger had not yet subsided, and as he witnessed the farce in the house, it raised its hood again. He heard Sundargauri wailing in anguish and climbed up the stairs.

The two women got up as soon as they saw Manchatura enter and tried hurriedly to wipe their tears and compose themselves. Manchatura enquired, 'Why are you crying, Sundargauri? Gunasundari, what is the matter?'

Sundargauri was silent and would not lift her eyes from the ground. But Gunasundari could no longer control her anger. This was also a good opportunity to let him know the truth. She said loud and clear, 'Pitaji, I do not know the cause of her tears, but I do know that she almost rushed into my room after the meal, followed moments later by Motabhai; but he ran up to his room as soon as he saw me. Sundarbhabhi has been crying ever since. She refuses to tell me what actually happened. I could ask the others; but it seems that even I have done some grievous wrong today as no one in the house is even willing to speak to me. Whom can I ask? If someone tells me what my fault is, I could assuage their hurt. But I am helpless when nothing is said to me. Sundarbhabhi, please stop crying.'

'I see. Now I understand everything.' Manchatura was livid. He did not know what to say to either of them. He stormed down the stairs, striking each step with his stick as he went and speaking aloud for the whole house to hear, 'That son of a rand! Couldn't he find anyone outside that he wants to wreak havoc inside the house!

Bastard! Don't you realise that she is like a mother to you! I suspected something all along!' Manchatura climbed up to Ganchatura's room and asked Chandika to leave the room. Ganchatura, taken aback, stared at his father. Manchatura raised his heavy stick and brought it down with all his strength on Ganchatura, who moved away, terrified. The stick struck the bed so hard that the bed cracked under its force. Manchatura had expended his energy; his anger had found a vent. He held Ganchatura by his shoulders and glared at his son, his eyes breathing fire. 'Isn't Sundargauri like a mother to you? Look here son, I will let you go this time. But if you ever bring her name to your lips or so much as glance at her again, I will finish you. I may be ill, but my body has strength enough for that.' Manchatura turned to leave and on his way out, he said, 'Remember, I will not pause to think that you are my own blood before I kill a son who is out to destroy the family. I am not afraid that the ruler will hang me. I gave you birth and truly, I will be the one to kill you with my own hands'. Manchatura had turned red with rage, his thick white hair glistened with perspiration as mogra flowers glisten with dew. His aged body throbbed with passion like waves in the sea. Dharmalaxmi, Chanchal and Dukhba had followed him as they saw him go up to Ganchatura's room. Seeing him come out, they all filed down as quickly and stealthily as they had come. Manchatura slowly climbed down the stairs. Just as people are petrified to face a king in his wrath, the whole family silently lined up to see the patriarch enter his room. He flung his stick away and sat down on his bed, exhausted. Dharmalaxmi turned meek in the face of his wrath. She sent Chanchal to Gunasundari's room. Chanchal, who had the rare ability to mask her true feelings, went in with a pleasant smiling face and brought both the sisters-in-law downstairs. Everyone hurriedly busied themselves in household work as if nothing in the world was the matter.

Manchatura watched them all. Having done its work, his anger had subsided somewhat. He was satisfied. He twirled his moustache and smoothed it down with pale, wrinkled fingers. He said to himself: Good. I should be grateful that this was enough. In some other houses—God save them—there are people as thick-skinned as asses who delight in rubbing themselves in filth and mud. For them, all means would fail. For now, it looks as if He still keeps an eye over my house. Lord, I am merciful. Manchatura was happy to see Dharmalaxmi moving about trying to please Gunasundari. He thought: It is because of this old woman that everyone has gone back to their chores. Just as Shivji Mahadev lay down in the path of Ma Kalika as she wreaked destruction, this woman comes forward whenever I am in a rage. It is true—everyone gets what they deserve. Since my youth, I have a quick temper like that of Durvasa. She is patient and forbearing; even if I kick her, she would ask if my feet hurt! If I had not found such a deeply religious soul like her, I would certainly have murdered one or two wives by now, perhaps. Her parents helped her cultivate this disposition. May their souls rest in peace. This conversation with himself eased his fraught mind and helped Manchatura wash out the dregs of his rage. At peace with himself, he finally lay down to sleep.

The rest of the day passed without incident. Everyone had had a heavy lunch and so were disinclined to have the evening meal. Only Gunasundari needed to eat, but she did not want a meal cooked only for herself. Once Manchatura went to sleep, the women began to make conciliatory gestures towards each other. They sought to explain and clarify their words and conduct and seemed eager to please, placate and show affection. Dharmalaxmi insisted that Gunasundari eat something. Chanchal offered to cook for her. Dukhba sat down with Sundargauri for a talk. Chandika sat on the swing and played with little Kumud, becoming childlike herself with the infant. The other children gathered around her and played. The constant daily friction, mistrust, resentment and conflict suddenly seemed to have passed just like an unpleasant dream. The family seemed peaceful and content once more, together and individually. Each one of them noticed this, but no one said anything.

Ganchatura was the only one who could not partake of this newfound togetherness, tranquility and joy. He was not innately evil. He was also not stupid or bereft of a conscience. He was raised by Manchatura. He had spent time with his father travelling to various places and was a witness to his father's debauched ways. The subordinates in Manchatura's office would invite young Ganchatura to join them. They spoke freely about all manner of things in his presence. The office staff was also required to travel to remote interior parts of the country. The bored and weary staff members often took Ganchatura along with them and made him party to their lowly and debauched fun. The young lad did not have the discrimination or experience to see the follies of the elders; he, in fact, saw their unrestrained debauchery as a virtue. The elders took bribes, delighted in foul language; the bachelors among them would tease women in the neighbourhood. Unafraid of social stigma and unhampered by any sense of moral propriety, they sought out adolescent girls, pursued women who were in bad marriages, wives of naïve men, debauched women, women looking for company, barren women looking for men to impregnate them, women who used other women to get their way, wives of subordinates and friends who trusted them; they also sought out women who were under the influence of debauched mothers, friends or even brothers. A witness to such conduct, a young impressionable Ganchatura soon came to believe that these men were brave and manly and that all intelligent boys must be like them. He was brought up in this impure environment and when he grew up, he sought the same environment. Manchatura wielded lowly authority, earned money through dishonest means and spent it on all manner of vices. He had an appetite for debauchery and bawdy behaviour. Manchatura lorded over a company of vice. His subordinates were government employees, but he treated them as if they were his personal servants. The son naturally came under the spell of the father's association.

Manchatura, however, also had some rare qualities and extraordinary strengths which he forgot to pass on to his son. He had a tremendously strong personality. He was not servile to vice and debauchery and could keep these proclivities on a tight leash. He indulged in them when he wanted to; but when he was determined not to, even Indra's divine consort Indrani could not entice him. Manchatura could will himself to be godly or satanic, and he took immense pride in this ability. He believed that religion and irreligion, merit and sin, his superiors and his subordinates were all inferior to him—and that he was servile to none. For him, manliness was to exemplify such behaviour. He was neither tempted by extreme happiness nor crushed by extreme pain; he was capable of laughter even when weighed down by immense sorrow. His passions were subject to his will; they surfaced when he desired and subsided at his command. He considered passions as insignificant as blades of grass. He enjoyed exercising power and displaying complete control—over his superiors, his subordinates, and over himself. If his superiors accepted his authority and gave him respect, Manchatura would use all the means at his command—intelligence, power and wealth—to help them in times of crisis and would not rest until he had succeeded. Some of his superiors had faced charges of bribery and similar misconduct; some had faced complex and knotty problems at work; some had to cope with criticism and machinations; some were sacrificed to the pride, vice or prejudices of their own superiors. Manchatura had shown them all a way out and saved them from a variety of complex problems by giving them real and timely assistance. Indebted and grateful, they all praised Manchatura's intellect and would become servile to him. On the other hand, if a superior were to become opposed to him or create obstacles in his path, Manchatura's intelligence and power were certain to trap him. He would consider it his great achievement in enticing the wife of such a superior and rest only when he publicly demonstrated his victory. The superior's family was certain to be embroiled in strife; complaints would be made to higher offices. Such opponents would lose their social prestige, face criticism, ignominy and suddenly find that they had thousands of enemies, even amongst friends. Such a person was always under the threat of a beating either at home or outside. He would find no respite until, utterly harassed and cornered, he would admit defeat and beg and plead with Manchatura, appease him. Should it be a matter of surprise then if a man capable of bringing his superiors down to their knees was feared by his subordinates? Manchatura treated his subordinates like goats; he thought it beneath him to put them through any harassment or humiliation. He considered protecting them or helping them in need a sign of his superiority. He was also never taken in by their flattery. Manchatura had a motto: if one must cheat, one should cheat a king, and if one must kill, one should kill an elephant. He never took a paisa from the poor, nor did he take money from wealthy but good, god-fearing people; he did their work for free. But if a cunning man came to him, he would suck him dry of his money and do his work only after the man had pleaded with him. He would ensure that such a person remained beholden to him for life. Manchatura believed that to entice women within the family or of friends and relatives was a debased thing, and he despised those who did. He considered it an act of great cowardice and stupidity to entrap a woman whose husband had reposed trust in him. Associating with debauched women was not for him because in such relationships a man was ensnared by a lowly woman. In his view such men were effete. He felt that infatuation for a beautiful woman and spending money on her was akin to suspending one's intelligence and a sign of utter stupidity. Manchatura's debauchery was the result of extreme pride, ego and animosity. If these two forces were absent, his passions were also reigned in. If a woman were to insult Manchatura, within days she was sure to approach him and become his slave. Wise and virtuous women recognised his power and never acted haughty in his presence, instead preferring to address him respectfully as kaka, mama or bhai; Manchatura also never looked upon them with desire. Not only that, if such women appeared to stray, he would show them the right path and save them from debasement. But if a man were to lock horns with Manchatura or act haughty, his wife was certain to be trapped by Manchatura.

Manchatura was a handsome man. Tall, broad, powerfully built and fair of complexion. In his youth, he cut his thick black hair short. They had a lustre all of their own. In his old age his hair turned grey but retained its lustre. He remained as attractive to women in his old age as he was in his youth. Women were drawn to him and submitted to his will. He spoke rarely, but when he did he spoke like a king, leaving his audience, even superiors, tongue-tied. He liked to exercise this ability of his, especially on women. Many debauched women infatuated with him would pursue him. He took advantage of their infatuation. Some who were not debauched but not strong-willed found him irresistible and willingly fell into his trap as moths fall into a lamp. Some intelligent women sought him out for his clever wit and conversation. Manchatura's image and words would etch themselves upon the minds of women with refined sensibilities and intelligence, who would hover around him as bees swarm around a hive. Manchatura would permit them to pursue him, encourage their conversations and allow them to nurture false hopes. He enjoyed setting traps for them, but more than that he enjoyed not being entrapped by them. He truly believed he was not a slave to his passions, that such instincts danced to his tunes, and that the whole world was subject to his will. Manchatura believed himself to be like Shri Krishna who could remain unaffected by the world even when completely immersed in it. He put in practice such ideas and marvelled at his own ability to attain them. It was a source of both immense pride and joy for him. He would thus bring a woman to a point of total surrender, and at that crucial juncture he would not take the final steps. Of a thousand such encounters he would bring only one to fruition, but give hope to the remaining nine hundred and ninety-nine women that they could have been the lucky one. Though dejected they would not lose hope. The arrogance of his youth did not entirely disappear with old age. But life taught him a lesson towards the end. At a time when he had almost given up his debauched ways, he contracted a disease from some woman, which proved incurable. All her life, Dharmalaxmi had borne with forbearance his vices and his wilfulness. She had remained silent hitherto. But in her approaching old age, she lost her patience. She sat weeping by his bedside and lectured him on moral conduct.

'Oh, I am ill-fated indeed! Some overeat, some steal, while others pursue women. If you were one of them, I would have said that like them you, too, are lowly. Just as we cannot control our bodies, the lowly and the inferior cannot control their instincts. The wretches may even recognise that they do wrong and repent, but fail to reign in their passions. But you, *you* have absolute control over your passions. You are capable of the self-control of an ascetic. Whatever you do, you do on purpose. Those who do wrong on purpose commit twice the sin—they cannot even repent.' She heaved a deep sigh and continued. 'We are partners in sin and merit in equal measure. I am and I desire to be religious—to be born a human is not easy and it does not happen repeatedly. But is my knowledge of any use? I realise this and you do not. It is like trying to put gloss on dust. You sin, and I too must share in your sins. The merit that I garner through my good deeds is washed away and the sin of others attaches itself to me. I will have to bear the burden of your sins even in the next life. I have borne this burden since my youth. I have never uttered a word or done anything, nor once chastised you. Did my heart not burn at the sight of your other women? Once, you suspected me of some wrongdoing and felt much the worse for it. Think of how they must have scalded me, how they singed me. May God keep you well. I shall undergo my share of suffering in this life. Good. If I have suffered enough, I will not be born again to suffer. But alas! What can I do? Everything flashes before my eyes—I see nothing but darkness. It breaks my heart to see you thus. Shiv! Shiv! Shiv! Oh my strong, clever and capable husband, won't realisation come to you even now? Won't these grey hairs of yours force you to reflect? Won't this illness teach you anything? I do not know how much more suffering is fated for me!' She was quiet for a while collecting her thoughts, then continued. 'By now you would have reached a pay of five hundred rupees. But we have to make do with little because of this one bad habit of yours. The body is here today and gone tomorrow. I am no longer worried about myself. But you have saved nothing. What will the children do? The younger one grew up with my brother and because of him, he earns something today. But the elder one has grown up in your shadow. You have found him a job and he carries on somehow. But your shadow is cast upon him. The merits and sins of parents must be borne by children as well. All your vices have flowered in him. He has neither your intelligence nor your abilities, but he imitates you. One day that boy is certain to fall, and that day there will be no one to help him rise. If I die before you, I would consider myself fortunate. But what will this boy eat? You are not going to leave him an inheritance. And whatever little is lying around in the nooks and crannies of the house will be spent on musical evenings or the children of debauched women will enjoy it. Throw it all into fire and let it burn to ashes! Each one must face what is destined for them. Even you will be born again. Have you ever considered what will become of you? Think about it. I am alive today but may not be tomorrow. This life will cease in a fraction of a second. Until then, I am bound to you by my destiny—thereafter what happens is not in my hands!'

Dharmalaxmi sat by Manchatura's bedside and kept talking, wiping her tears intermittently. When she started speaking, Manchatura's anger rose and he was about to tell her: Rand! Is this the time to say such things? But he stopped himself and waited for her to finish. As Dharmalaxmi narrated how his impure life had cast a shadow over his family, how his elder son had followed in his footsteps, like a warrior who leads his forces into the hands of the enemy by his own wilfulness and folly and comes to despise himself for it, Manchatura, too, began to despise himself. For years, he had deluded himself that what he had done was an act of courage and defiance. But as he realised that his actions had also planted the seeds of a noxious weed in his own family, his anger gave way to repentance. Shaken by disease and remorse, his conscience rose as arrogance and pride made way for thoughts of morality. His mind opened like the doors and windows of a house uninhabited and locked up for years. Just as one cleans the house with a lamp in one hand and a broom in another, Dharmalaxmi's words on moral conduct entered his mind and gradually began to cleanse it and change it. These changes taking place within him were evident in the crease on his forehead, his eyes that blinked rapidly, in the colour of his face which turned crimson and then pale in succession, in the involuntary movement of his lips and in the unease of his body. As he realised his wife's infinite forbearance and forgiveness towards him since the days of their youth, Manchatura recognised his evil, and he burnt within like a hair singed to its roots. It suddenly came home to him that he had no recognition whatsoever of any wrongdoing, and that his achievement was limited to wounding the hearts of women. In the dark night that his mind was in, Dharmalaxmi's patience and forgiveness flashed like lightning. He knew that he deserved no mercy from her. Manchatura had never shed a tear since he was a young boy. A few tears now glistened in the old man's eyes. He looked up at her finally and said, 'You speak when it is too late. You give me counsel when I am on my death bed. Of what use is it to me now? Why didn't you say this when you first came into this house as a young bride? Why did you decide to dig a well only after the fire was well and truly raging?' His sleep-laden eyes were wide open as he spoke. They remained open as he kept looking at her, as if to capture her response with his eyes. His hand came to rest in Dharmalaxmi's lap, as if seeking forgiveness. Dharmalaxmi took his hand in hers.

'I know this is not the best time for me to say these things to you. If I were certain that you are never going to be cured of your disease, I would have said nothing. But my conscience tells me that tomorrow morning you will leave this bed. I am not so ill-fated. I am destined to die with all the auspicious signs of marriage intact on me. All that I have said today will prove beneficial to you once your health is completely restored. Hitherto, I never said anything because even if I had, you would have discarded it as useless. And if I had waited for you to get well, you would not have heard a word from me. I am old now, my desires have died; but your passions will be rekindled. Right now your eyes are open, and hence you are willing to see what I show you; your ears are alert and hence you hear me out. I know I cause you great pain by saying these things, but if I do not say them now, then when? Have you ever granted me the right to speak for your good and my good and the good of our family? How could I have said anything to you before now? This right which I have given to myself will last only until the day you get well. After that I will lose this right. This pinprick will save you from the agonies of death and ignominy—it is only in this hope that I have wounded you with barbs. My words must hurt, please forgive me! This is the most opportune moment for me to say these things, because it will protect your dharma and mine, and our family's welfare. If I miss this opportunity, a second one of this kind would not present itself during my lifetime. I have seized the moment and I have been harsh to you. Please forgive me!' The pious, devoted and loving wife capable of great forgiveness clasped her husband's feet and wept, 'Forgive me, please forgive me! I am hard as vajra and heartless as a sword. But what else can I do? I am married to a man as strong-willed as you. In my life I have come across many men big and small; but I found them all to be weaklings with little or no self-control. They all talk wisely until the moment of trial arrives; but at the first available opportunity, all men without exception are shaken from their resolve like children tempted by the sight of a toy. They entice innocent and virtuous women and are driven mad by their passions. The mind of man is effete, it melts in a moment, it rolls away like mercury. Men have no shame, no religiosity, recognise no relationships; they are not in possession of their senses, they do not understand the feelings of others; they relate to women only through bodily passion and desire, they seek nothing but the fulfilment of their desires. I have observed men who follow social customs and perform religious acts. I know well the conscientiousness of men of conscience, be they men of learning, ascetics or devotees. The authority of high officials is confined only to their offices, their power is only in their words. They are all slaves to their passions. Their greatness is false. And then there are those who come to us with their English learning. They say one should not accept bribes; they decry religion and insist that truth is the only religion. They criticise our religion and observances as mere superstition. We women are a thousand times better than these men who have received English education. You, too, are not ignorant of their base intentions with regard to women. If one were to even lightly squeeze a wet cloth, water would drip from it—their resolve is only as firm as that water. I have seen you make such men dance as if they were your puppets. Men are weaker and lowlier than women. I have hitherto seen only one man truly powerful and possessed of firm resolve and will. I have that man for my husband. I am proud of his manliness. I am proud that I am the wife of such a man. Women sing during the garba: My husband is equal to fifty-two brave men. At such moments, I am delighted. For I say to them, albeit in my mind, that all of you are lying—only I have such a husband. You possess the self-restraint to disregard a woman whose beauty entices the world as if she were disfigured and ugly. You can control your desires. I know from experience that all other men are made of straw; you are the only true man!' As she praised her husband from her heart, Dharmalaxmi was filled with gladness. Her tears dried. The pride and joy she had once known in her youth came back to her in her old age.

Manchatura, too, was overwhelmed to hear true praise from his wife. He sat up erect, looked at her affectionately and said, laughing, 'All right, I understand everything that you have said. Now tell me what is it that you want from me? I will grant your wish. Tell me what is your desire? All your life you have kept my word, my honour, my whims and wishes. Do you think I am incapable of granting you this one wish?'

Dharmalaxmi quietly said,'Once you decide, the matter is entirely within your grasp. I only want you to make up your mind about things that are already within your grasp. The rest of mankind may resolve a thousand times but will not be able to keep it. But you, my husband, have only to make a resolve, and I know you shall keep it, always.'

'All right, from today onwards I make the resolve.' With these words Manchatura lay down again and closed his eyes. Dharmalaxmi felt that his pledge was a fulfilment of both his and her life. She knew that his pledge would not be false. This certainty gave her peace at last. She felt reborn and closed her eyes to fully experience the profound peace and joy that she felt within her. The devoted wife softly asked, 'Is it a firm resolve?'

'Yes, it is a firm resolve,' he spoke like one in deep slumber and his right hand raised itself as if in promise and fell into her lap. Manchatura had fallen asleep. She held his hand for some time, gazing at his imposing features, his closed eyelids and his silver moustache and hair ruffled gently by the breeze. She carefully placed his hand back on his bed and got up noiselessly. She stood there thoughtfully for a while, a hand on her heart. She willed and prayed with all her being that her husband's body be restored to complete health by the power of his newfound purity and resolve. Thus reassured, she left him in the care of sleep. As she came out, quietly closing the door of his room behind her, Dharmalaxmi engrossed herself in domestic matters.

Pious Dharmalaxmi reformed Manchatura; but their eldest son was not to be reformed. Ganchatura possessed not even a fraction of his father's will and self-restraint. He was incapable of grasping the power of his father's intellect. Bereft of Manchatura's formidable mental strength, the vices magnified a hundred fold in Ganchatura; they crushed all sense of discernment and forced their way just as the Niagara falls forcefully make their way through rocky terrain. Dharmalaxmi considered Ganchatura to be a lowly being. Tired of trying to reform him, she eventually gave up and left him to his fate. She would tell Manchatura that their son's vices were because of him and that he should reform him. This was not easy. The father tried every trick he knew, but succeeded only partially. Manchatura was never fully cured of his disease, though he recovered enough to rejoin his post. He worked for three or four years. Then the disease that lay dormant resurfaced. Finally, he resigned from his post and came to live with his younger son. During these years, many opportunities came his way to tempt him to break the pledge he had taken at his wife's insistence. Several women who had relations with him previously tried their utmost to lure him back into a relationship. He had many occasions to wield what he had hitherto considered to be manliness. But Manchatura now sought fulfilment and channelised his not inconsiderable energies elsewhere. He now considered it a blot upon his manhood and a sign of weakness if Dharmalaxmi were to believe that he was once again lured by lust. He was eager to demonstrate that he was not weak, and that he had the power to uphold his pledge. In his old age, he was enthused and possessed by the idea of being faithful to his devout and virtuous wife and of leading a pure and blameless life. He wanted above all to prove that he could control his demons and passions effortlessly, that his willpower was so strong that nothing was impossible for him. Dharmalaxmi had told him, 'You have only to make a resolve, and I know you shall keep it'. Manchatura proved that her faith in him was not misplaced. Dharmalaxmi's pride in her husband grew even stronger. She told everyone that her husband's fidelity was as steadfast as Shri Krishna's detachment and the asceticism of Rishi Durvasa. She felt that her husband had at last broken free from his cage of lust. She saw him like a lion break free from bondage and roar to celebrate his newfound freedom. It was as if the joys of old age had repaid all the agonies and uncertainties of youth. Dharmalaxmi had only one more aspiration. She told Manchatura, 'Ganchatura is caught in a trap even stronger than yours. But he possesses not an iota of your strength. You have only one more duty to perform—set him free from his bondage'.

Old Manchatura, experienced in such matters, made a great many efforts to reform his son. Initially, he tried to keep Ganchatura so occupied with work that he would not have the time to indulge his vices. But Ganchatura found the time as easily as water slips through a sieve. Manchatura found for him good friends; but he made his friends take to his ways. Manchatura tried to isolate him from his friends; Ganchatura met them secretly and cheated on his father. Manchatura tried to show him that a life of vice may result in incurable disease and the poor physical condition that he himself had been reduced to. Ganchatura was aware of the dangers of disease, but he was blinded by lust and could not free himself from this ghost. Manchatura pointed out other dangers; he told Ganchatura he might lose his job, face criminal charges, ignominy, bring disrepute to the entire family and meet an untimely and gruesome death. He pointed out thousands of such dangers, but to no effect. Manchatura pursued his son with determination. He spread rumours that the women Ganchatura associated with were diseased, that the husbands of some of these women had hired killers to murder Ganchatura. He even sent hired thugs in pursuit of his son who threatened Ganchatura in the name of the husbands. He had armed men chase Ganchatura right up to his bed room; they would return without harming him and report that Ganchatura had a lucky escape that day. Manchatura would berate and abuse him saying, 'Rascal, don't you know you are being pursued by your death!' Frightened for his life, Ganchatura grew weary. In face of extreme fear, his lust seemed to subside. Manchatura felt that his ploy had paid off at last. Ganchatura lost his job and some modicum of sense seemed to dawn upon him. His body grew feeble, which also affected his lust. Jobless, he was forced to seek shelter with the younger brother, which he resented. He felt confined and dependent. His lust seemed to evaporate. But Ganchatura was innately weak of mind and so the impulses that lay dormant suddenly raised their head. He did not have the discrimination to recognise that Sundargauri was his brother's widow. Moreover, he had also kept his hand on Gunasundari's shoulder—that was the ultimate mistake. Everyone in the family now knew what they should have never known. He had crossed his limits and consequently, Manchatura's patience had also run its course. To add insult to injury, his wife Chandika had wailed and beaten her breasts before him as if he were already dead.

After his father left with a dire warning, Ganchatura was left all alone in his room. He felt that death was preferable to a life of such disgrace. He was incapable of earning his livelihood and everyone, including his wife, was behaving as if they were strangers. Ganchatura thought: I have no one I can call my own. With what face can I go to my family? Who needs me anyway? Besieged by such gloomy thoughts, his mind was in a whirl. He sat alone in his room from two in the afternoon till late in the night. No one thought of bringing a lamp up to his room after dark. No food was cooked, hence no one came to ask him if he wanted to eat. Ganchatura felt that the neglect was intentional. As he sat brooding in the dark room, hours passed. He thought of ending his life by pulling the sacred janoi around his neck. He folded the thread three or four times to strengthen it, looped it around his neck and pulled. But he lacked the courage to pull it hard enough to strangle himself. He tried to muster the will to end his life. Just then, Ganchatura saw a light reflect on the wall opposite his room. He could also hear the footsteps of two persons. Who were they? What was their purpose?

Manchatura had gone to sleep after giving Ganchatura a tongue-lashing. The women had patched up and were busily chatting away and working. Ganchatura was the only one who could not forget what had happened. That evening after dark, Dharmalaxmi went to talk with Manchatura. Gunasundari, Chandika and the others were in the courtyard. They could overhear snatches of the old couple's conversation.

A worried Dharmalaxmi asked Manchatura as to what had really transpired earlier in the day. She wanted to know what he intended to do with Ganchatura. As he narrated to her the details, Manchatura's voice rose in irritation. 'I cannot reform him. Even if he could be reformed, I shall make no further attempts. I am tired of him. I give up. His vices will only go with his death. Only his wife could have reformed him. When a woman goes astray, her husband must be blamed; likewise when a man takes to vice, his wife, too, is to be blamed. If for nothing else, they are to be blamed for not attempting to reform the other. I am not going to live as long as he does. He will never realise his options; hence he will never reform himself. What can we do? If he does not mend his ways, his wife will have to bear the brunt. Therefore, if she knows how, she should try and change him. If she does not know, it is her funeral. Vidya Chatura and Gunasundari, in the goodness of their hearts, provide for Ganchatura and Chandika—but can they do so all their life? You changed me, didn't you? Similarly, Chandika should try and change him. Or else the two of them can go jump into a ditch.' Manchatura said nothing more. Dharmalaxmi did not want to excite him any further. She got up and came away.

Chandika heard this conversation from the courtyard. She was somewhat foolish, but she was naturally jealous of Ganchatura's affairs with other women. Like Dharmalaxmi, she too had faced these experiences ever since her marriage at a young age. But she did not have Dharmalaxmi's patience and forgiveness. Lifelong jealousy and insecurity had turned her into a cantankerous nag. Over time, jealousy and a perpetual irrational irritability became part of her nature. Chandika was well aware of this, but she lacked the strength to fight back envy. She was envious of Sundargauri because Gunasundari was fond of her. She burned with envy because Gunasundari had a house, a good husband who loved her, while she lacked both. She would beat her breasts and lament when alone; she would berate and abuse Ganchatura, beat her children. She would not extend any help to Gunasundari with household work and feel pleased whenever Gunasundari encountered any problem. If someone scolded Chandika, she would pay no heed. If Manchatura praised Gunasundari, she would make faces at him. If Gunasundari did something for their mother-in-law, Chandika accused her of sycophancy. The only person she was not envious of was Dukhba—because Dukhba had nothing that Chandika could be envious about. When she overheard Manchatura say that she was also to be blamed for her husband's vices and her own misfortune, it was the last straw. Chandika lost her temper. But she could not respond to Manchatura, so her anger and distress found no outlet. Not knowing what to do, Chandika went to Gunasundari and suddenly broke down. She said, 'Bhabhi, did you hear that? Even this fault lies with me! What can a wretch like me do! How can I reform others of their vices? I would accept the charge if I had done wrong. They should pity me and my wretched plight. Instead, they call *me* vile! All right, let them say what they want. I was ill-fated to be married into this house, so everyone's wrongs become my fault. That must be so. Why did I not die!'

Gunasundari knew that what her worldly wise father-in-law had said was not without substance. But if she were to point this out, Chandika would have turned against her. Chandika had hitherto always remained distant and cold. Now she had come to her of her own will, unexpectedly opened her heart, wept and sought advice. Gunasundari knew that another opportunity like this was unlikely to present itself to gain Chandika's affection and trust and to draw her nearer. She said to console her elder sister-in-law, 'Bhabhiji, let it be. Don't cry. What are we to do? He is an elder of the family. How can men understand the workings of a woman's mind?' They spoke for about an hour. Gunasundari wisely allowed Chandika to unburden herself first. Chandika felt new affection for such a patient listener. This was the real achievement of this small gesture of Gunasundari. At length, she also showed Chandika a way out of her predicament. Chandika's envy slowly made way for trust and affection and she listened attentively to Gunasundari.

'Bhabhiji, it is within your power to reform Motabhai. Let me tell you how. You should fulfil his desires. You know him well; you should anticipate his wants. Once you take him into your hands, you can pull the strings like a puppeteer. It is not something you cannot do. Once you fulfil his desires, he will be your slave.'

Chandika snapped, 'No, that is not possible for me! He wants that I should ignore all his philandering with lascivious women. I cannot do that—absolutely not!'

'Why do you fume and fret? What we want is to cut these women off. I will show you a way. Motabhai will not even look at them and you shall be the focus of all his attention.'

'That will only be in my next life for sure!'

'Bhabhiji, the way those women please him, you should, too. You should keep him under your control to the extent that he won't set eyes on anyone else.'

'My attempt to control him would inevitably result in a quarrel.'

'No, why should it be so? You should act wisely and calmly and always be sweet of tongue. He can get angry only if you lose your temper. We are concerned here with the fruits of our actions. You should willingly agree to all his suggestions, but get him to do exactly what you want.'

'I do not know how to do these things.'

'Bhabhiji, but you are intelligent and most capable! Tell me, is there anything that you cannot do if you really want to?' Gunasundari said with a laugh. Chandika was surprised and pleased to hear her own praise; no one had ever praised her before. Gunasundari chatted pleasantly with her, distracted her with jokes, and they went up to her and Ganchatura's room. The three of them spent a few hours talking. Gunasundari generously praised Chandika and gave her due respect, acting as if she were subservient to her elder sister-in-law. And like a mother who overlooks her son's follies, she also pretended to have forgotten Ganchatura's transgression. In the few hours that she spent with them, Gunasundari sucked out the poison of envy from Chandika. They became like friends. Even Ganchatura, who until a little while ago had felt utterly alone, unwanted and bereft of family, began to look upon Gunasundari as a motherly figure. By the time Gunasundari finally went down, happy and content at what she had been able to achieve, it was almost midnight. Everyone else had gone to sleep. Sundargauri had slept off on the floor of the store room with her head resting on the raised threshold. Gunasundari gently woke her up and sent her to bed. Then she lay down in her own bed. But sleep eluded her. The next day, her period of impurity was going to end. She thought of all the many tasks and challenges that awaited her. She must reorganise the household, keep everyone happy and be a source of joy for her husband. All these thoughts did not allow her to sleep. The clock struck twelve; then one; then two, but there was no trace of sleep in her eyes.

So Gunasundari talked to herself. Oh God, guide me through this ocean! Until the other day, I believed that a joint family was a boon, a source of endless joy. But this is no joy—only conflict and endless blood-boil! Each one has a mind of their own; their true colours are different. Each one has a bad habit as large as a tree; and when their bad habits are curbed, I get all the blame! I have to care for all their desires, but there is no one to care for mine. No one considers what my feelings are. My condition is like that of a washerman's dog that belongs neither to the washing ghats nor to the washerman's house. This world has been likened to a stormy sea, and the comparison is not futile. I have already had such varied experiences. Who knows what more lies in store for me. Pitaji, Mataji, Chanchalbehn, Dukhba, Chandikabhabhi and Motabhai Ganchatura—all of them have one quality and one vice. This Sundargauri sleeps so soundly! Sleep, my sister, sleep. You are far happier compared with me. You need worry only for yourself. But I must worry for all of you. And now this girl! Who knows what concerns she will bring me once she grows up? But my beloved Chatura, you have far greater worries than I do. And I cannot share them. Oh, how his face withered today! Just a word from me, and his face fell. He had come to spend just a few moments of joy with me after months, and he went away looking dejected. Who knows what he thinks and feels? Wretch that I am, I did not even ask him. But what do I need to ask? It is apparent. He is worried about the family. He says nothing. But he has eyes and ears, he sees and listens. And he is concerned about me as well. He earns little, but the expenditure is huge. He would be less concerned if all these problems were to disappear. If I cannot even manage that much, then I am of little use, am I not?

Pitaji is stern and prone to fits of rage. He could turn even a wedding celebration into a funeral. But apart from him, who else takes pity on me or even thinks of me? But of what use is his compassion to me? I do not want to be honoured and feted and praised. What I do is for the love of God. The family of my Chatura is my family. However they might be, whatever they might be, can he get rid of his family? Hence, what is his is also mine. Pitaji will care for me. My Chatura will care for me. But how am I to care for him? He must have gone to bed with who knows how many worries.

It is true that an irritable, nagging nature turns one into a beast. Chandikabhabhi almost crushed Sundarbhabhi in her rage. She also silenced Motabhai. But how can one blame her? What a source of infernal pain her husband must be! How can she just watch in silence? But Jethji truly knows no limits—how his lust has blinded him! How lascivious, how weak can a man be? How he must repent now. He has been punished. But how much more punishment must lie in wait for him. Lust is a terrible thing, and however strong we are, we all submit to it. Oh my Chatura! We were barely together for a few moments. So be it. This social practice of segregation after childbirth is not such a bad thing after all. A rain-laden cloud finds no relief in solitary thunder. Similarly when we are alone together, mere talk does not satisfy us.

All passions are bad, be it lust, anger or any other. When passions rule, humans cease to be human and become animal. They can think of neither their own nor of the good of others; a person loses sight of everything else. Or else why would Motabhai mistake me for Sundargauri? Poor Sundar, her condition is a hundred times worse than mine. Isn't she a human being? Doesn't she have needs and desires? But God snatched away what He gave her, and so young. I am blessed. His blessings upon me are far more generous than on Sundar and both my sisters-in-law. Or else, my Chatura, without you ...

Without you ...! Why did such inauspicious words, why did such an inauspicious thought even occur to me? What if they were to come true? How desolate my life would be! How could I live without my Chatura? How would I pass the days? Sahasrai is alive, but without him Dukhba has turned sour. Is it surprising that Dukhba's nature has become what it is? What state would my Chatura be in if I had died? Gunasundari imagined herself dead and pictured a lonely and vacant Vidya Chatura. Tears filled her eyes. She tried to shut her eyes and go to sleep. Infant Kumud suckled at her breast; with her mother's milk she also drank her melancholy thoughts. Gunasundari sought refuge in the wooden plank of the bed. She slept close to it, touching it. When at last she fell asleep, she murmured in her sleep and wept softly.

The night progressed quickly. The whole house slept. As the hours moved on stealthily, the night was no longer young. And just as old age creeps in after youth, dawn was about to break. The morning dew cooled the world. Gunasundari was an early riser. She opened her eyes and sat up in bed. The silence was total—not a whisper could be heard in the house. She stared at the lamp that still burned. The myriad concerns of the previous night sprouted in her mind like seeds. She was to take her ritually purifying bath and take over the reins of the household today. She eagerly thought of ways to put her experiences to good use. In a short while, she had thought everything through. She asked herself: What was there to think of? It was simple—I must take all responsibility. I must get the daily provisions so that Sundar is not required to go up and face Ganchatura. The provisions, which were required often, should be stored downstairs. I must prepare well before sitting down to cook. The one who serves food has the position of a queen who provides; someone else must be given this responsibility. All other sundry tasks should be completed while others take their meals. Cooking does not require the use of speech; hence all instructions to servants and children should be passed on while I cook. Sundar will look after my daughter; this will also keep her happy. I must rest for an hour after lunch—only if I care for my body will I be able to care for others. If I keep feeling sorry for myself like Dukhba, suffering will attach itself to me for life. Why would I want that? I must also get back to my studies—my Chatura would be very happy for it. After studies, I must go to the temple and take the children with me. This would give me exercise and help digestion. On my return, I must prepare for dinner. In the evening, I should spend time with the family. And the night shall belong only to me and my Chatura.

Until then Gunasundari had not seriously thought of what to do. That morning she applied herself and found a way out. Sometimes one has to remind oneself to think. Gunasundari had understood how to economise on her work and learnt how to work without taking help from others; she also knew the advantages of being large-hearted. Through her diligence and acumen, Gunasundari quickly set the household smoothly on sail. Her quiet forbearance stitched shut all bickering tongues. Her generosity gave no scope for envy to flourish; starved of fodder in a short while envy died out. Her cheerfulness and affection ruled over the family. She set everyone free and accepted regimentation for herself. Her virtues enslaved everyone and they regarded her as superior to themselves. Vidya Chatura regained his peace and his happiness. He credited Gunasundari for this.

Gunasundari's responsibilities did not end with assigning all the work to herself and apportioning her time accordingly. It enabled her to run the household efficiently without having to ask or expect any help from anyone. Gunasundari took upon herself the burden of the man of the house, that of alleviating difficulties for everyone without their having to ask for it. She aspired to serve everyone selflessly and gain their trust. She hoped to keep them happy and entertained. She also aspired to lead them on the path of noble virtues. The expert in household economy sought to minimise expenses and maximise happiness.

She read the *Ramayana* and the *Mahabharata* during the day and in the evening. She gradually weaned the conversation away from domestic matters and gossip to introduce the insights of seers like Valmiki and Vyasa. She would narrate interesting and illuminating episodes from these texts and explain them, enabling the others to share and appreciate their teachings on life in this world as well as the next. In her role as teacher, there was a newfound respect for her in the family. Gradually a situation developed that people were hesitant to speak vengeful, angry or distasteful words that might hurt others. What others fail to achieve by anger, deceit, force and punishment, Gunasundari achieved through her kind and gentle words. People felt hesitant to act contrary to her wishes, albeit unspoken, and if they did, they were rebuked by someone else, not her.

Ganchatura was without work. Vidya Chatura did not know what to do about it. He tried to get him a job wherever there was an opening, but failed. Many a times he requested Jarashankar to find his brother a job. Jarashankar had grown weary of Ganchatura's vices. Every time Vidya Chatura broached the subject, Jarashankar was quick to retort, 'In the rule of kings like Mallaraj, his employees have to be as careful as one is while walking on a sword's edge. Your brother's vices are such that he would rob us all of our jobs and food. The wise thing therefore is for you to provide for him from your earnings so that the rest of us can feed our families and retain our employment. In a few years he would be considered too old for employment. Your father earned his "pension" and left his job, but this one lost both his pension and his job. If you are looking after one, then look after the other as well'. Vidya Chatura was unable to share such responses with anyone else. No one knew of the real reasons for his failure to find employment for Ganchatura and remained dissatisfied with him.

Gunasundari took upon herself what her husband had failed to do. One day with this intent she visited Jarashankar Mama's house. She spoke to his wife and with her help broached the subject with him. Jarashankar was amused that Gunasundari should plead the case of her elder brother-in-law, but his response was the same as he had given Vidya Chatura. Gunasundari had an answer ready. She said what her husband had been unable to say. 'Mamaji, what you say is true. But just as the ignorance of adolescence is remedied by old age, the remedy for vice is experience. A person does not remain unchanged for ever. My plea to find Jethji a job is not because I want them to leave my house and set up their own. Being gainfully occupied reforms even those who have taken the path of vice—Jethji is already on the path of reform. Mamaji, you cannot escape your responsibility. Children may turn against us, but can parents decline to be parents?'

Jarashankar laughed at her advocacy. 'Beta, you may give your jeth a 'certificate' of good behaviour out of your generosity and enthusiasm, but I do not believe it. If Ganchatura is not reformed, do you take the responsibility of reforming him? If you accept to be a guarantor for him, I may consider.'

Gunasundari was prompt to respond, 'Is that all? All right, I take it upon me. But you have given me your word, Mamaji, and you must be true to it.'

Jarashankar could not refuse Gunasundari. In a few days, a position appropriate to Ganchatura's abilities was found for him in Ratnanagari. Some days later, Jarashankar's wife told Ganchatura and Chandika how the job was found for him. Both of them felt beholden to Gunasundari and repented their past behaviour towards her. Ganchatura was deeply ashamed that he had inadvertently touched Gunasundari. If the earth had opened up and accepted him, he would have willingly disappeared into it, such was his guilt and repentance. Ganchatura wanted to change Gunasundari's opinion of him, especially with regard to his conduct towards Sundargauri—this became his primary objective. The man who could not be reformed by his own father was changed by Gunasundari and by his own sense of shame. Gunasundari was destined to do more for him and his wife.

There was a time when Chandika would haughtily say, 'What do I need Gunasundari for?' But times changed. Gunasundari had to look after Chandika's children, too. Chandika's elder son Hariprasad was a good-natured boy; his wife Manohari was older than him. When Ganchatura had lost his job, Manohari had gone to live with her parents. Manohari was tall, intelligent and beautiful. She was in the bloom of adolescence while her husband was still childish; he was also less intelligent than her. She was youthful and passionate and her beauty attracted a lot of young men. It was well known that Manohari and Hariprasad were a mismatch. Some lascivious men saw this as an opportunity. People sang bawdy songs about Manohari. Her name was scribbled on public walls. Every time she ventured out, lewd comments would fall on her ears; she could sense eyes staring at her. Every time she danced the garba a crowd would gather around; some even threw pebbles at her to attract her attention or pulled at her clothes. If she walked alone, some men would brush against her on purpose or follow her while others would walk ahead and turn their heads to watch her. Manohari was exasperated and frightened by such harassment. She would ignore such advances and unwanted attention. People sent anonymous letters to her and her husband. Even at the temple, people never missed a chance to say a few lewd words to her, and if she was in a crowd, some took even greater liberty with her. When she joined the community feast, people spoke in whispers about her; some spoke openly. Over time, Manohari, too, became brazen. She was no longer bothered by these remarks and lewd gossip. The gossip was not without substance either. She invariably had a tryst with all the romantic men who passed through town. She reasoned that with a husband like hers, she had a licence for some promiscuity. She wanted her husband to grow up so she could be freed from such promiscuous tendencies. Hariprasad invariably got to hear of all the gossip about his wife. In anger, he took to beating Manohari. But she became immune to his beating and sometimes she would even hit back. Sometimes she would mock him and say, 'Come on, beat me. I take your beating because I want to. Or else you can't even raise a finger at me.'

Manohari had driven Chandika mad. The mother constantly egged on her son to reform Manohari and suggested various ways of doing so. Manohari felt that her mother-in-law was turning her husband against her and so she tended to disregard everything her husband said. Sometimes she complained about Hariprasad's beatings to her paramour, who would beat up Hariprasad either in the school or in the streets and would take an undertaking from him that he would not beat Manohari in future. Chandika was hugely relieved when Manohari decided to go and live with her parents. But when she chose to come back and live with the rest of them in Vidya Chatura's house, Chandika grew anxious and apprehensive. God knows what new woes await me now, she thought. One day all the women had sat down for lunch. Gunasundari was busy with something and had not joined the others for the meal. Little Kumud was in Manohari's care. Manohari sat playing with Kumud on a swing on the first floor, singing aloud as she swayed on the swing.

Going, going ... going away
This youth of mine is going
Like trickling water
Like the arc of a star
My youth is wasting away
A woman with a boy husband
Is in an ill-starred match—
Her youth wastes away
Like she whose husband is away
She is married yet a widow—
Oh, her youth wastes away
The mother-in-law nags her
The husband is mother's pet—
Oh, her youth wastes away
Such a wife weeps; the widow weeps, too
Oh, their youth wastes away

The song infuriated Chandika. But what could she do? Manohari was sharp of tongue and quick to retort. Everyone else laughed when they heard the song and exchanged furtive glances. Gunasundari also heard the song. Manohari began to sing a new song more suggestive than the previous one. She sang lustily and full-throated in rhythm to the swing.

I can't bear it, I can't stand it
I can't bear this youth of mine
I see all my friends carousing and
I can't stop these eyes from staring
This mismatch has made of me a
A jealous woman: my boy-husband holds no charm
I'm promised that in four years, he'll become a man
But by then I will be an old hag
My untamed youth won't wait
But I contain myself somehow

Chandika could bear it no longer. She left her food and got up. Gunasundari realised that she had lost her temper. To prevent a confrontation, she quickly intervened, cajoled Chandika and sent her back to her meal, promising she would speak to Manohari herself. The song had stopped. Manohari was playing with Kumud, holding her high up in the air, rocking her in her arms and showering kisses on her. Gunasundari came up and silently stood watching. Manohari had her back to Gunasundari and so was not aware of being watched. Seeing her mother, little Kumud smiled, extending her arms and kicking her legs, wanting to go to her. Manohari realised that Gunasundari had come up and that she might have heard the bawdy song. She felt somewhat ashamed then. She got up from the swing and came towards Gunasundari, her cheeks flushed. Seeing that Manohari still possessed a sense of shame, Gunasundari felt that all was not lost and she was pleased. Gunasundari was hardly five or seven years elder to Manohari. Despite being an aunt-in-law to her, Gunasundari could take advantage of her age and talk as friends. Sometimes the advice of peers is most effective. Gunasundari felt that Manohari may have taken to bad ways, but that she was intelligent and could grasp the message quickly. If Gunasundari were to speak to her affectionately as an equal, Manohari could be influenced and reformed. Gunasundari thought: If I were to confront her and point out her errors she is sure to take affront; she is still a child, wilful and petulant. Hence, the best way would be to befriend her and make her realise her follies herself. I should say nothing by way of advice but wait for her to admit her mistakes. This mismatch is the outcome of social custom. She is young and her youthful passions have found an outlet. Her child husband behaved childishly and Chandika's responses are characteristic of her nature. What can poor Manohari do? No one guided her to the path of virtue, so she took the path that her youthful passions dictated. As Manohari shyly approached her, Gunasundari quickly thought of a response. She sat down with her on the swing and said appreciatively, 'You have a good voice. What is it you were singing?'

Manohari blushed and looking down at Kumud who was in her lap, replied, 'Nothing, just a few lines'. Manohari could retort brazenly to her mother-in-law, but in presence of Gunasundari who was her aunt-in-law she was tongue-tied. She felt restrained. She thought: Why did Kakiji have to hear my song? What am I to tell her? Intelligent and capable of recognising goodness, Manohari was aware of Gunasundari's virtues. Chandika had none of Gunasundari's qualities and therefore her attempts to reform Manohari had only made her more defiant. Manohari got up from the swing. She played with Kumud, kissed her and pressed the child to her bosom and said to divert Gunasundari from any talk of her singing, 'Kakiji, how did this little one recognise you? You are not even paying attention to her. She is delicate as a petal. She compels us to love her'.

As they sat talking on the swing, Gunasundari slowly coaxed Manohari to open up. She also advised Manohari during the course of the conversation, but in a manner that it did not clash with the girl's nature. When Manohari finally spoke up, it proved that Gunasundari's advice had found its mark. 'Kakiji, tell me what wrong have I done? But ask my mother-in-law how often she has filled his ears with stories about me? It was my fate that I should be in such a mismatched marriage. He is just about to grow out of childhood, but his mother wants him to be completely devoted to her. I am young, am I not? I might have some desires, too, isn't it? But she can't bear it even if he buys me a comb worth a few paisas. She calls him weak and unmanly. If he comes up to my room in the afternoon even for a glass of water on his return from school, she calls us shameless and brazen in the presence of outsiders. My husband is after all her son—why should she be envious of us? It would be another matter if I were to talk to someone else. She behaves as if she has forgotten her own youth. Kakiji, you do all the household work, all the drudgery; Kakaji does the work of the state. But when you are alone for a few moments and spend time gazing into each other's eyes, it would not be a sin, would it? And if someone were to object to that, their eyes should be plucked out, isn't it!' Manohari gesticulated animatedly as she spoke, made angry faces and pursed her lips. Gunasundari was amused and laughed at the sight. Young Manohari who kept the company of lowly people did not realise that she should not be saying such things to Gunasundari. She was slightly taken aback by Gunasundari's laughter. The girl realised that her words were inappropriate, and that if she had spoken such words to her mother-in-law, by now they would have quarrelled.

Gunasundari said in jest, 'You are clever, one has to admit. You thought if you take my example, I would have nothing to say. But your mother-in-law is your elder; she knows something more of the ways of the world than you. She must have thought that she should teach you the ways of our family. And hence she would have told you certain things. I will try and see to it that she does not speak harshly to you henceforth. But Manohari, your conduct should also be such that she has no opportunity to say anything unpleasant to you.'

Manohari replied, 'All right, but you will see that she will not be able to restrain herself. If she does not scold me, she will scold her son. Kakiji, you do not know her nature. If I spend time with you, she will tell me to carry my complaints to you and say that she has nothing more to do with me. You do not know that her eyes are full of envy. You will realise it only when you yourself face it. Nandi the bull knows the true nature of Mahadev; similarly only a daughter-in-law knows the true character of her mother-in-law.'

Gunasundari realised there was some truth to what loquacious Manohari had said. She affectionately placed her hand on Manohari's head and said, 'All right, but what if she were to stop saying things about you to Hariprasad or anyone else?'

'So what? How do I know what she likes? She does a thousand vile things which I can neither imagine nor tolerate. I am not her slave. I will never be her slave,' said Manohari with a toss of her head.

Gunasundari gently persisted, 'Let that be, but you will do what I ask of you, won't you?'

'All right, I will. But Kakiji, let us be clear, I am not going to follow my mother-in-law's dictates. That will never happen, never ever. I don't even like looking at her face. She has stopped short of nothing while harassing me. I will do what you ask me to do because you know my pain. If you tie me with a cotton thread, I will gladly accept that bondage. But if she were to tie me with thick ropes, I will wriggle free and make a scene to top it all!'

Gunasundari gradually took Manohari in her hands. She also spoke to Chandika and she told her a thing or two. She taught Chandika to be happy at the joy of her son and daughter-in-law and to set them free, within certain limits. She proved that young ones cannot be reformed by scolding. She told Chandika that she must always praise Manohari in presence of her son. She gave Chandika the assurance that she would reform Manohari and that Chandika would have her way with Manohari, but only through Gunasundari's mediation. It took a lot of effort over many days for Gunasundari to accomplish this. She ensured that Manohari spent as much time with her as possible; she took her with her whenever she went out and urged her to dress up; she fulfilled some of her youthful desires. Manohari began to understand which of her desires could be fulfilled and which she would have to learn to suppress for the time being. Gunasundari did not prevent Manohari from expressing her youthful desires but taught her to impose limits on herself. If Manohari were to speak about men, Gunasundari would cleverly change the subject to Hariprasad and his qualities. Gradually, Manohari, too, grew fond of her husband. She did not become completely submissive, but her haughtiness was restricted to her dealings with outsiders; she was quick to pounce on anyone who spoke ill of her family. Gunasundari kept Manohari's youthful exuberance under control until Hariprasad attained maturity. As the couple become more compatible in age, body and mind, Gunasundari made it possible for them to cohabit happily.

Chandika used to take pride that she was not beholden to Gunasundari for anything. But Gunasundari's conduct made Chandika profoundly grateful and obliged to her. Earlier Chandika had fought hard to retain her pride; now pride was replaced by repentance and humility. Though she was younger, Gunasundari had proved more mature in terms of her abilities and qualities and had assumed the role of the elder between them. Chandika often went to Gunasundari for help and succour. 'How shall I ever thank you?' she would say. 'Your Jeth has completely changed—it is as if a man who could not live without meat now drinks only milk. It is easier to capture and subdue a snake, but Manohari could not be subdued by anything. Even if she were confined to the nether world, she was capable of jumping up to the skies. But you have made her as compliant as a snake charmer's snake. How will I ever repay your gratitude? My own temper was so harsh—and let me admit, I was given to envy as well—but you have changed me. What praises can I sing of your virtues? The one who gave you such an apt name truly deserves praise.' In response, Gunasundari would simply smile and change the topic. If she had to respond she would say, 'How have I done anything at all? You have all these qualities and hence you have taken these things positively. If you have changed, it is because of your own abilities and efforts.'

Gunasundari's responsibilities to the family were not yet over. She was concerned about the condition of her two sisters-in-law. Dukhba was a permanent source of heartburn to her parents. Her husband Sahasrai wandered from place to place and never even wrote a letter to Dukhba. Their daughter Kumari had attained marriageable age. Over time, Gunasundari befriended Dukhba. But the resolution of her problems required money. Vidya Chatura's limited income was entirely spent on his large household. Gunasundari knew this well. She found a way out from resources that were within her means. One day when she saw Vidya Chatura in a balanced frame of mind, she broached the subject of Dukhba's problems. He heard her out. He, too, felt that something should be done and sought Gunasundari's advice on the matter.

Gunasundari looked around to make sure they were alone, and said, 'Kumari's marriage must take place. There is no option. No one speaks about it, but don't we know of its necessity? If we don't take the responsibility, who will? I feel that to incur a debt is not right. You deposit my gold and jewels as security and borrow money against it. We shall save money over the next four years or so and reclaim it on payment of dues. We shall be able to invite Sahasrai for this occasion. All the money will not be spent on the marriage; what remains can be used to repay his debts.'

Vidya Chatura could not help but smile. He said, 'Gunial, you speak as if gold and jewels are just lying around waiting to be picked. What will you do once your ornaments are pawned?'

It was a question about the future. A ponderous question. Gunasundari thought about it for a moment, trembling inside. Then she put her hands on her hips, looked up at him and said, 'If I am ill-fated, what use would ornaments be for me? If my destiny turns against me, what is the guarantee that these ornaments will also not prove unlucky? If I am destined to suffer, how will human effort help? But if I have trembled at the thought of sin, even God will not forsake me in times of sorrow. Don't I have Sundarbhabhi's example before me? Therefore please do as I ask you. As long as you are there with me, I possess the equivalent of countless priceless ornaments. Why should I even think that you shall not be with me for ever? Won't I have the good fortune to die before you? Why should we think of our own future while doing good to others? So rise, my Chatura!'

Vidya Chatura was reminded of the generous Raja Bhoj, and of the king's response to his minister who urged caution as Bhoj prepared to make generous gifts.

> Save wealth for difficult times, o King.
> But Minister, how can the wealthy have difficulties?
> My King, if one squanders wealth, one will eventually lose all accumulated wealth.[5]

Vidya Chatura posed another question to test her. 'All right, let us forget about the future. But have you thought of the present? I have not been able to give you a single ornament. You have nothing except what you came with from your parent's home. If you give away all the ornaments from your body, what will you wear?' He assumed that even educated and wise women tend to be fond of ornaments, and that Gunasundari would be no exception to this.

'Oh! I did not know that you have failed to know me hitherto. This is a failing on your part, my Chatura.'

'What is it that I have failed to know?'

'You assumed that like other women I, too, am married to gold and silver. No. Not in the least. Why does one wear ornaments? So that others look at us and feel happy? No. Can we see the ornaments

[5] *Niti Sara*, Verse 45, translated for this volume by Arindam Chakrabarti.

that we wear? No. Do I wear ornaments because there is a lack in my beauty? Do I want to please my Chatura with ornaments?'

'Ah! So you do not feel obliged to please me any longer?'

'How can I say that I do not feel the need to please you? But we have to help Dukhba, it is our joint duty. And I know well that nothing would give you more pleasure than the performance of our duty. Now tell me, my Chatura, aren't you caught? You must admit you have been defeated and I have won!'

'Does defeating the husband also form part of a wife's duties according to you?'

'Not in everything, but certainly in love and play. Don't you remember what Rati said?

> Dost thou remember, O Cupid, my binding thee with the strings of my waist-band whenever I was addressed with a wrong name by thee, or my beating thee with lotuses used as ear-ornaments, hurting thy eyes with pollen-dust dropping from them?[6]

'Even without the lustre of ornaments, I am your Rati and you are my Kama. I must win over you and I must also bind you! Now do you understand, my Chatura? I win over you every time I utter your name.'

They moved from domestic matters to their mutual love and desire. Their conversation delighted them. Vidya Chatura immensely enjoyed conversing with his learned, intelligent and comely wife. For an instant, he distanced himself like a witness and gazed upon her face unblinking. He remembered the saying:

> An ideal wife will have these six virtues—she will be like a counsellor in dealing with various situations, like a maid servant in serving her husband, like Goddess Lakshmi in beauty, like earth in patience, like a mother in giving love, and like a courtesan in the bed chamber.[7]

'O' bharya, the one who bears burden, you took my family under your care, you held them close to your heart. Gunial, only you could have

[6] M. R. Kale's trans. *Kumarasambhava of Kalidasa*, Canto IV, Verse 8, 2nd ed. 1917 (Delhi: Motilal Banarsidass, 1981) 185–186.

[7] *Niti Sara*, Verse 14, translated for this volume by Arindam Chakrabarti.

done this. It is because of you that this family is together and happy today. But for you, it would have been a bed of thorns.' This one thought proved to be a distraction in their joyful conversation. Gunasundari found it pleasant to be a distraction. Vidya Chatura resolved that he must help find a way out of Dukhba's woes. He asked his wife many things during their conversation which helped him make up his mind. He also posed to her many questions to ascertain her capacity to negotiate hurdles. He never hesitated in having a frank discussion with her and delighted in gauging the depth of her intelligence and also if she were really capable of following her words with action. Vidya Chatura decided he would be guided by Gunasundari in this.

Gunasundari decided that she would arrange Kumari's marriage, and with the consent of her husband, she took the entire family into confidence. Everyone was pleased and praised her decision. But not Manchatura; he was in fact greatly annoyed. Sahasrai was wandering about who knows where. Vidya Chatura was already shouldering a huge burden of responsibilities. Manchatura was not pleased at this further addition to his burden. I am not anxious that some old woman would die, he thought, but this is like showing Yama the road to their house! Moreover, Manchatura did not want this to become a habit with everyone. Chanchal's children were also unmarried. Manchatura made his displeasure known to Gunasundari in no uncertain terms. 'Gunasundari, you have no mercy for yourself. You are still childish. You will have other children of your own. Vidya Chatura does not earn so much that we can spend lakhs. If you take on new responsibilities, you will not be able to fulfil them in times to come. And if you are unable to bear these burdens in future, whatever you have done in the past will also be abused by others while their expectations will forever remain unfulfilled. Hence, do not take on this responsibility. If Sahasrai is not concerned about his daughter, why should you be? You want to take credit for your good deeds—but credit can also become a noose around your neck. Credit is not going to bring food to your house. If you are so concerned, ask Dukhba to call Sahasrai. If you are going to feed the brahmins by keeping your children hungry, you and I will not get along. If daughters are so dear to their mothers, mothers would rob their sons to fill their daughters' houses, and the sons-in-law would get all the good things while the daughters would come back and sit on our heads. By doing this you will endear yourself to your mother-in-law. But if you want my affection, have some pity on my son who works hard day and night to feed the house. Your sister-in-law has a right to be fed in your house. But Gunasundari, if you take on the responsibility of arranging the marriages of their children, even the gods will turn against you.'

The whole family, including Dukhba, was present when Manchatura expressed his annoyance. Dukhba could not bring herself to tell Gunasundari, 'Why do you worry so much?' She was meek; her sorrow had made her greedy and self-seeking. She had not parted with one piece of her gold to help Sahasrai in all his troubles. Instead, she opted to live with her brother and sister-in-law. But Dukhba had no sense of gratitude towards them. She believed that they had the means to arrange for Kumari's marriage and therefore they were doing it. She heard her father, but she could not bring herself to say, even insincerely, to Gunasundari, 'But why should you take on this burden?' She felt if she were to say anything of the kind, Gunasundari would do exactly what her father wanted. Dharmalaxmi did not like the charge that she was robbing her son to fill the houses of her daughters. She kept quiet because she knew that Manchatura was angry. Everyone eagerly awaited Gunasundari's response. They all looked towards her.

Gunasundari gravely listened to her father-in-law. Then she spoke with a smile, 'Pitaji, have we ever disregarded your words? Why would we, the women, trouble ourselves about where the money for Kumari's marriage will come from? You are there for it; so is Sahasrai, and so is everyone else. You will do what is appropriate. You have no objection if we call back Sahasrai. You also have no objection if we look for a suitable groom for Kumari. Once the marriage is fixed, the celebration will take place in whichever house you decide. You do not discriminate between your five fingers. The expenses will be borne by whosoever you decide. Why should we think of that now? Pitaji, now tell me, do you still object?'

Manchatura was thoughtful for a while, then said, 'No, there is no objection in doing that much. But I know your tricks. Be careful. And know that for me all fingers are of varying length; some are longer than the others. Each one does its work. Don't bind me to it. And don't take this as an assurance for the future'.

Gunasundari replied, 'Pitaji, how can we tie you down to anything? Is it appropriate for us to seek assurances from you? We needed your permission, which you have given. The matter ends there'.

Gunasundari busied herself with household chores. Everyone else also went their separate ways. Left alone, Manchatura thought to himself: This daughter-in-law of mine is virtuous and equally clever. I will not be able to have my way with her. She has made up her mind and she will conclude this her own way. She got me to agree to those things about which I cannot possibly object; the rest she has kept hanging. Who knows what shape she will give it when the time comes? Was I right in saying what I did? She works so hard. The rest are like animals; they don't lighten her burden even for the sake of form. Sahasrai has incurred big debts; he is unlikely to return for the asking. How is he going to spend on the wedding? He knows quite well that Vidya Chatura will spend for his nieces and nephews. He must have written to Dukhba. And Dukhba must have got Gunasundari to agree to the idea. Gunasundari wants credit. But she does not know that the axe will fall on her feet. She is not so dumb that she wouldn't understand this, but God has made her generous and forgiving. If my son were the Karbhari of Ratnanagari, her generosity would have brought him even greater glory. Manchatura's anger gradually subsided as his mind turned to more positive thoughts.

A search was mounted for a suitable groom for Kumari. Dukhba liked an old but rich man. She was tempted by his wealth. There was another proposal, but that was an obvious mismatch. And with Manohari's example before Dukhba, she was against such matches. Manohari also chipped in, saying, 'Only the ill-fated would agree to such a match'. Gunasundari was against the marriage with the old man. 'We cannot decide by looking at the old man's wealth,' she said. 'A man's body is fit to enjoy the pleasures of marriage for long years, but by the time men turn fifty they become useless. In this Kaliyug one lives only for sixty years. So when a man turns fifty, he should be considered as good as dead for some things. His wife should also forsake worldly pleasures. From the age of fifty to sixty, our daughter will be a closet widow, and after sixty she will be widowed in any case. Therefore, this idea must be dropped.'

Unknown to Gunasundari, Manchatura overheard this conversation and his eyes widened in surprise as he thought: How does she know of all this at her age?

But Manohari could not restrain herself. She burst out laughing, caught hold of Gunasundari's shoulder and loudly butted in, 'Wait, Kakiji, wait! How do you know all these things? I don't deny that you speak wisely. But please tell me from where did you learn all this? Now you are caught good and proper. Tell me, please, you have to! I won't let you speak of anything else'.

Dukhba caught hold of Manohari and said, 'Go away! Why do you interfere in things you don't understand?'

'Why, Foiji? Can't I even ask? Kakiji doesn't mind in the least. So what is your problem?' Manohari sharply asked her elder aunt-in-law.

Dukhba persisted, 'No, Gunasundari merely keeps quiet, so don't assume she doesn't. And think before you speak, Manohari. All you can do is bark! Do you even have the brains for anything else?'

Manohari saw her point and kept quiet. Gunasundari turned to her and smiling, said, 'Even those who are yet to marry have attended marriages. I might have asked someone knowledgeable like you, and therefore I know these things'.

'Happy? Got your answer? What did you gain by butting in? Even my tongue grew weary of warning you not to take on your Kakiji. Now take what she dished out to you and hold your tongue!' Dukhba said.

Manohari felt sheepish. 'Foiji, I am still a child, so I can ask such things. You said it is inappropriate to ask these things, so I won't ask again. But I don't know what it is about Kakiji that every time one opens one's mouth, she responds so sharply that we have to shut up. But what Kakiji said is not wrong at all. A woman soon to be widowed by marrying an old man has no future. But the kind of problem I have was short-lived. By the time we are twenty-twenty-two, these problems vanish. And with an old husband, one gets some pleasure till he turns fifty, after which the woman has to roam around, doesn't she? Will his money satisfy our hunger? I am much better off!' This was not something that should have been said openly. Manohari was immature and brash, but what she said reflected her own experience. The other women blushed at her blunt talk and laughed her off. But Manohari nevertheless brought home to them the truth of the matter. Eventually, Kumari was betrothed to a boy ten years her senior and of average means.

Sahasrai returned. Kumari's marriage was fixed. Some days prior to the marriage Gunasundari took out all her ornaments and gave them to Vidya Chatura. Vidya Chatura did not accept them. He reasoned with her, 'If I take away your ornaments now, someone will come to know of it and there will be a lot of unnecessary discussion. Also, on the day of the marriage if you are seen without any ornaments on your person, it will look bad. We are going to bring the necessary things on credit. I will need money only when the accounts are to be settled. We shall take a decision then'.

No one asked the question of money and expenditure until the time came for the accounts to be settled. No one even mentioned it. Sahasrai had assumed that Vidya Chatura would bear all expenses. Gunasundari had assured Manchatura that, 'You will not have to pay'. Manchatura's response was, 'We will see'. Only the two of them were worried about the expenses. Gunasundari was worried that Vidya Chatura might hesitate while taking her ornaments. Manchatura was worried that eventually Sahasrai will wash his hands off and Vidya Chatura will have to bear the entire expenses. Gunasundari's assurance to Manchatura was some comfort to him; but he was still apprehensive that ultimately Gunasundari will be cheated and Vidya Chatura will have to pay either out of social compulsion, or out of pity for Dukhba and Sahasrai. Gunasundari had indeed said that Manchatura will not have to pay. What she had not said was that: 'I will pay—I will give my ornaments'. Manchatura had not understood what she had deliberately left unsaid.

Some days after the marriage, the creditors brought the accounts to Vidya Chatura and sought payment. Neither Gunasundari nor Manchatura were unaware of this development. Gunasundari went up to her room and confronted Vidya Chatura, 'Have you thought of a solution?' Vidya Chatura laughed and said, '*You* have to think of a solution. Why do you ask me?'

Manchatura was quick to realise that Gunasundari had gone up to her room to arrange for the payment. He got up. Hitherto, he had never spied upon his son and daughter-in-law. But that day he stood at the bottom of the staircase and overheard their conversation with eager anticipation. Manchatura found Vidya Chatura's question rather strange; he failed to understand it.

Just then Gunasundari said in response, 'My dearest Chatura, today you have finally said the right thing. Kumari's marriage was a source of great joy. Dukhba is relieved. And I, too, shall feel relieved once my promise is fulfilled. I am fortunate that my ornaments will at last be put to some good use'.

Manchatura was shocked. He chewed his lower lip, pulled on his moustache pensively and muttered: So the expenses will be paid from Gunasundari's jewellery!

Vidya Chatura was heard speaking in disconcerted tones, 'I don't know if this is good fortune or ill fortune, but I have no cash to spare at present. I undertook this responsibility only upon your insistence and your steadfastness, Gunial'.

Manchatura slapped his forehead and stamped his foot in anger. Shame on a son who accepts his wife's ornaments! Oh, such is my fate that not one of my sons proved worthy of anything. I was wrong in my estimation of this son as well. This daughter-in-law is the light of the family. All the rest bring me nothing but discredit and pain. ... Her ornaments!

But Gunasundari's response did not allow Manchatura to express his anger. She said, 'You speak to me in honorific terms. You sound depressed. This is new'.

Vidya Chatura forced a smile. 'No, it's nothing, really. What can I do? If I go out to seek money on loan, it might be refused. We would also lose our prestige. Till date I have never asked anyone for anything.'

'Why do you need to do so now? It is almost night. Tomorrow morning I will give you the ornaments. Go and sell them off; you will have all the money you want and you won't need to ask anyone for a loan.'

'But everyone will notice if there are no ornaments on you. We will lose our prestige either way.'

'You will earn merit if the ornaments are used for a good cause. This merit will bring good times and I will have a hundred fold more jewellery to use. If we give our jewels for your sister, our prestige will increase by a hundred-thousand fold.'

'But if I try to sell them, I will get a lower price. Instead of a hundred rupees, I will get only sixty.'

'God will make up for such losses.'

'It is not a sign of wisdom to invoke God in practical matters.'

Gunasundari could not help but laugh. 'Should we then invoke God only in useless matters?'

Vidya Chatura was defeated. 'I think that we should pawn the jewellery, not sell it.'

'Then do so.'

'But it is not a good thing to pawn jewellery.'

'Why so?'

'The world will call us foolish.'

'Let the world go to hell. We are not doing this to earn praise.'

'If someone were to know about this in the family, they would never let us do it.'

'We should not worry about that now. They will know only after the matter is resolved.'

'It is neither my duty nor my morality that I should take away your ornaments. I will find some other way.'

'Do you consider me separate from you?' Gunasundari asked, pain writ large over her face. Vidya Chatura got up. 'No, I don't. But we shall see.' He began to change his clothes. Gunasundari, still seated, held on to his hand and stopped him. 'If this is not separateness, then what is?' He wriggled out of her grip and began to wear his angarkha. 'No, no. Why do you think such ill thoughts? I have to go to the palace soon. Everything will be fine, Gunial—all at the right time.'

Gunasundari got up and brought him his pagdi. She placed it on his head and said, 'There is no such thing as the right time. Everything must be done by tomorrow. I will not allow you to have your way'.

'We shall see,' Vidya Chatura said, moving towards the staircase. But Gunasundari held on to his angarkha and stopped him, 'No, there is nothing more to see. Give my life or your word'.

'Let me go, Gunial. Pitaji is downstairs, he will see us.'

Gunasundari let go off him and said, 'All right. You are going away just now. But I will have my way ultimately. There is a night to pass before tomorrow comes'.

Vidya Chatura hurried down the stairs thinking to himself: Such a good wife is an act of God's grace. But a woman who is virtuous and also cares for the family is so rare to find! Gunial, your thoughts are lofty and do well unto others. Your steadfastness and strength with regard to your own aspirations for others defeat us all. You always get your way. You win over everyone with your virtues, intellect and deeds. I have you for a wife, and that is a sign of God's grace on me. Why should I, a husband of a jewel like you, not take pride in you and prize you more than wealth or a position in the state? He recalled the lines of a poem.

Sweet stream, that winds through yonder glade,
Apt emblem of a virtuous maid—
Silent and chaste she steals along,
Far from the world's gay busy throng;
With gentle yet prevailing force,
Intent upon her destined course;
Graceful and useful all she does,
Blessing and blest where'er she goes;
Pure bosomed as that watery glass,
And heaven reflected in her face.[8]

[8] Author's note: William Cowper, 'To a Young Lady'.

My Gunial, too, is a heavenly blessing, thought Vidya Chatura as he left the house.

Gunasundari followed after him. But Manchatura accosted her on the way and asked, 'Gunasundari, these creditors have been doing the rounds. Who is going to pay them? Your sister-in-law or her husband? You had said that we won't have to bear the burden.'

'No, of course not. You will not have to pay.'

'Then who is going to pay? Are all the creditors just going to give up their claims?'

'Pitaji, you will know when it is done. Even if Dukhba and her husband do not pay, the burden will not come upon your family.' Gunasundari did not want to answer any further questions, so she quickly went inside and got busy with chores.

Manchatura stood there stroking his chin thoughtfully. She is determined to give away her ornaments. They are those that she got from her parents' home at marriage. That is why she said the burden will not fall on my family. Gunasundari spoke the truth. She can't be accused of lying. She spoke the truth and she tricked me as well. How was I to imagine that she would give away her own ornaments? What I could not imagine she is intent on doing. Her virtue is limitless. It is something without a precedent. That a daughter-in-law would give away her own ornaments for the marriage of her sister-in-law's daughter! My old eyes will see something unseen! I am not going to let this happen. She is capable of such generosity, and these asses in my family are so selfish they can neither comprehend nor appreciate it! I have now understood. And if I pretend otherwise, I would be labelled the leader of a pack of asses! Our ancestors made this custom of giving gold ornaments to our daughters for their own protection, so that if widowed, they would not be left without means. And this wretched rand of a daughter of mine! Her husband is hale and hearty and yet she is a burden on her brother. What would she not do if he were to die! But Manchatura checked himself, he did not want to pursue such inauspicious thoughts and consume his energies needlessly. What is Dukhba going to do with her ornaments, he wondered. She will keep them. But Gunasundari will give away hers to pay for Kumari's wedding! Oh, the absurdity of it! Darkness seems to have descended on Brahma's house. If Gunasundari were to starve to death someday, will Sahasrai find it within himself to give her even a pie to buy poison? What is Dukhba doing with her gold, rubbing it on her boils to soothe them? No. I am not going to let this happen. Such a practice should not be encouraged. Even Chanchal has children who need to be married. God, will these children ever bring any light to my family? Gunasundari is still young. Poor thing, she is accursed!

Manchatura withdrew to his room. After everyone had gone to sleep after dinner, he called Sahasrai to his room. He told him of Gunasundari's decision to give away her ornaments and scolded him. Sahasrai was ashamed to tears. He said, 'What am I to do? I don't have money enough to buy myself poison. I feel ashamed. I will do whatever you suggest'.

Manchatura suggested that Dukhba's ornaments be pawned to pay off the expenses. Sahasrai sighed deeply and said, 'As if that is within my power. When I had asked for it to save my pride and prestige, she refused to part with it. If I could have used her gold, I would not have come to such a pass today. My creditors are generous; they are even willing to settle for less. If I had Dukhba's ornaments, I could have re-established my business without anyone's support'. Manchatura felt pity for Sahasrai. His dislike and anger for his meek yet unfair and selfish daughter intensified. He called Dukhba and told her of Gunasundari's decision. He berated her more harshly than he had Sahasrai and shamed her, saying, 'Wretch, at least now make an offer, however false! She is not the one to accept. But you are found wanting even in pretence! Where have you kept your ornaments?'

Dukhba said nothing. 'Oh! So you won't say anything? Anything at all?' Manchatura barked, nearly hitting her. Suddenly he said, 'Sahasrai, get up. I know where she has kept them'.

Dukhba was frightened. She quickly went and stood with her back towards the tin case where she had kept her ornaments. Manchatura realised that she had hidden her ornaments in that case. He suddenly leapt up, caught Dukhba by her throat, clenched his teeth and said with eyes bulging in anger, 'Will you hand them to us, rand, or shall I take them?' Terrified, Dukhba opened the case and gave all her ornaments to her father. Father-in-law and son-in-law went away. Dukhba spent the whole night crying. She did not sleep. Early morning, Manchatura and Sahasrai went into town, pawned the ornaments and got the money.

Around the same time, Gunasundari took off all the gold ornaments from her body and handed them to Vidya Chatura. He kept them safely in his case. He looked at his wife, completely bereft of any adornment. 'Gunial, is there not even a trace of unhappiness in you? Sorrow has cast a shadow over your face, pain is writ large on it. You finally had your way. You gave your word without really meaning to, but you did keep it. You make a brave show of being unruffled. So be it. But I am glad that you kept your word. You may deny it, but I know it pains you deep within. I don't want that. I am happy with your gesture. Take them, put them on. You don't look good without them.'

Gunasundari smiled in response. 'If my state was really the way you describe it to be, your words would have singed me. I have done nothing to please you. I had decided to do something. I did. That is all. Kumari's marriage has been celebrated, and I have given my ornaments to you. I had resolved to do this. This was not done to please you. You may be right that I don't look good without any embellishments. Ornaments enhance the beauty of a woman bereft of both virtue and beauty. But my Chatura, you are so clever and yet you make a mistake. We were married as children. You did not marry my beauty, my virtue or even my ornaments. You were married to me. Ugly, foolish or without virtues, you only have me.'

Whatever I am, I am yours
Ocean of compassion, bear with me

Gunasundari looked alluringly beautiful as she sang and danced joyfully to the song. Her only adornment was a bangle on her wrist, a sign of her married status, a simple clean sari wrapped around her, and a crescent moon-shaped mark on her forehead. Her long black hair gleamed. Not just her face but her entire fair unblemished body seemed to smile at him enticingly. Her radiant forehead, her bright mischievous eyes, her dimpled cheeks, full smiling lips, pearl-white teeth; her bare neck seemed longer without ornaments, her bare arms delicate and smooth as lotus stems looked even more beautiful for she had not worn a blouse; her breasts trembled ever so slightly under the translucent cloth like a pair of love birds, enticing and inviting; her flat stomach, her firm legs visible from under the cloth and even the delicate soft heels of her feet radiated a sensual joy. Vidya Chatura, who had enjoyed the pleasures of that virtuous body, forgot everything else and drank in her beauty without restraint. Gazing into her laughing eyes, he put his arms around her shoulders and sang to himself.

> Clad in a white silk raiment, decked only with ornaments indispensable to auspiciousness, ... her hair marked with the holy *durva* grass, [she] appears to be reconciled with me from her very person, with its haughty deportment given up under the pretext of (the observance of) a vow.[9]

He held her in a close embrace for moments. Then he led her to his cupboard, opened it and showed her a bag full of money. He looked at her and smiled. 'Gunial, all this was done to see the limits to which your virtue extends. I also wanted to see your beauty without any embellishments. God has given me enough money for the wedding expenses. Now put on all your ornaments.'

Gunasundari bashfully hid herself in his arms and gave no response.

Eventually she went down, but without any ornaments. Manchatura called Vidya Chatura for a talk and gathered all the information about the wedding expenses and the amount due to each creditor. After lunch, Vidya Chatura went out. Manchatura and Sahasrai went to each creditor and paid the amount due to them on behalf of Vidya Chatura. The accounts were settled. Surprised that his creditors had not sought payment of dues from him, Vidya Chatura made enquiries. He was then told that Manchatura and Sahasrai had

[9] M. R. Kale, trans. *The Vikramorvasiyam of Kalidasa*, Canto 3, Verse 12, 11th ed., 3rd reprint (Delhi: Motilal Banarsidass, 1967, 2012), 159.

made all the payments. Manchatura had his way. His ego was satisfied. Everything that happened was conducive to his nature.

Gunasundari performed all her familial duties as always. The life of the family settled into a routine. Occasionally, there was some friction. If Gunasundari got something for herself, it was invariably exhausted in sharing with the family, but her generous heart never failed to take delight in it. Manchatura was the only one who disapproved of such generosity. He was reminded of the proverb: A good daughter-in-law cooks and a worthy son goes to a foreign land to earn. He clearly foresaw that Gunasundari will never be able to experience the real joys of life as long as she was entrapped within this family web. He believed it was a sign of ingratitude to keep her embroiled in family affairs at such a young age. Manchatura thought: I have enjoyed my youth. She must also have some desires. Gunasundari is generous to a fault and does not take the deprivation to heart. A string of flowers meant for her hair were claimed by Manohari; she got a ring which Dukhba took away; a bed meant for her went to Chandika's pleasure suite—that rand has grown up children and still desires a new bed! She got glass chandeliers which the old woman claimed for her gods. Everyone needs everything. Old and wise Gunasundari needs nothing—she has no desires! Ganchatura does not realise that he now earns and he should lead his own life and reduce his younger brother's burden. They all want to crush their brother to the ground. That Ganchatura thinks if he were to have his own house, it would look bad in society! Not any longer. Sahasrai has re-established his business; I will pack off Dukhba to her husband. And I will drive all the remaining asses to Manoharpuri and live there. It is a village, expenses will be less there, and this one here will get some respite. Yes, that is my final decision. If I don't understand her plight, who will?

Manchatura went about his task tactfully and adroitly. First, he sent Dukhba off to Sahasrai. Manchatura argued that it was difficult for Sahasrai to live alone in a foreign land. Sahasrai had learnt some useful tips from Manchatura. His business was doing well; he could easily bear his wife's additional expense. After this Manchatura convinced Ganchatura to start living independently. Gunasundari objected but Manchatura brushed her objections aside. A house adjacent to Vidya Chatura's was rented for Ganchatura and Chandika. Gunasundari shifted from her house as much furniture as could be fitted in that house. Manchatura did not keep very well. He used that as an excuse and went for a change of climate and fresh air to Manoharpuri. Dharmalaxmi also moved to Manoharpuri along with Chanchal and her children. Thus, just as birds go their separate ways at the break of dawn, one by one everyone left Gunasundari's house. Only Sundargauri stayed on. Bereft of family, Gunasundari felt lonely in that vacant house and initially she even wept for them. She visited Manoharpuri often.

As the days passed, Gunasundari gained in experience. Two years after Kumud Sundari's birth, another daughter was born to her, Kusum Sundari. She had no more children after that. For some years, Gunasundari had desired a son. But Vidya Chatura helped her to alleviate this discontent; her own good education and intellect also helped her. Then came those years when one after another members of the family died. First Dharmalaxmi, followed by Chanchal, then her children, then Dukhba, followed by Ganchatura and finally Chandika, they all passed away. Gunasundari dealt with their illnesses and deaths and subsequent rituals. She had to make her heart stony.

At the present juncture in our narrative, Gunasundari and Vidya Chatura lived alone in Ratnanagari. Kumud Sundari was with her in-laws in Suvarnapur. Manchatura, despite all these hard blows, lived on. He continued to stay at Manoharpuri. Sundargauri, almost on the threshold of old age now, lived with Manchatura and cared for him; she had adopted a widow's garb and shaven her hair. Hariprasad had given up studies and taken up a job. Manohari, now caught in the responsibilities of family life, no longer behaved petulantly. They lived in another town. Manohari occasionally wrote letters to Gunasundari as a daughter would to a mother. Gunasundari's heart had grown a thousand-fold more tender and loving with all these myriad different experiences. The rich memories of days gone past came before her often, and they prepared her for the barrenness and loneliness of death.

That loving mother was now anxiously waiting to meet her daughter at Bhadreshwar. Standing on the high raised platform of her rest house at Manoharpuri, for a moment Gunasundari forgot that she was the wife of the Prime Minister of Ratnanagari. As her eyes strained to look beyond the village outskirts, her heart was filled with memories of family life. She wondered: So many have left me for good. Which of them will stay with me forever? What lies in the fates of my two daughters? Her eyes brimmed over with tears. All the people who had gathered to receive and welcome her seemed to float in her tears.

6 A Night in Manoharpuri

Compared to other houses in the village, Gunasundari's house in Manoharpuri was spacious and comfortable. There were separate rooms for Manchatura, Sundargauri, Gunasundari and Chandrakant. Each of these rooms had all the required conveniences and the rooms were well furnished. There was a kitchen, a dining room, a water room and a bath room. There was a veranda through which one entered the house. There was some land at the rear of the house which was fenced.

From the time that Sarasvatichandra lay wounded in the forest till dusk with Aarthdas for company, Gunasundari remained in the veranda of her house, her eyes riveted on the road that led to the village. The sun had not yet set. In the distance, the taad trees caught the last rays of the sun. Leaning against a ladder for support, Gunasundari was responding to the queries and concerns of the villagers who had gathered to meet her, but her mind was elsewhere. Her attention moved from the road to the history of her family. The sun finally set. As darkness descended, Gunasundari saw two riders approaching the village. She followed their progress as they made their way through the curious crowd. Even from a distance, their dress identified them. As they came closer, it became clear that these were the two armed guards—Abdullah and Fatehsinh—who had been sent to Suvarnapur. They rode up to the veranda and Fatehsinh, still astride his horse, handed a note to Gunasundari. She quickly tore open the cover and read the letter.

> Mother, pious as a shrine, may the auspicious signs of your marriage remain forever. I shall leave this evening and embrace your feet tomorrow morning. The riders will give you other news as well. My revered father-in-law has become the Karbhari of Suvarnapur. The old administration has changed. Mother-in-law and sister-in-law invite you here. I am happy here. But today my heart feels heavy. I will unburden myself when I meet you tomorrow. Please convey my dandavat pranam to Dadaji and Kaki. My blessings to the sister. Father must be in Ratnanagari.
>
> Dandvat pranam of Kumud, the dust of thy feet.
>
> Chaitra Sud Bij

As Gunasundari read the letter, Manchatura, Sundargauri, Kusum Sundari and Chandrakant came and stood around her in anticipation. Kusum took the letter from her mother and read it out aloud. Each of them took turns to read it, including Chandrakant. He had last seen Kumud's letters in the hands of Sarasvatichandra; that memory now caused a desolate sigh to escape him. Gunasundari was worried by the words, '... my heart feels heavy. I will unburden myself when I meet you tomorrow'. She speculated over what Kumud could have possibly meant. She put many queries to the two riders, asking them about Suvarnapur, Buddhidhan's family, her son-in-law and her daughter. Finally, Abdullah and Fatehsinh sought her permission and left.

Night descended upon the world. The lamps were lit, spreading their light. The villagers also sought leave of Gunasundari and left for their homes, talking amongst themselves about the goodness of their minister's wife. For some time their chatter, and the sounds of children playing their last games before being called home, pierced the falling dark. Everything became quiet after that. Only the dark of the night persisted. It was time for dinner. Manchatura decreed that everyone, including the women of the house, should sit down to dinner together. He wanted to savour the togetherness. Everyone sat down. Gunasundari had raised an orphan girl who lived in Manoharpuri; she, too, sat down with them. Manchatura was fond of hearing village songs. He asked her to sing. As the others ate their dinner, the girl sang for them. 'Gunasundariba,' she said, 'Listen to this message sent by a daughter from her in-laws' house.'

Go tell mother and father that,
Banished to a faraway marital home,
Their daughter is dead
Sister-in-law taunts me; mother-in-law gives me grief,
My husband, his mother's boy, tears my heart to shreds
To whom do I unburden my soul?
I'm confused: do I jump into this well or that pond?
I have no more will to live, mother
But I long to see you again, mother
Why have you forsaken me?

Kumud Sundari's letter still fresh in her mind, the simple plaintive village song pierced Gunasundari's heart. Tears welled up in her eyes. She grew restless. She turned to Sundargauri and said, 'Such is the plight of a daughter sent to her in-laws. She has no one to share her pain with. Sundarbhabhi, my heart is not in my control ever since I read Kumud's letter. Sing, my daughter, sing!' The girl said, 'Gunasundariba, listen. A girl sits at a window in her in-laws' house. Her gaze is fixed in the direction of her parents' house. She heaves deep sighs and sends messages with passers-by. Listen ...' Gunasundari listened, absorbed, and the morsel of food remained uneaten in her hand.

This road leads to my house
But my eyes can't see that far
Today my heart longs for home
O' traveller, if you go by my house
Tell my mother, tell my father
That their daughter yearns for them

Gunasundari suppressed a sob. The girl continued her song.

O' sky farer, go take wing: you will
Find shelter in my home; stay there awhile
At break of dawn, go sit on my roof
My parents will be in the courtyard
Waiting

When father goes to the village square
Mother will tell him: Ask is she well and happy?
Having told him so, she will weep

Gunasundari could no longer contain herself and she cried out: 'Speechless bird, watching this even you shall weep!'

The girl said, 'Gunasundariba, just the other day Kumud behn and I were sitting in the veranda and singing this song. I said to her that you, too, will go away to Bombay and leave your parents' home.' The atmosphere turned solemn and sad. Gunasundari was reminded of Sarasvatichandra. She asked the girl to sing the last two lines again, and she wept her heart out.

Kusum Sundari had also sat down for dinner with her mother. Hitherto, she used to eat with her grandfather. She was thirteen now. Her body had begun to change. Her mind, too, was maturing. Her marriage had not yet been fixed. This did not prevent youth from dawning upon her adolescent body. As a child she had been naughty, unabashed and independent. Her parents had given her an education. Kusum proved to be an intelligent and keen learner of new skills and arts. She taught herself through observation. She heard attentively, watched carefully and imitated to perfection, resting only when she had mastered the skill she had set her mind to. Kusum was still innocent and she neither knew nor recognised passion. And yet, unknown to her, Kama the God of Love had not failed in his duties to teach her his art. She still had naïve and romantic notions of love and was too young to know anything of the art of lovemaking. And yet, unseen and unknown passions flowed through her veins, through every hair on her body. This change had gone unnoticed. People who saw her were still under the impression that only her body was changing, not her mind. No one could discern the intense new energies flowing through Kusum. A new sense of shame restrained her. She tried to hide her growing body. Shame made her dress differently, walk differently. Those who observed her and believed that Kusum had not changed at all were not entirely misguided either. In the grip of something she could neither understand nor control, she held on fiercely to her childhood, to what she knew, swaying under the pull of dual forces.

Kusum was seated between Gunasundari and Sundargauri. She saw her mother weeping. She turned to Manchatura and said, 'Dadaji, did you see, Gunial has tears in her eyes and she is crying.'

Her unexpected question broke the spell. Old Manchatura smiled and told his granddaughter, 'Kusum behn, your prestige is at stake. You are with her, and still she weeps.'

'No, no, that is not true. When we were in Ratnanagari, Gunial was critical of Sarasvatichandra. She said he was childish and that he should not have been so offended at a few harsh words from his father. And now Gunial is weeping at a song that describes a daughter's plight. Is Gunial not being childish? Sarasvatichandra's hurt was personal, but she is crying at a song! I was telling Gunial the other day that before criticising Sarasvatichandra, we should consider what we would have done if we were in his place.'

'You intend to say that you have won the argument and that Gunial has lost, isn't it?'

'Of course! Not once but a thousand times over.'

'Kusum, we shouldn't desire to defeat our mother,' Sundargauri said gently, caressing Kusum affectionately.

'No, that is not true, Kaki. The young always win over their elders. You have often told me that Gunial would win over everyone in the family and to such an extent that no one, not even Dadaji, not even Moti Ba nor any of the aunts could contradict her. If she won over everyone, why should I not win over her?'

Everyone, including Chandrakant, laughed. Chandrakant felt like joining issues with Kusum. He asked her with a smile, 'Behn, how can you take sides with someone that your mother is critical of?'

Part of Kusum Sundari's face glowed in the light of the lamp while the rest was in shadow. Chandrakant's eyes were focused on the part of her eager and joyous face lit by the lamp. As he looked at the girl who still defended Sarasvatichandra, Chandrakant's mind was filled with mixed emotions. He said to himself, but more to his absent friend: Sarasvatichandra, Kumud Sundari is meek. This one is a more suitable match for you. Because she will be equal to you. She will change your grave and peculiar character. But when will that day come? Chandrakant sighed and looked at Kusum expectantly.

Chandrakant was a stranger. Kusum was not accustomed to talking to such men. She was a little taken aback at his unexpected question. She felt shy and looked down. Then assuming a gravity beyond her years, she said, 'Chandrakantbhai, Sarasvatichandra left my sister. But you, a friend of his, still have affection for Kumud's family. Why is that so? Just as you have affection for us, we are also partial to Sarasvatichandra. This is also a heartfelt relationship.'

Chandrakant was won over by her response and choked with emotion. 'You are right, behn. May such feelings last forever.' He again thought: Sarasvatichandra, you deserve her. But where are you?

Manchatura butted in, 'Kumud was raised by Sundar, and Kusum by Manohari. If Manohari cannot be defeated by words, how can Kusum be? Isn't it so, Kusum?' Gunasundari changed the topic. Buddhidhan had become the Karbhari of Suvarnapur—this was important news. There was much speculation about Sarasvatichandra's sudden departure from Suvarnapur and his probable destination. Chandrakant was worried. There was much talk of the presence of outlaws. Kumud Sundari was scheduled to travel the next day. Everyone grew increasingly anxious about her safety. They talked through the meal and finally retired to their respective bedrooms.

Chandrakant was to share Manchatura's room. They continued to talk late into the night. Manchatura asked about Sarasvatichandra's decision to leave home. Chandrakant spoke at length. As he described Sarasvatichandra's qualities, his achievements, Chandrakant's narration grew animated. He described Sheth Laxminandan's feeble-mindedness, Guman's jealousy and insecurity, Dhurtalal's machinations and the tragic outcome of these forces. His hatred for them was evident. His voice was sad as he described his friend's disappearance. He also spoke at length about Vidya Chatura's disapproval of Sarasvatichandra. He did not care that the one listening to his narration was none other than Vidya Chatura's father. Chandrakant refuted Vidya Chatura's charges with passion and eloquence. Such levels of eloquence and lucidity eluded him during intellectual debates in Bombay. He did not realise that Gunasundari had entered the room. His love for his friend had made him articulate and he argued like the lawyer that he was. He asserted that ministers and high functionaries of native states were way below the calibre of his friend Sarasvatichandra who possessed qualities which were unique to him.

Chandrakant's ardent speech had the desired effect on Manchatura, Gunasundari and others who heard him. Gunasundari repented that Vidya Chatura had been so harsh in his criticism of Sarasvatichandra. Young Kusum leaned on Sundargauri's shoulders and listened with bated breath as Chandrakant passionately defended his friend against the world. Old Manchatura heard him indulgently as if it were his duty to solace a wounded heart. He drew upon his past experiences to sit in judgement upon his own son, clarify his own position and absolve Sarasvatichandra of any wrongdoing. In conclusion Manchatura said, 'Chandrakant, all things considered, Sarasvatichandra's decision was not wrong. There can be no doubt that Kumud would not have been happy with a mother-in-law like Guman. Vidya Chatura is unlikely to understand such things. He is fortunate to have Gunasundari as his wife. She has always shielded him from the lashes of the world. He cannot even imagine how the world can hurt you. By now Gunasundari would have forgotten. She was just twenty-two or twenty-three years old then. Our family was more or less harmonious, but still there were daily dramas. I still clearly remember how she, even at that young age, worked tactfully to bring peace to the house. That girl of just twenty-odd years bore the burden of the whole family as lightly as if she were carrying a flower. That burden would have crushed even mature experienced elders under its weight. But her dainty frame moved around the house as swift as a silver lamp—she spread her light in every corner. Her patience, her equanimity was praiseworthy. An old man like me found it difficult to keep my temper in check, but she would never utter a word. And when she spoke, she spoke slowly, in a calm voice. She soothed everyone. Not only that, she never took anything to heart. There are some people who feel the hurt but conceal it. But this young girl was something else. If someone came to bite her, she loved them even more. She would not confront them but would be accommodative and win them over, as if nothing was the matter.'

Manchatura's praise made Gunasundari coy. She was about to give an appropriately modest response when Manchatura, shrewd as he was, sensed it and was quick to stop her. Looking at her fondly, he laughed and said, 'Gunasundari, don't be so impatient. Don't feel so proud at my praise. It is not you that I praise. Many years ago there was a girl called Gunasundari in this house. It is her I praise. You may not even have seen that girl. Tell me did you ever see another girl like her? It is possible that you may have seen her in the mirror.' Everyone laughed at this. 'You I am going to criticise. And that you will have to hear patiently. When an elder criticises, one must listen, isn't it?'

Gunasundari smiled beguilingly and said, 'Yes, of course. Whatever the elders say must be right', and she touched her forehead as a sign of deference.

Manchatura continued his narrative. 'Chandrakant, what shall I tell you? The house was full of people. Someone must have said something untoward, spoken something by way of a taunt, would have been ungrateful, refused to bear the burden, even made her dance to their tune. Someone would have taken things away from her, harassed her, accused her wrongly, and all this went on for years. But Gunasundari never uttered a word. She also ensured that Vidya Chatura knew nothing about it. She kept him completely ignorant of everyday domestic matters. She never allowed the poor man to experience the pains of being in a family—not even in his worst nightmares. What is this? Is this conduct worthy of a woman? Any other woman in her place would have wept daily and robbed her husband of sleep. She would have given him an object lesson in the pains of domesticity, and the man would have repented the day he married. A woman is one who makes her husband an equal partner in her sorrows. But our Gunasundari was extremely selfish. She bore all the suffering, did not share it with anyone, she drank the poison alone. She wanted all the suffering for herself. Do you understand? As a result, throughout his life Vidya Chatura was denied any knowledge, any experience of suffering. And so he failed to understand Sarasvatichandra's pain. He could not understand the anguish of harsh words spoken by a father ensnared by a younger woman. And the reason for Vidya Chatura's failure to do so is our Gunial. When I talk about it, she feels coy. How is she to share her failings? She gave my Vidya Chatura only joy and denied him any share of pain. No other woman should ever do such a thing. A woman who does not allow the husband to experience pain, does not harass him by weeping and complaining is not a woman. Therefore, Chandrakant, you should disregard what my son said to you and blame it all on Gunasundari that she did not allow even a whisper of suffering to reach him. All these are her failings.

'Yes, my son's fault is that he assumed that every house has a Gunasundari. Because he had her for a wife. He assumed that it was child's play to be a Gunasundari. Those who eat sweets know nothing of the plight of those who eat coarse grains. But I have experienced more than he has, and understand these things well. Sarasvatichandra was anguished by Laxminandan's harsh words. And rightly so. He is delicate as a flower. How can a flower like him withstand snowy blizzards? His assumption was also not faulty. My meek Kumud would have been oppressed and tormented by Guman and she would have died suffering. Even my Gunial cannot withstand a Guman, how could poor Kumud be a match? Guman needs someone brazen—someone like my Kusum. What do you say, Kusum? Will you put Guman in order, or will she straighten you out?'

'You think I am so gutsy?' Kusum said. 'Dadaji, you are very clever. You praised Gunial again!'

'Is there anything wrong in being clever?'

'No, why should it be so? If the grandfather is clever, the granddaughter must be clever, too. We got diverted. Let us hear you.'

Manchatura took up the thread once again. 'All right, I will neither praise your mother, nor will I point out her follies. But Chandrakant, even you will admit that Sarasvatichandra's diagnosis was correct, but not his remedy. He left home and became a wanderer. His intellect failed him. He should have lived independently from Laxminandan.

If you ask me, I see much wisdom in the customs of the white Sahibs. They have the wherewithal to maintain a separate household. They marry and live separately. Our customs are not all wrong, but they work only when everyone lives together with affection. It works as long as there is harmony. Among the Sahibs, they have the joys of a couple, but they know nothing of the joys of our family life. My family is around me. We have so much fun together. I know and appreciate these joys, and so does my Gunial. But the Sahibs cannot imagine them even in their dreams. Among the Sahibs, the wife's mother and sisters are welcome but the man's old parents have to fend for themselves somehow. Among us, an old man like me and a poor widow like Sundar have insurance without ever having the need to take out insurance. Our blessings are with Gunasundari and she will always be happy. Old, lame, unproductive people like us have been a burden on Gunasundari for years, even when Vidya Chatura earned a low salary ...'

'What are you saying, Pitaji! Have some pity on us!' Gunasundari interjected.

'Listen to me. What I said is not without substance. It is also true that we might have been of some help to you at some point, your service will bring you glory in this and the other world; but till such time comes, the person who can endure the burden is only one, and that is Gunasundari. And this Gunasundari is in this house—she is matchless, not found anywhere else. What could be crueller than being dependent upon the income of poor and struggling sons, to belabour good and industrious daughters-in-law to the bone, to imprison them by our presence in a way that their youthful aspirations find no expression, and to suppress their intelligence and creativity? I speak from experience that many parents and parents-in-law have either consciously or unconsciously acted in a way that is cruel. Everyone knows the sufferings of daughters-in-law who speak out and fight back. The world knows of the misadventures of worthless sons. But there is a saying among us that a good daughter-in-law cooks while a worthy son goes to a foreign land to earn. If we were to go by that, who knows about the plight of sons and daughters-in-law who do not complain?

It is the duty of parents and parents-in-laws to know the plight of such children and not subject them to punishment; it is not good to uproot trees that bear sweet fruits. Parents do not subject their children to punishment wilfully, but even when it is done unconsciously the one that is crushed is as delicate as a flower. I speak from experience. I believe it to be the duty of parents and siblings to work for the freedom of others. One may not always have the means, but gradually one must work towards separation and independence. If Laxminandan had worked out an arrangement whereby Sarasvatichandra could have lived separately and yet maintained togetherness, such a day would never have come. It is a sign of wisdom and foresight to work out the separate arrangement when the family is still harmonious. One should not wait for discord to set in. It is foolish to consider possible social disapproval. Eventually, every generation and each branch of the family has to live separately, but to do so at the right time is a sign of social wisdom. Sarasvatichandra could not even conceive that he could have lived in his own house, separate from his parents. This inability proves that although learned, he was not made wise by experience. Was this a big issue? It is the societal norm that eventually each one must live separately, why must one hesitate? Sarasvatichandra felt ashamed of taking this decision because he is still fundamentally a child. I have set forth some principles. The first of which is at no point should two women be made to live in the same house. The second is that everyone—man or woman—should be allowed to live their separate lives in their own households. For my own self I have adopted the model of the sun. The sun is far away from the earth and provides light and heat, but the sun does not bother as to what humans do under the roofs of their houses, nor does it want to see what we do in nooks and crannies where its light does not reach. I should be the sun of the family. The happiness and welfare of all will be secured by this. This is the duty of elders, and all elders must abide by this duty if we truly love our families and desire happiness for all. If the elders follow this norm, their old age will be as happy and fulfilling as mine. But those who act contrary to this will have to abuse their sons and sing that song: Who sent me old age? All of you will attain old age someday. And therefore,

I say this to you. There is a lesson in it for your conduct in the present as well. If some action is imperative, do not act like Sarasvatichandra, or like a woman ask yourself: How can this be done? Do not hesitate or be shy. Do what appears to be correct; act patiently, deliberately and consciously. Do not harbour any hesitation or doubt. Those who are frank about food and social conduct remain happy.'

Gunasundari was not in the habit of interrupting her father-in-law. She heard him out patiently and then asked, 'So this was the reason why Jethji was sent to his own house notwithstanding all my protests? And this is why you came to live here, pretending that you needed a change of air and water?'

Manchatura looked up straight at her and twirling his moustache, smiled a wicked smile and triumphantly said, 'Yes.' His monosyllabic answer silenced Gunasundari.

Chandrakant had felt enraged at Vidya Chatura's criticism of Sarasvatichandra. Manchatura's forceful, even if somewhat inconsistent argument, drawing upon his diverse experiences left Chandrakant spellbound. He was surprised and stunned by his sharp intellect. He felt that Manchatura was much sharper than his minister son and he found himself in awe of the old patriarch.

It was late into the night. Everyone retired to their bedrooms and sooner or later, they fell asleep. But Gunasundari's natural and characteristic patience and calm deserted her. She was anxious and apprehensive. Kumud Sundari's letter and her impending journey filled Gunasundari with trepidation. Sleep eluded her. At some point Sundargauri woke up and found Gunasundari awake and weeping silently to herself. Sundargauri gathered her wits about her and asked, 'Gunialbhabhi, what happened? Why do you cry?' Gunasundari rested her head on Sundar's bosom and wept. 'Sundarbhabhi, today I have a sense of foreboding and I cannot but cry. Kumud's letter fills me with apprehension and pain. I can no longer bear it.' Kusum Sundari, ever so alert, also woke up. As she was about to get up from bed, someone was heard knocking at the door and calling out, 'Gunasundariba, Gunasundariba, please open the door!' They strained their ears to ascertain the voice. Kusum recognised it and said, 'That is Fatehsinh's voice! Gunial, shall I open the door?' Gunasundari nodded and Kusum opened the door. Fatehsinh entered with a lantern in hand. He kept the lantern on the floor and sat down at some distance from Gunasundari. He held his sword in his hand and spoke, 'I could not have shared this with others. Hence, I have come back.' Everyone grew anxious. Fatehsinh informed Gunasundari of what Kumud Sundari had told him regarding Sarasvatichandra. He also told her that the outlaws had abducted Sarasvatichandra and that Harbhamji had gone in search of him.

'What! Sarasvatichandra was found and then lost again? Have the outlaws abducted him? Oh, Sundar! He was a guest of Buddhidhan. Do you now understand the meaning of Kumud's letter? She wrote about unburdening her heart. What else could it be? Shall we wake up Pitaji and Chandrakant and give them the news?'

Fatehsinh said, 'No, no, there is no need to wake them up so late in the night.'

Sundargauri interjected, 'But Chandrakant is a friend of Sarasvatichandra. He has come only in search of Sarasvatichandra.'

Gunasundari tried to calm herself. She thought for a while and said, 'What news is to be given to him? He has finally gone to sleep, tired. Let him sleep. What can he do even if we wake him up now? If he hears this, he will lose both his sleep and his peace. And nothing can be done until Harbham comes back with some news. Fatehsinh, you can go now. We will wake up the others only in the morning. But bring Harbham as soon as he returns and wake us up.'

Fatehsinh left. Kusum latched the door. Gunasundari said, 'Who knows what news the morning will bring. Chandrakant will never see Sarasvatichandra's folly. Oh why should Sarasvatichandra bring such things upon himself?' Sundargauri replied, 'It is his destiny. What can he do?'

Kusum remembered the lines from a song:

What is destined cannot be altered.

Sundargauri hugged Kusum. Just then there was a knock on the door. They were startled. 'Who is there?' asked Gunasundari. The silence of the night was pierced once again.

As soon as Fatehsinh stepped out of Gunasundari's house, he saw two human forms approach. He could not ascertain whether they were thieves or good men, ghost or human, friends or foes. Fatehsinh walked on, his hand ready to draw his sword. He called out loudly, 'Victory to Maharaja Maniraj! Who goes there?'

From a distance both forms responded in unison, 'Victory to Maharaja Maniraj!' They recognised each other's voices. The outlaws had met under the banyan tree where the three roads met. It was the first quarter of the night. Harbhamji, hidden in the tree, had heard their plans. He had rushed to meet Mukhi Patel, the village headman, and they were now on their way to inform Gunasundari and Manchatura when they met Fatehsinh. It was dark, faces could not be discerned.

'Is that Harbhamji?'

'Yes. Is that Fatehsinhji?'

'Yes. Who is following you?'

'Mukhi Patel.'

'Good. Gunasundariba awaits us.' Fatehsinh led the way. So it was he who knocked on Gunasundari's door once again that night and replied, 'Ba, it is us, Harbham and Fatehsinh. Please open the door'. Even before he had finished speaking, Kusum appeared carrying a lantern. The masculine faces were brought into focus by its light. The three came in and closed the door behind them. Gunasundari and Sundargauri sat on a cot. Kusum squeezed in between them. The lantern was kept on the floor. The three men sat at some distance on the floor. Harbhamji sat on his haunches and narrated the sequence of events. He informed them in detail about the outlaws and their plans to capture Kumud Sundari. He said, 'Ba, do not be afraid. Buddhidhanbhai's authority is immense. The world trembles before Maharaja Maniraj's power. Anyone who dares lay his hands on Vidya Chatura's daughter will have no future.'

The three women were terrified. Sundargauri wept. Kusum Sundari trembled. Gunasundari finally overcame her numbing fear and said, 'Fatehsinh, wake up Pitaji at once'. They rushed towards Manchatura's room.

Manchatura and Chandrakant woke up by the rustle of their feet. They opened the door and came out. Manchatura asked, 'What is it, behn? What has happened?'

Gunasundari hurriedly appraised them both. Chandrakant went cold the moment he heard that the outlaws had captured Sarasvatichandra. But what had happened to Sarasvatichandra was no longer the primary concern. Right now, it was far more important to save Kumud Sundari. Concern about Sarasvatichandra's plight faded from their minds just as the moon fades at the first light of dawn. Chandrakant's mind churned in helplessness and fury. He was furious at his obdurate friend and he berated himself for his own stupidity: I sent him that letter, and that is why he left Suvarnapur! Now where on earth shall I look for him? Until Kumud Sundari reaches home safe and unharmed, how can I even speak of a search party for Sarasvatichandra? Questions like these circled relentlessly in Chandrakant's fraught mind. But outwardly, he remained concerned about Kumud Sundari's fate.

Manchatura put some quick questions to Harbhamji and consulted the Mukhi Patel about possible courses of action. He heard the Mukhi and the two soldiers, considered their suggestions and thought quietly to himself for a while. Then he began to issue rapid instructions: 'Mukhi Patel, you claim there are about forty riders ready in the village. That is fortuitous. Make the following arrangements. We will divide them into five groups. We shall send the maximum number of soldiers to the spot where they intend to capture Kumud. One group should be stationed in the village; another group should patrol the area where the three roads meet. A third group should be positioned near the bridge on the river; they should hide in the ravines. Where shall we keep the fourth group? Yes, they should be on the other bank of river Subhadra which is where the forest is. They should be as close to the Suvarnapur border as possible. The last group should meet Kumud and her group on the way and escort her to safety.

'Mukhi Patel, you have extra responsibility. You are familiar with all roads. Therefore, you should patrol the terrain between the banyan tree and the river. You should move about with your men with due pomp and show. The outlaws must realise that you are alert and prepared and the rascals won't dare to make any mischief. I am certain that you will be more than a match for Chandandas and Vaghji. The group that will stay on in Manoharpuri should comprise ordinary men, but they should remain completely alert and ready.'

Harbhamji agreed, 'Yes, this is perfect. No one can point a finger at Vidya Chaturabhai's security arrangements. The entire area is in awe of Maharaja Maniraj's power. And in Manoharpuri we already have an army of people, so there is no need to deploy soldiers. Even so, it is good to have a few men guard the village in case of any eventuality; they could be anyone from among the troops.'

Manchatura was pleased to hear his son's praise. He said, 'Harbham, Mukhi Patel will keep watch over the entire stretch between the tree and the river without any trouble'. Manchatura wanted Harbhamji's opinion on this; but he also wanted to test the Mukhi's courage. Mukhi's hand went to his sword at once; he clenched his teeth which sparkled in the light of the lamp. Manchatura saw this as a good omen. He continued, 'Fatehsinh, you will hide in the ravines and keep a close watch over Bhimji and Pratap. That is something you will do easily'. Fatehsinh twirled his moustaches in response. 'Harbham, the most important task will be assigned to you. Will you be able to do it?'

'Thundering clouds do not rain,' replied Harbhamji. 'Do I need to thunder?'

'So be it—go and pour over them! You must right away ascertain the whereabouts of Sursinh. You and your group must ensure that Sursinh's associates are unable to send him messages. You should not allow him to cross over to the other side either by the river or by the road. He should find you as his shadow whenever he turns, wherever he goes.'

Pleased at this responsibility, Harbhamji promptly responded, 'Consider it done! But you still need to deploy one more group.'

Manchatura said, 'You are so impatient, Harbham, that you don't let me finish. Abdullah will lead that group.'

Harbhamji said, 'Abdullah is an expert swordsman. But we need someone with intelligence. Pratapsinh is certain to try and snatch Kumud behn away. He will play some vile tricks. Abdullah will not be a match for him.'

Manchatura's chest expanded with pride as he said, 'I will go with Abdullah and his men'.

Harbhamji replied, 'Yes, that is best'.

Gunasundari grew alarmed and immediately said, 'No, Pitaji, you cannot take that risk! Your body is old. This is not your work'.

Manchatura laughed. 'Gunasundari, just watch your father-in-law. You were not even born then. The Sahibs had just entered the country. At that time I used to wield a sword along with the Rajputs. My Kumud is in danger, and am I to be a mere spectator? If that happens my life itself would be futile. Harbham, now pay attention. Abdullah and I will leave forthwith. We and the soldiers will cross the Subhadra and keep going till we meet Kumud. We shall escort her back. She will also be accompanied by a few soldiers. We shall go now and come back fast, having made all the arrangements. Gunasundari, have someone take out a pyjama from my old clothes. I will tell you what other clothes I will need. Fatehsinh, find me a good sword and fetch a rifle as well and ...'

Before Manchatura could say anything more they had all dispersed, eager to carry out his orders. The women went in to get his clothes. In the olden times, before the advent of the British, the entire country used to carry arms for protection against thugs and bandits. Even brahmins and women were required to be prepared for self-defence. Manchatura had passed his youth in such dangerous times. He was often required to use arms and was skilled at wielding a variety of weapons. The country was disarmed following Nana Sahib's revolt. But the courage, valour and expertise required for the use of arms had not deserted Manchatura. It was after many years that he had this opportunity. A lion awakened from sleep is still a lion—Manchatura felt his old valour reinvigorated and new blood flow in his old veins. He turned to Chandrakant and said, 'You stay at home. You will be safe here with the women. The English Bahadur took away our arms. So along with women, men like you are freed from this burden.'

Chandrakant, deep in his own thoughts, was startled by this statement. He felt angry at the British government for having disarmed the country.

Manchatura continued, 'Don't worry. I am not going to get into a debate with you right now. You will achieve nothing by coming with us. The outlaws will have no patience for your legal debates. I could give you a gun, but you can't stuff books in it and fire. It needs gun powder. I have no time for further talk. I am going fully armed and prepared. By the time I return, do write an essay about it'. And without waiting for a response, Manchatura disappeared outside to oversee arrangements.

Angry, ashamed and stunned, Chandrakant kept sitting there. Soon, many more people assembled outside; he could hear their urgent but low voices indistinctly and the clink of their weapons. Finally he heard Manchatura's rousing command, 'Let us go!' Once the armed contingent had set off for the encounter, the night turned silent once again. Chandrakant realised that he was left alone with the women of the house. He sat there, trying to collect his disparate thoughts. At about three in the morning he at last fell asleep, exhausted.

7 Forest, Dark Night and Sarasvatichandra

Aarthdas, who was moved purely by self-interest, was incapable of comprehending Sarasvatichandra's selfless generosity. He disappeared with the ring that Sarasvatichandra offered him without once looking back. The night was upon them. The sky seemed to be in the throes of labour, uneasy and on the verge of losing consciousness. Sensing the liminality of the twilight hour as if by instinct, birds small and big flew back to earth and disappeared into the branches of trees that sheltered them. The play of light and dark, the moving shadows and the shroud-like silence of the forest were capable of unnerving a lonely, forlorn heart. A distant feeble moon rose uncertainly in the sky. The moon seemed frightened by the world and wished to hide with the sun and the constellations in the dark caves of the mythical Astachal which lay in the west. It was at that twilight hour that Sarasvatichandra regained consciousness. As he lay on his back, his open eyes took in the sky, the forest and the shrieking night. The last vestige of human presence, Aarthdas, was nowhere to be seen. Sarasvatichandra sat up and looked around, his eyes searching the swiftly falling dark for the path that Aarthdas would have taken. He realised that he searched in vain. He looked up at the night sky. All around him, the forest breathed and rustled in the wind as if it were alive. Sounds of wild animals coming from deep within the forest startled and frightened him. He stood up at once, his heart pounding. His agility suggested that he was neither hungry, nor feeble, nor even melancholic. The faint moon had disappeared as if in fright. Darkness, impenetrable, soft and heavy, descended as suddenly as a tiger jumps on its prey and it enveloped Sarasvatichandra. Face to face with that all-encompassing dark, his heart stopped beating for moments. He cupped his hands over his ears to stop the blood rushing in his ears. Suddenly, his eyes began to glow with an intense delight. He cried out aloud: Oh, at last!—the vision of the Great Night that I have long sought! Oh, Kumud, at this moment I erase you from memory. You belong to the world of day, and I to the world of night. This vision allows me to imagine the dark night of death. Chandrakant, you had wanted to save me from this vision, to redeem me! Gumanba, all this was possible because of you. Pitaji, you stopped loving me and freed me from the bondage of love. Today I stand freed of all bonds—of illusion, society, family, love and wealth. Free at last, I can experience this ultimate sublime state. I am surrounded by this dark, dense forest bereft of any human presence except myself. Here I am amidst the beasts of the night. God is my only succour. I have attained the condition that one attains at the end of one's life. I have moved from being a millionaire in Bombay to a destitute guest of Buddhidhan. And now I stand in this blind forest. It is certain that I shall go further down.

While the sound whirls around,
Down, down!
As the fawn draws the hound,
As the lightning the vapour,
As a weak moth the taper;
Death, despair; love, sorrow;
Time, both; to-day, to-morrow;
As steel obeys the spirit of the stone,
Down, down!
Through the gray, void abysm,
Down, down!
Where the air is no prism,
And the moon and stars are not,
And the cavern-crags wear not
The radiance of Heaven,
Nor the gloom to Earth given,
Where there is One pervading, One alone,

Down, down!
In the depth of the deep,
Down, down!
Like veiled lightning asleep,
Like the spark nursed in embers,
The last look Love remembers,
Like a diamond which shines
On the dark wealth of mines,
A spell is treasured but for thee alone.
Down, down![1]

Sarasvatichandra was unaware of his own speech. The forest echoed his words back to him like so many answers. As he stood there in that impenetrable darkness, his arms crossed over his chest, he felt a profound silence surge within him, a sense of contentment. He felt at peace with himself. Not one thought clouded his mind. He stood there motionless, as if waiting for the light that would pierce the dark and the song that would drown the sounds of the forest.

At that moment when Sarasvatichandra stood still, almost lifeless, lost in a dream world in a deep meditative silence, like him the night, too, broke free of all constraints, it erased all concerns of the world, all its joys and sorrows and desires. It stood lifeless, eternal and vast—extending itself from one end of the universe to the other. It destroyed all sense of duty and obligation, right and wrong, good and evil. Under its inexorable sweep, those who wore crowns submitted to the charms of women; diligent scholars grew stupefied with sleep; those under oath of celibacy and asceticism were enticed into the world of dreams; those who were rational and clever came under its sway and behaved irrationally. The world gripped by night was bereft of light, of consciousness, even vesture. People lay lifeless like dead bodies in a crematorium. Owls and jackals howled as eternal solitude burnt on the pyre of time. Darkness enveloped all ten directions. Forests, hills, cities and beasts were enfolded by the unseen limbs of darkness. The night merged the world of consciousness into the unconscious.

[1] Author's note: *Prometheus Unbound*, Percy Bysshe Shelly.

The roars of lions and tigers were part of its dream world. The myriad machinations and decisions of the day were swallowed by the unfathomable dark. Sarasvatichandra's mind became imbued with the presence of something omnipresent—and the darkness merged with it. He had abandoned home, wealth, father, friend, Kumud, and love itself. As all these veils were lifted one by one, Sarasvatichandra could see the unseen. He stood surrounded by the infinite night and the forest in a state of absolute thoughtlessness.

But this condition did not last long. Soon, like rocks that break the flow of a mighty river, the body reasserted itself—it broke his solitude. The mind grew aware of the body once again. When a resurgent body asserts itself, even the power of yoga pales before it. Hunger devoured his mind; his mind turned blank and thirst lodged itself in his parched throat and drank up knowledge and Sarasvati herself. His eyes rendered useless by the dark closed as his frail body could no longer bear their sightless weight. Sarasvatichandra fell to the ground and lost consciousness. Intellect that produces remorse lost anchor; consciousness that experiences fear and sorrow was lost. Arrogant men make lofty claims but lose courage the moment they are to be tested. But not Sarasvatichandra. Many submit to their passions, act thoughtlessly, and later, as hindsight prevails, try to undo what cannot be undone. It was no longer possible for Sarasvatichandra to undo what he had done unto Kumud Sundari—this was his only regret. And so he had run away from Chandrakant and sought refuge in the forest; he had sought peace and meaning in a rootless wanderer's life. The curtains came down on this strange drama quite abruptly. Sarasvatichandra could no longer consider if he had acted foolishly or wisely and attained some higher purpose. Time and space also did nothing to awaken him.

Darkness like an army moved swiftly and brought all ten directions under its sway. The night was filled with sounds like those of galloping horses. The branches of trees swayed and grazed and collided with each other like the clashing of swords. The wind rustled and whistled through the trees, branches and leaves like so many arrows from the bow of a great warrior. The shrill buzz of insects filled the forest air like clarion calls fill a battlefield. Deer, rabbits and other defenceless creatures captured by predators cried out in anguish of death. Their cries and moans were like those of fatally wounded soldiers who lay waiting for death, trampled under the feet of their warring comrades. Predators and prey ran amuck in the forest; teeth and claws tore into warm flesh. Jackals howled like cowardly soldiers deserting the battlefield. Tigers moved swiftly and stealthily through the forest like mighty warriors on their steeds. A lone lion, just by his roar, stamped his authority over all other beasts. His roar—like the deafening thunder of clouds or cannons firing—silenced even tigers and elephants; wild buffaloes and deer ran helter-skelter; monkeys chattered and shrieked excitedly; birds asleep in the trees woke up startled, squawking. His roar reverberated through every nook and glade of the forest and reached the caves of the distant Sundargiri mountains. His fiery eyes glowed like embers, mocking anyone who dared approach him. The undisputed king of the forest roared time and again, silencing even the constant buzz of forest insects. As the lion sat alone and regal in one part of the forest, Sarasvatichandra, master of his own mind and destiny, lay lifeless in a place where any other heart would tremble and palpitate with fear.

No human being would have the heart to enter the forest at that hour. Even the bravest of the brave would not dare face the predators of the night. Even when the outlaws met, they preferred to meet under the banyan tree on the way to Manoharpuri. The spot where Sarasvatichandra lay was at some distance from the banyan tree. As he regained consciousness and opened his eyes, his senses were once more assaulted by the dreadful darkness saturated with the roars, cries and howls of the wild. Even the distant stars in the sky seemed to him frightful like countless fiery eyes. The awe-inspiring grandeur of the wild would have driven a feeble-minded person mad. All thought deserted him; poetry did not dare come near; all knowledge was swallowed by oblivion and amnesia; parents, Kumud Sundari, Chandrakant—he could see no one in his mind's eye. At the hour of death, one is utterly alone and lonely. Sarasvatichandra lay orphaned, face to face with mortal danger. Like in a nightmare, he lay paralysed without the strength to move, get up or call out. Running away was out of the question. Where could he have run to? The forest was dark, dense and unfamiliar. Death seemed intimate and near. If hunger and thirst did not claim him first, some wild beast certainly would. He felt it was time to bid this world farewell. A pained visage of his father, of Kumud, of his dearest friend Chandrakant now flashed before his eyes; they all seemed to be weeping inconsolably. Sarasvatichandra could not speak but his soul cried out, he sought their forgiveness, he pleaded with them. He remembered that he had slain Kumud's love, a crime as heinous as the murder of a brahmin. Tears flowed from his eyes and were absorbed by the dust. He felt cold convulsions rippling through his body. If he had any strength left, he would have cried aloud, but he couldn't. His limbs went numb. Laxminandan, Kumud Sundari, Chandrakant—these three names got caught in his breath and his chest heaved as he tried to exhale. He opened his mouth so his breath and, with it, his life could escape his body. A fire raged in his belly. He heard footsteps, footsteps of the messenger of God of Death. There was no one to cremate his body, no one to mourn him. The forest enveloped him just as a tiger pounces on his prey, ready to devour it.

Just then a sound came from the bushes and a great black cobra came out hissing. It moved rapidly towards Sarasvatichandra, unstoppable as the waves of the sea. Its hissing and sinuous movement infused his numb and feeble body with some energy and he moved his neck to watch death approach him. He took his eyes away and stared up at the sky. In a flash, all thoughts of near and dear ones, all remorse, sorrows, tears and all other worldly matters vanished. Sarasvatichandra prepared himself for the most auspicious moment and waited with bated breath for the cobra to bite him. For him the world was about to end. He was filled with peace. In that moment of calm, the fear of death also disappeared. The only thing left in him was the 'instinct of self-preservation'. This instinct taught him that it was better to appear dead and allow the cobra to pass over his body. As it came closer, Sarasvatichandra stopped breathing. The cobra slithered up to him, saw an obstacle in its path, went around the inert body and finally climbed on top of him. It was thick, black and about five to six hand-spans long. The serpent coiled itself over Sarasvatichandra's chest and raising its hood, began to sway to its own slow deathly rhythm. Its gleaming round eyes and the white pattern on its hood glowed like jewels in the light of the stars. Sarasvatichandra's patience had its limits. Numb with fear, he felt crushed by its weight. The cobra seemed to grow heavier with every passing moment. The knife-sharp agony he experienced was akin to the bite of the cobra itself. His lips, nails and teeth must have turned black with fear, but this was difficult to discern in the dark. His body went cold as ice, his ears turned deaf, the blood stopped flowing in his veins. Only the soul remained a mute witness in his lifeless body. The cobra remained on his chest for five to seven eternal minutes. Then quite abruptly it turned around, lashing its tail on his face as it did, slithered down the length of his body and went away. At that moment, Sarasvatichandra felt the pain of the cobra's bite, which fearful possibility flowed through his veins like venom. His heart stopped beating and he lost consciousness. The forest was unchanged. The darkness burnt like a body in funeral pyre. The forest, the wild animals wailed in mourning. Their cries pierced the sky. The lion roared but his roar was like the wail of death, powerful enough to melt the stoniest of hearts. All other sounds drowned in this roar. As Sarasvatichandra lay in the lap of death in the forest enshrouded by night, there was no reason to believe that there was any other human being present even in the vicinity of a few miles to witness his final journey. The forest, the earth, the sky and all the ten directions called out to the ebbing life. Sarasvatichandra! O' Sarasvatichandra!—this cavernous wail escaped the tall forest trees and pierced Chandrakant's heart in Manoharpuri. They reached Suvarnapur and drove out sleep from Kumud's eyes and filled them with tears. Pramaddhan's bedroom, his abode of lustful pleasures turned as desolate as a crematorium for her.

At an hour when it was impossible to hear a foot fall in the forest, Sarasvatichandra lay lifeless. The wild beasts roared even louder as the owls and jackals joined them with their dreadful calls. The dogs of Manoharpuri barked furiously in response. Except for a lone wisp of cloud that had lost its way, the night sky was studded with stars, but their solitary light filled one with trepidation. Dew had started to form. It clung to the frightened world like beads of perspiration. The night was cold. The world shivered. It was about eleven. Just then, some ghostlike apparitions seemed to materialise from the east. They were not the outlaws, who had long dispersed after their meeting.

Some of them carried torches of bamboo. These long torches burnt without oil, their orange-red flames leaping and dancing as they strode briskly through the night. These torches looked like the flaming tops of the surrounding trees in the dark. When the burning bamboo splintered, sparks and embers would fly. Each member of this group had long black matted hair coiled into a large bun or left to hang like snakes from their shoulders. This was a group of ascetics. The cobra had heard their footfalls and, sensing lights approach from a distance, had vanished into the safety of darkness.

This group of sadhus soon arrived at the spot where Sarasvatichandra lay. There were thirty or forty of them. At the centre of the group was a carriage, not pulled by bullocks but by the sadhus themselves. Some carried a variety of musical instruments which they played as they walked. Some were torch-bearers. Some carried unsheathed swords, alert and ready to protect the carriage. One of them carried a large saffron flag; the red and ochre of the flag glowed in the light of the torch flames. They had smeared ash, sandalwood paste and vermillion on their bodies; their torsos were laden with beaded necklaces; their dark, sinewy bodies gave an inkling of their strength; their song was robust and could match the piercing roar of the lion. They walked effortlessly to the rhythm of their song. This group of carefree ascetics who had vanquished the forest presented a sight no less fearsome and awe-inspiring than the sight of lions and tigers. They walked with long strides. Their voices boomed. Fire leapt from their torches. Each of them carried long black tongs which gave the appearance of black snakes hanging from their bodies. A boat-shaped vessel for seeking alms was slung over their shoulders. Each of them also carried a saffron cloth bag. They looked like a group of tigers or the dreaded gana of Shiva as they approached Sarasvatichandra.

The man who walked in front suddenly saw a body lying inert in his path. Startled, he stopped. The entire group halted in its tracks, stunned into silence. Vishnudas, their leader who rode in the carriage, shouted, 'Mohanpuri, what is it?' A group of sword-wielding ascetics surrounded Mohanpuri and the unconscious body. Mohanpuri bent his stout frame, examined the body in the light of the torches and replied, 'Guruji, there is a human body lying here as if dead. If you permit, I could ascertain by touch if he is alive or dead'. They examined the body and resolved that he was neither killed by animals, nor was he in fact dead. Guruji closed his eyes in silence for a moment, then commanded, 'Child, lift him up! Our Lord Shri Jagadish desires that this man will be the saviour of our Sundargiri muth and that the sadhus will one day follow him. Child, protect him with your life. He shall be a great soul one day and be worshipped even by sadhus'.

Vishnudas was said to possess knowledge of all three times—the past, the present and the future. This unexpected declaration stunned them. Mohanpuri lifted the unconscious Sarasvatichandra onto his shoulders as easily as one would a child. And the group walked away, singing. Some distance away a forest fire raged. A dense thicket of bamboo had caught fire; the bamboo cracked and split and the flying embers spread the fire. Animals large and small, predator and prey alike ran amuck to escape the flames. Birds asleep in their nests were caught unawares and charred to death. They gave one last shriek of horror before being silenced forever. The skies were filled with smoke. The night sky itself seemed to be afire. The group of sadhus made their way through this inferno, disappearing right into the scorching heat and tree-high walls of fire. Sarasvatichandra lay lifeless on Mohanpuri's broad shoulders. For a fleeting moment the terrible heat caused him to open his eyes. He thought he was looking at a painted dream. He asked no questions, he thought no thoughts, and his eyes closed once again.

8 Kumud Sundari Leaves Suvarnapur

Navinchandra was none other than Sarasvatichandra himself, and Chandrakant would take him back to Bombay where he would live a life of glorious fulfilment. These and similar other thoughts had filled Kumud Sundari with hope and joy. But the morning had crushed all her hopes. Sarasvatichandra left Suvarnapur. And all she could do was to helplessly watch him leave. She was not allowed even a word with him. Could any pain be more agonising than this? This unseen wound was inflicted upon Kumud at a time when Buddhidhan's household was waking up to celebrations. She had fallen down unconscious in presence of everyone, as you may recall. Dear reader, this part of the story we know.

Kumud Sundari decided to share everything with her parents. She resolved to find Sarasvatichandra. She was determined not to fail. She sent Harbhamji, Fatehsinh and Abdullah back to Manoharpuri with this news. Her departure for Bhadreshwar was delayed by a day.

Krishna Kalika and Pramaddhan rejoiced at Kumud's decision to visit her parents. But Buddhidhan had been informed of their liaison. This spoilt their joy. Pramaddhan was gripped by fear when he realised that Buddhidhan was intent on punishment. Navinchandra refused to be of any assistance. This was also a cause of worry. There was no one else who could have advised him; therefore Pramaddhan sought Krishna Kalika's counsel and he called her to Rajeshwar Mahadev. She in her wisdom suggested that he should accuse Kumud Sundari of an amorous alliance with Navinchandra. She further advised that Pramaddhan should present her as a witness and also suggest that the accusations of his illicit conduct were of Kumud Sundari's making. Pramaddhan went home, but on second thoughts realised that no one would believe his accusation. He paced up and down in his room searching for a plausible defence. His eyes fell on some tiny scraps of paper lying under his desk. Kumud Sundari had torn and burnt all her letters, made marmadarakbhasma of them and kept the remains in a bottle labelled 'Soul Ash'. But some tiny unburnt pieces lay under the table. On piecing the scraps together, Pramaddhan immediately recognised Navinchandra's handwriting. He deciphered a line which read: 'I once had wealth, a father, a beloved and a friend'. Pramaddhan was overjoyed at this discovery. Navinchandra wrote the word beloved! What more could be required as proof? His joy swiftly turned to anger as he thought: Such are the ways of the educated! I never knew that you were Navinchandra's beloved. At that instant Kumud Sundari entered the room. Observant as she was, she immediately discerned a change in Pramaddhan. But before she could ask anything, Pramaddhan went berserk, 'So my wise, most clever and learned one, ultimately this is who you turned out to be!'

Kumud Sundari was already numbed by her grief. She was also still weak from her faint. But this unexpected shower of flower petals startled her. She looked at her husband, calmed her nerves and asked in a soft yet steady voice, 'What is it?'

Pramaddhan shot back at her in even greater rage, 'What is it? Why, you were the one who was a beloved of that fellow Navinchandra, isn't it so? Read this and pluck out your eyes!' He flung the scraps of paper at Kumud Sundari who stood trembling.

Poor Kumud Sundari! It was as if fuel was added to raging fire. It was a blow to one already fallen. Her face grew lustreless, her legs threatened to give way, she broke into a cold sweat, her gaze was fixed to the ground and tears flowed from her eyes. In that moment, five hundred different thoughts flashed through her overwrought, unhappy mind. Her heart wrenched. She thought: To whom shall I tell the truth? Who shall believe me? All that I lacked was this dark blot upon my character. Am I to tell a lie? How can I deceive him? My condition is like that of Damayanti whose necklace was stolen, and worse. Dear God! You know the truth. I submit to You. Do what You must with me. Guide me to the path that is destined for me. I have done no wrong. And yet I am not entirely blameless. What can I tell him? She said nothing and returned the scraps of paper to Pramaddhan.

Pramaddhan was enraged. 'What? Do you admit that this is true or not? Tell me!' He slapped Kumud Sundari hard. She did not raise her hand to shield her face. Her tears dried up. She stopped sweating and no longer trembled. She looked up calmly at her husband and said, 'Why do you hesitate? Why end it just with a slap? Oh my warrior, lift that sword from the corner and put it to my neck. Why get into this futile exchange of words? If you kill me, I will find redemption. When else would I get a death by your hands?' She fetched the sword and placed it by his side. She stood before him, lowered her neck and quietly repeated, 'Do not hesitate. Lift the sword. It is my good fortune to receive this death from your hands.'

Kumud Sundari believed in earnest that her enraged husband would kill her and free her from all her agony and misery. She stood there with her head lowered, waiting anxiously for the sword to fall. She kept waiting. After a while she looked up and found herself alone in the room. Stunned and taken aback by this gruesome suggestion of Kumud and not knowing what to do, Pramaddhan had pocketed the scraps of paper and silently walked out. He was at his wit's end; he had no courage to say or do anything else. In deep quandary and in anguish, Kumud sat down on a chair and wept.

Pramaddhan immediately went in search of Krishna Kalika and told her what happened. She counselled him, 'It is not advantageous to prolong the matter with Kumud Sundari. Tell her that this was only a drama to test her. Tell her that you are assured of her good character, show affection for her, deceive her and quickly send her off to her parents. Once she goes, a thorn from our side will have been removed. If she suspects that you harbour any suspicion at all, she will not go and come in our way. If your father brings up the matter about us after she is gone, show him the scraps of paper and tell him that Kumud spread the rumours about us to conceal her illicit liaison. But all this is to be done only after she is gone.'

Pramaddhan liked the suggestion and executed it to perfection. Kumud Sundari was deceived. Late that night, she sat in her carriage ready to depart for her journey, escorted by the soldiers sent by Gunasundari and few others assigned by Buddhidhan. Her mother-in-law and sister-in-law embraced her and wept. Buddhidhan, too, choked with emotion. Everyone except for Pramaddhan was sad to see her leave. As the carriage slowly began to move, her family tearfully bid her farewell. 'Kumud Sundari, come back soon! Bhabhi, please don't stay a day more than fifteen! Daughter, your parents will be overjoyed, but my house will be vacant without you. Come back soon, my daughter, take pity on your mother-in-law. Bhabhisahib, take care of yourself and return soon! Go in God's care.' Buddhidhan, Saubhagya Devi and Alak Kishori stood at the threshold with tears in their eyes along with the household servants, watching anxiously as the carriage disappeared into the night. Inside, Kumud Sundari, too, sat weeping. The night was dark and still. In a while, the creaking of wheels and the trotting of horses could no longer be heard. Even the light of the torches carried by the soldiers grew smaller and finally disappeared. No one in the household of Suvarnapur's new Karbhari went back to sleep that night. They talked among themselves, sang praises of the wise, virtuous and affectionate daughter-in-law. Pramaddhan was hugely relieved. He happily went up to his room and dreamt of Krishna Kalika.

Before Kumud Sundari's carriage had left the town, it was brought to a halt near the outskirts. By chance, Vanleela had witnessed Pramaddhan's meeting with Krishna Kalika and had heard their entire conversation unobserved. But she did not tell Kumud about it, not wanting to add to her distress. She also had no opportunity during the day for a private conversation with her. But finally when she realised that there was no way that Kumud would know unless she herself told her, Vanleela could no longer keep it a secret. She wrote down all that had transpired on a piece of paper. She had stayed awake and kept a watch from a window. Unknown to anyone else in the family and unobserved, Vanleela had followed the carriage at a distance. Once it reached the outskirts of

Suvarnapur, she caused it to stop and got into it. She gave the letter to Kumud Sundari and asked her to read it at daybreak. 'Kumud behn, I cannot ever forget your affection. There is no one else I can talk to. I will write to you—do respond. Oh, this love is not a good thing—I just can't bring myself to leave you! You have imprisoned me by your qualities. Convey my regards to Gunial. Do not forget me, dearest Kumud behn, and do not stop loving me.' Vanleela said many such things as she held Kumud tightly in her arms. Both of them wept unabashedly. 'Oh, my Vanliladi, I could have relieved my heart of its burdens if I had just a night to spend with you. But now what is to happen will happen. Come to Ratnanagari. How can I ever forget you! Keep loving me. And go back home safely,' Kumud said to Vanleela, embracing her. At last they separated. Vanleela, still weeping, walked back to her house. Kumud was unaware of the grave nature of the letter; she assumed that it contained some light-hearted banter and rumours going around the town. She kept it inside her blouse without another thought. The carriage moved on. Thoughts of her parents, of Sarasvatichandra, Pramaddhan, her parents-in-law and sister-in-law crowded her mind. Finally, exhausted from all the exertions and excitement of the day, her fragile body and tired mind surrendered to the rhythmic movement of the carriage and she fell asleep. Even as she slept, tears streamed down her cheeks. Her innocent and hurt mind had only a momentary respite from the machinations of the evil world when the world of dreams caught up with her. Sleep like a mother took pity on this virtuous daughter and drove away all her nightmares. At last, Kumud Sundari fell into a deep and dreamless sleep.

The soldiers moved alongside the carriage, talking softly amongst themselves. The night was dark but stars shone in the sky. The torches they carried spread light. It was pleasantly cold. They emerged out of the gates of the capital and moved onto the forest path. Even the wild animals took pity on this young woman harassed by the world of men. As the last quarter of the night moved towards day, the animals became quiet; the forest was free of fear for Kumud. The wind rustling through the leaves and dry blades of grass brought with it the sweet fragrance of wild nocturnal flowers, the coolness of ponds, streams and the vast star-studded sky. It gently ruffled the curtains of Kumud's carriage, driving out all her dreams to soothe and to calm her troubled heart as she slept.

9 Preparations for the Morning

To go from Suvarnapur to Manoharpuri one had to cross a bridge on river Subhadra. The river flowed under the arches of this stone bridge. The sea was near. Hence, even during the summer months of Chaitra the water in the river was deep, almost as high as a full grown man. The river was even deeper around the pillars of the bridge. The water came rushing down to be halted by the arches of the bridge only to emerge with greater force, cutting through the deep ravines on either bank. A stranger to these parts watching the river from the top of the ravines was quite likely to fall and drown in the river if not extremely cautious. The force of the flow was such that even expert swimmers dared not swim across the Subhadra.

Since midnight the stone bridge had been the focus of stealthy but urgent human movement. Exactly at midnight Shankar Maharaj was seen running towards Suvarnapur, carrying his long thick staff in hand; he was heading for a village within the territory of Suvarnapur. The brave brahmin warrior feared neither wild animals nor Sursinh; anyone watching him would imagine that he too was a tiger or lion in human form. A few hours later a group of riders from Manoharpuri were seen approaching the bridge. They halted at the bridge and divided themselves into two groups. One group led by Manchatura and Abdullah moved on while Fatehsinh stayed back with the rest. Three or four of them got down from their horses and got busy preparing large fires. The men sat around these fires, exchanging stories of past valour among themselves, alert to the slightest movement and sound. Within a quarter of an hour, the riders from Manoharpuri had covered the entire area from the banyan tree to the stone bridge and beyond. As they went, they shouted out: 'Victory to Maharaja Maniraj! Run! Run, all enemies of Maniraj, run!' The forest and the skies reverberated with their calls. On the southern end of the bridge the fires crackled merrily, their crimson flames leaping up to the skies, dispelling the dark, while on its northern end, Maniraj's victory was hailed aloud. All this hectic nocturnal activity was not witnessed by other people. But the forest was silent as if in awe of Maniraj's power. Even the lions and tigers had retreated to their lairs as if to signal that a new day was upon them. The gushing waters of the Subhadra reflected the glow of the fires and the echoes of the soldiers hailing victory to Maniraj. They removed all shadows of inauspiciousness from Kumud Sundari's path.

On the other side, Sursinh's men had also taken up their positions. Each group with its leader had reached the remote villages located on the peripheries of the forest. Some of these villages had no human presence except for abandoned and denuded houses, some were sparsely populated, but none of them had the wherewithal to resist and deny shelter to the outlaws. The outlaws slept where they could. Some slept on the floor, others managed to make beds of hay, a few even managed to get sheets to cover them with; they rested their heads on stones or the shields that they carried. Each man kept his weapons within reach as he slept. Their swords hung by their sides, bows and arrows next to them and spears and clubs at their feet. Pratapsinh, Vaghji, Bhimji and Chandandas accompanied by their men tried to catch a few hours of disturbed and anxiety-filled sleep while remaining vigilant. Some of them lit small fires and sat around them, smoking, alert to the slightest movement or sound. They chatted among themselves to keep sleep at bay. As the night progressed, they looked up at the stars to determine as to when they should wake up their companions. On either side, the men were anxious, impatient and sleepless. Sursinh's men were somewhat more carefree as they had no inkling that someone had overheard their plans. They were prepared for any eventuality, but they did not anticipate the kind of organised resistance that awaited them.

One of the principles of Vidya Chatura's statecraft was that he ensured that he was kept apprised of all matters. Those who were assigned a given task were required to apprise themselves of all issues relating to the task at hand. It is often the case in native states that subordinate officers are untrustworthy; hence their superiors do not repose any trust in them and do not give them any autonomous responsibility. The tendency of the subordinates, too, is to deny all responsibility. They are often seen eager to please their superiors instead of doing the task assigned to them. No minister or ruler can do all the work by himself, work that ought to be done by subordinates. Consequently, work suffers. Ultimately, some lifeless wretched individual is blamed for the disorder. The British administered areas had vast territories and were thickly populated. It was not possible for the rulers to keep all functionaries under close observation; therefore, reliance upon laws and administrative hierarchy became imperative. But in smaller native states, it was possible to keep all functionaries under observation, to assign them responsibilities, and thus create conditions that permitted a certain degree of autonomy in exercise of authority even at the lower levels of administration. Vidya Chatura was convinced that it was possible to create such a mechanism of governance. He was also convinced that a state administered on these lines would far better secure the people's welfare as compared to a state under British rule. Vidya Chatura believed that it was equally inappropriate for rulers to either mistrust all functionaries as also to repose full faith in all of them. This principle applied not only to the ruler but also to his ministers. Vidya Chatura's own conduct, therefore, was in conformity to these principles. His counsel to young Maniraj was: 'O' glorious King! Why should we not be able to find trustworthy men? Those whom we cannot trust are not fit to be in your service. If they are worthy of our trust, they also deserve the autonomy to serve you well. We are concerned with work. We should not expect our servants to rise and sit at our command. Everyone in your service should know as to what ways and means are undesirable to you. It is your and, in turn, my responsibility to find capable, intelligent and independent persons who can accomplish the tasks assigned to them efficiently using good means, while keeping their distance from undesirable methods. Servants unworthy of trust and incapable of independent action work without enthusiasm. Lack of enthusiasm achieves nothing; it only spoils the work. When people are given the freedom to work, they work with a will and develop their intellect and capabilities, and intelligent servants are capable of recognising what is unacceptable to their superiors. Even ordinary men are capable of ascertaining the true worth of gems. It is a king's duty to ascertain the true worth of his men. Gems adorn the king's crown and his ornaments, but priceless and rare individuals are the true gems of a kingdom; such men bring light to a state, cause poverty to disappear and their light dispels darkness. Maharaja! No state can be without such sterling men, but only wise and intelligent rulers can find them, test them and nurture them.' Vidya Chatura counselled Maniraj without taking away anything from the king's authority. He not only gave him advice but put it in practice by his own conduct. Just as a magnet attracts even the tiniest of metal pieces, Vidya Chatura found capable men from remote parts of the state, observed them minutely and gave them prestige and responsibility commensurate with their abilities. He trusted them, gave them autonomy, and they in turn proved true to his trust. Every servant of the state could take pride in knowing that he was a pillar of strength for the state; and yet he also remained free of false pride in his dealings with his superiors. Both superiors and subordinates learnt from each other and accomplished the assigned task. They grasped the norms of righteous and good statecraft through example and discussion. Just as an army moves at a signal from its chief, Vidya Chatura's administration functioned similarly. His administration itself was a place for learning.

The plan prepared to protect Kumud Sundari was also a result of such experience. Fatehsinh, Abdullah and Harbhamji were low-level functionaries of the state but well-versed in the task assigned to them. It would not be an exaggeration to say that the qualities and capabilities they possessed were to be found in most officers of Ratnanagari. Vidya Chatura had not personally appointed them, but the chief of police, following his minister's principles, had selected them. They were assigned their responsibilities and shown the way, but the decision as to how they should implement them was left to them. Their judgement was trusted. Their superior officers ensured that this trust was not misplaced. Thus, the reins of power were in the hands of all functionaries of the state—together they wove the tapestry of statecraft. The alert servants of an all-seeing king now moved rapidly as one to protect their minister's daughter who was in danger. Old and experienced Manchatura became their guide. His strategy was to put a powerful display of strength and force on the borders of three states. He wanted to frighten the enemy without the use of arms. He was conscious that his men should not use arms in the territory of another state lest they are made answerable in the court of law of that state. The enemy was certain to be discouraged faced with a large force, while the protectors were conscious that force should be used with discrimination. The troop leaders understood the intent of Manchatura's plan. They moved swiftly not requiring further instructions. Manchatura's instructions were executed as effortlessly as music that is produced by pressing the keys of an instrument.

Abdullah, Mukhi Patel and Fatehsinh were eager to show off their prowess, but the opportunity to do so had not hitherto presented itself. Harbhamji had sought out the opportunity for himself. He had heard the plans the outlaws had hatched early that night. He was given the task of shadowing Sursinh. Harbhamji enjoyed the combination of valour, the test of his wits and intelligence-gathering that his work entailed. Manchatura and others headed towards Suvarnapur, while Harbhamji with his chosen men moved in the opposite direction. He moved towards the villages under British territory on the eastern side of the mango orchards. He entered some villages himself; in others he sent his men to spread messages; he met brave men who ventured out at night; he spoke to thieves, robbers and beggars as well. He sent messages, received information and dropped hints. He not only sought information about Sursinh and his band but he also spread the rumours that Sursinh's activities were known to the armies of both Ratnanagari and Suvarnapur. He spread word in the villages and hamlets that armies of the two native states along with British forces were lying in wait for Sursinh and that they would capture him early that morning before he could do what he intended to do. It was difficult to locate Sursinh in the forest at night. But news of Harbhamji's activities reached Sursinh. Sursinh and his men lost some of their determination and courage. The mukhis and guards of all the surrounding villages became alert to the imminent danger and prepared themselves to meet any eventuality.

Harbhamji, devoted to Vidya Chatura, was fearless enough to move among the wild animals of the forest at night. He was also cautious and farsighted and could strategise and plan like an expert chess player. He spent most of the night moving from place to place. Finally he selected a perfect spot near the river which allowed him to receive messages under cover and, when necessary, join the other parties. Harbhamji knew that Sursinh would also locate himself at a place from where he could coordinate the movements of Pratapsinh, Vaghji and Bhimji. Shrewdly anticipating Sursinh's movements, Harbhamji selected a cluster of ruins from where he could shadow Sursinh. It was already four in the morning when Harbhamji and his men came to halt in the ruins. They lit a small fire and rested their mounts. They put fodder for the horses and massaged their tired bodies. The men lit their bidis to refresh themselves and sat talking softly among themselves. Harbhamji sat on a boulder at the entrance of the ruins. As he sat massaging his horse and occasionally joining in the conversation of his men, his eyes scanned the horizon. Everyone waited anxiously for the day to break. As if also impatient to meet them, as they spoke, the first rays of the sun prised open the doors of night and the first light of day coloured the eastern sky.

10 An Encounter with the Outlaws

The carriage moved on at a steady pace with the mounted soldiers riding alongside, encircling it in a protective cordon. They had covered a distance of about four miles when the reign of night came to an end. Except for the creaking and lurching of the carriage on the uneven dust roads, the sounds of the bullocks' hooves and the trotting of horses, the rustling and snapping of dry branches against the moving carriage and the crowing of roosters in distant villages, the forest was silent. Kumud Sundari was in pleasant and deep sleep. The carriage driver held on to the reins and the prod firmly, but he, too, seemed to be dozing. The soldiers were alert and talked in low voices among themselves. A soft light spread upon the earth. In this first light, the colours of leaves and flowers could not yet be discerned, but their silhouettes were taking shape. As light slowly began to spread across the sky from the east, the stars could no longer be seen.

At that hour, the soldiers accompanying Kumud Sundari were surprised to see Manchatura approach with some other riders. Abdullah apprised them of the situation. Both parties merged and moved forward with the carriage. Old Manchatura gently raised the curtains of the carriage and peered inside—Kumud Sundari was still fast asleep. He lowered the curtains and joined the group of riders. The soldiers grew more alert now; their hands rested impatiently upon their weapons, ready to draw them. As night lifted its veil of darkness to usher in the day, the dramatic reality of the forest burst forth. Shrubs laden with red, yellow and white flowers swayed in the dawn breeze. Fields on either side of their path were harvested.

Fields which had exhausted their fecundity seemed to be in repose, regenerating themselves like women exhausted after childbirth. As the gossamer light of dawn spread through the forest freeing it from the slumber of night, the tops of the tallest trees caught the first rays of the sun. The dreaded nocturnal predators disappeared and beautiful, delicate birds of bright plumage took their place. They flew from tree to tree, chirping and singing melodiously. The male and the female of the species played their own games of love and desire. Mother birds fed their young ones; their doting love was an example for other animals.

It was a new day. The sky was clear and the forest no longer appeared impregnable. The soft breeze and morning light entered through the drawn curtains of the carriage and played on Kumud's closed eyelids. She opened her still sleep-laden eyes. Raising herself up a little on her elbows, she rubbed delicate fingers on her eyelids. She was fully awake now. Kumud took out Vanleela's note from the folds of her blouse. She read it hurriedly at first—the letter was a true reflection of ever affectionate and playful Vanleela. Kumud read the letter again, this time pondering over each word. She re-read important parts for the third time. The note described in detail the plan hatched by Pramaddhan and Krishna Kalika. She was pained by her husband's deception. Kumud realised that Pramaddhan, incapable of any reflection, not only suspected her of infidelity but that in his desire to take revenge and punish her, he was ready to commit even greater crimes. And that he was still under Krishna Kalika's evil influence—this whole plan was a part of their illicit alliance. This knowledge pierced her like a thorn. She was so far from him, but the searing pain was immediate.

Oh, he indulges himself unrestrained, and yet he suspects me and wants his revenge! Is this justice? Has he decided to discredit me once I am gone? What will Devi and Alak behn think of me? What will my father-in-law make of all this? This news will also travel to Gunial. Should I turn back and return to Suvarnapur? Will not truth emerge triumphant? In her distress, Kumud remembered these lines from Nalakhyan:

O' Lord, You are the herald of truth
But I am not part of that truth
Lord, what are the deeds that caused this birth?
What could be worse than being a thief?

I will be accused of a crime much worse than what Damayanti had to face, thought Kumud. How will I face anyone after this? God, You are my last resort. She wiped her tears and parted the curtains of the carriage. She saw new soldiers and then to her surprise, she saw Manchatura leading them. Alert to any movement inside the carriage, Manchatura immediately drew up his horse beside the carriage.

'Behn, are you well?'

'Yes, Dadaji, but why are you here?' Kumud held up the curtain and craned her neck out to converse with him.

'Gunasundari and Sundar are at Manoharpuri. There was some danger in your path, and so I came with some men to protect you.'

Kumud was surprised. 'Danger! What kind of danger?'

'Don't be afraid, behn. We have so many men protecting you that they would not dare come near you.' Manchatura changed the topic and asked, 'Are your in-laws well?'

'Yes, father-in-law has been made the Karbhari. Yesterday he was presented with the robes.'

'Oh, that is very good! You must also be feeling proud and acting haughty?' the old man laughed.

'Dadaji, do your children understand what it is to be haughty? My parents-in-law send their pranam to you.'

Suddenly, a loud shout was heard from the banks of the Subhadra. The soldiers drew their weapons at once and stood like a fortress around the carriage which had come to a halt. Their faces were flushed with rushing blood. Manchatura sat up straight on his horse, his old frame trembling with rising valour as he drew his sword and raised it in the air. 'Be alert, men. We shall send them to hell. Do not be scared, Kumud behn, I will be close by you. Abdullah, look around for a place, we shall halt here.'

They took out their guns and loaded them. Kumud Sundari was now visibly frightened, yet mustering all her equanimity she asked,

'What is it, Dadaji, what has happened?' even as her eyes searched in all directions for signs of danger.

'Nothing. Do not be scared. Withdraw your head inside the carriage and don't look out. It's just some people shouting in the distance.'

The shouts grew louder, the noises came closer, gunshots were heard, their smoke rising above the tree tops; animals ran helter-skelter and birds took flight, squawking shrilly. Kumud shivered and broke out in cold sweat, her heart beat faster and she felt her limbs going numb.

Abdullah rode ahead and looked closely in the direction from which the sounds of skirmishes were coming. He could see a rider approaching them at a gallop. Abdullah recognised him; he was from Fatehsinh's group. The soldier rode up to Abdullah and breathlessly gave him the news. Abdullah took him to Manchatura. The rider greeted Manchatura with a salute of his right hand. 'Victory to Maharaja Maniraj! His authority is stamped all over this forest. The outlaws recognised the extent of our readiness in the morning. Every village, including those in British territory, is on the alert. Those rascals have not been able to come together. Mukhi Patel is patrolling the path between the banyan tree and the river. Chandandas saw him and ran away; the bania realised he was outmatched. Vaghji has not ventured anywhere near the banyan tree and is still hiding among the mango trees, waiting for his chance. Fatehsinh encountered Bhimji and his men, but they did not confront Fatehsinh and disappeared into the taad forest. We, too, decided not to confront them. There was a man with a drum stationed near the bridge. We captured him. The man began to beat his drum. Bhimji and Pratapsinh responded to his call and rushed out. The drummer was in the territory of Suvarnapur. We came face to face with Pratapsinh and his men.'

'Was there a fight?' Manchatura asked impatiently.

'Pratapsinh demanded to know why we had captured the drummer. Fatehsinh retorted, "Go away! Who are you to ask us questions?" Fatehsinh said that Sursinh and his two sons had turned outlaws and that we had warrants for their arrest from the British and from Bhupsinh. He said, "We are authorised to move freely within the territories of all three states. This drummer is a companion of the outlaws and therefore we have taken him into our custody".'

'What happened next?' Abdullah asked in Hindustani.

'Fatehsinh told Pratapsinh, "You fellows also appear to be outlaws. Tell me who you are, or else I will have to arrest you as well".'

'Very good, Fatehsinh!' Abdullah said, twirling his moustache. 'Phir kya hua?'

'Pratapsinh turned mellow and said, "We are on our way to Bhadreshwar. We do not know any outlaws. This drummer is with us and we are going to make an offering of the drum to Mahadev".'

Manchatura laughed, 'Hah! Just hear that scoundrel!'

'Fatehsinh said, "Whatever it is, we are not going to release this man or return his drum". Then he shouted out his command to us: "All of them are from the gang of outlaws—capture them alive or kill all the scoundrels!"'

'Very good, Fatehsinh. Your deeds truly justify your name,' said Abdullah. 'Phir kya hua?'

'Our men rushed in and fired a few gunshots. Pratapsinh's men ran away.

'The cowards!' exclaimed Manchatura.

'Pratapsinh was enraged. He was left alone, but he drew his sword to face Fatehsinh. The duel was about to begin when a few of his men who had run away came back and dragged him away. We allowed them to escape and I rushed to give you the news.'

'All the women have fled. Coachman, let us move on,' said Abdullah.

Manchatura said, 'Patience, Abdullah. They will collect their forces. It is not good to move the carriage until they disperse'. He turned to the messenger and said, 'You may go now. Send me a message if you have any news about Harbham and Sursinh. Also let me know when Vaghji retreats. Be careful, Pratapsinh is certain to strike back. There is no danger on this side of the river now. We will move on slowly but remain on this side of the river. Our men will be ready to assist you.

But you must ensure that when the scoundrels resurface they must be pushed inside Suvarnapur's territory, so that in event of a battle, we are safe. Do not allow anyone to cross the river. We shall cross the bridge once the other side is secured and safe'.

The messenger rushed back. The carriage moved on cautiously towards the bridge. Manchatura muttered to himself: If we were to fight them in the British territories, their courts will hold us guilty; the thieves will sit in judgement on the police! Whatever happens must happen inside the taad forest. He lifted the curtain and found Kumud shivering with fright.

'Behn, half our worries are over. The scoundrels have run away. We are just being cautious.' Manchatura was old but his vision was sharp. Towards the west, he saw a cloud of dust rising. He would need Fatehsinh and Mukhi to face the new danger. At his command the group moved swiftly and reached the bridge. Fatehsinh had secured the bridge from the opposite side and called out,'Don't worry—all the flies are gone'.

Manchatura signalled towards the west. They saw a lone rider approaching them. Buddhidhan's soldiers accompanying Kumud Sundari immediately recognised the man. One of them asked, 'Maharaj, what are you doing here?'

Shankar Maharaj replied, 'Do not worry. Some men from my village will come following me. We are going to meet Sursinh. Understood?'

'Proceed. May victory be yours! Return soon.'

Manchatura, who understood nothing of what was said, quietly asked Buddhidhan's soldier and was satisfied. Shankar Maharaj and his men crossed the river.

Sursinh had nothing but bad news. Chandandas was the first to abandon. Bhimji was separated from the rest, and the other groups retreated without Vaghji and Pratap. Every village knew that forces of Buddhidhan and Vidya Chatura had come together to pursue the outlaws. If Sursinh were to stick to the plan, his destruction was certain. Just then Shankar Maharaj came and joined him. Sursinh felt somewhat reassured to see him. Sursinh, Vaghji, Pratapsinh and Shankar Maharaj accompanied by their brave men moved swiftly. Their force was awe-inspiring. Shankar murmured to himself:

As he breathes, the mountains crumble
Clouds roll into the abyss
As he walks, the earth quivers
We have seen such a man fall
Praise the Lord!

Look at these men! Despite such hardship, the earth trembles when they move. They have had nothing to eat for four days, their clothes are in tatters, and yet they move with such pride! They are my friends. If I serve the King, I shall be a traitor to my friend. But do I have a choice? Will I be able to feed myself otherwise? No. But then I have also eaten the salt of my King.

Sursinh abruptly came to a halt, stood still and asked, 'Shankar, do you hear horses in the distance?' Everyone stopped. They strained their ears and peered closely in the direction Sursinh pointed.

Shankar Maharaj said, 'We are hallucinating. What are you scared of? Come on, let's move.'

'No, no, Shankar ...'

'Forget your nays. There is no one. The carriage is on the other side of the bridge. All we need to do is capture Kumud Sundari. I have seen everything myself.'

Pratap was happy to hear this. 'It is true. Let's not delay.'

Everyone moved ahead, but Sursinh kept glancing at his back; he was not convinced.

Shankar Maharaj drew his horse close to Sursinh and said, 'Bha, your apprehension is not unfounded. These young boys don't know anything. Fatehsinh and Mukhi Patel are waiting for us. We should take a detour towards the south, cross the road and attack the carriage from behind. Oh, yes, and we might also meet Bhimji', Shankar added.

Sursinh was drawn to the idea as iron is drawn to a magnet. 'Yes, let's move on, it's broad daylight now.'

Sursinh galloped ahead, followed by his family and associates. They took a detour towards the south, crossed the road and entered the territory of Suvarnapur. None of them realised that they were now in territories administered by Buddhidhan. Shankar Maharaj had led them away from the British territories and was pleased with himself.

Manchatura saw them approaching from a distance and immediately alerted all the groups. Fatehsinh guarded the northern and the eastern sides. A cloud of dust followed Sursinh at some distance—it was Harbhamji and his group. They came galloping to catch up with Sursinh and his band as Sursinh entered the territories of Suvarnapur. In no time at all, Harbhamji stood with his men between Kumud Sundari's carriage and Sursinh's band. Sursinh realised that his plans were botched. Any attempt to capture Kumud Sundari now was certain to result in death. He whispered to Shankar Maharaj, 'Let us turn back. We have lost the game. We could have engaged them in battle after capturing Kumud Sundari. It is futile to imagine that we can engage them in battle, overpower them and also capture Kumud'.

The logic of the experienced outlaw was accurate. But Shankar's intention was to thwart him from acting upon it. Only if Sursinh were to attack the carriage with his men would the defenders respond; only then could Shankar reveal his true loyalties and help realise Buddhidhan's strategy. Vidya Chatura's men were unlikely to make the first move if Sursinh refrained from attacking the carriage; without their help, Shankar was powerless to capture the outlaws. He pretended not to have heard Sursinh, and raising his sword, he called out to Sursinh's men, 'What are you waiting for? Never again will we get such an opportunity. There are only a few of them guarding the carriage—just drag her out. Come, let's charge!' and Shankar suddenly charged towards the carriage. Seeing him, Sursinh's companions also charged forward. It was too late for Sursinh to rein them in, so he followed them. Shankar fired blanks from his gun; the other outlaws followed his example and fired bullets. Astride their galloping horses, they felt the blood rushing through their veins and could no longer be restrained. Sursinh's eyes searched desperately for Bhimji, but saw no one coming to his aid. As Abhimanyu caught in the Chakravyuh had called out to his uncle, Bhīma: 'Kaka Bhimsen, where are you? Come!' Sursinh searched for Bhimji and Chandandas, his heart pleaded with them, but no one came to his rescue. Before he knew it, he was surrounded by enemies. Fatehsinh and his men faced him, while Harbhamji with his men blocked his path from the rear. The carriage was beyond reach of even a bullet. Some soldiers of Suvarnapur flanked his right side.

In a climactic moment, even cowards turn brave and the brave are filled with valour. The Rajput saw that victory was but a distant dream—at this moment, nothing but his own valour would come to his aid. As he braced himself, Sursinh's eyes bulged fearfully, his brows creased, blood rushed through his throbbing veins; he was ready to jump down from his horse and charge on foot. He raised his sword high and gave the clarion call: 'What are you waiting for, brothers! Charge! It is victory or death! Charge!' Sursinh's valour caught on like a forest fire. His companions shouted in response, ready to attack. With his sons Vaghji and Pratap flanking him on either side, Sursinh attacked Fatehsinh. The blow of his sword was so powerful that if Fatehsinh had failed to protect himself with his shield, he would have been cut into two. There was a deep cut in the shield.

As soon as Sursinh had made the first strike, Shankar Maharaj called out, 'Victory to Maharana Bhupsinh!' and he and his men separated from the outlaws. His loyalty was revealed like a flash of lightning. 'Sursinh, you and I are friends. But I must be true to my salt. I befriended you to serve the King of Suvarnapur. You are surrounded. You are like a mighty elephant that has fallen into a ditch and is waiting to be chained. Either you court death, or you surrender. There is no third option. Your valour is undisputed. No one can deny you the glory that is rightly yours. Bhupsinh did not take over your garas, you have no animosity towards him; he, too, recognises your worth. Even Shathrai, now fallen, knows of Rana Bhupsinh's generosity. You are a citizen of Bhupsinh's kingdom. Even if you shed a drop of blood in his territory you would be committing a crime; you would forfeit the right to obtain pardon from our compassionate Rana. I am not a traitor. But

I must serve my Rana. If you surrender, I will fall at his feet, sing your praises and prove that my friendship was not deceit. If you choose not to surrender, I am free to act. By not surrendering, you will also commit a crime towards your associates. Your actions will also deny them the chance of a pardon. You will be responsible for their futile death. The curses of their wives and children will haunt you for births to come like the sin of killing a brahmin. These two are your sons—they are in the prime of youth, they too will meet a pointless death; you will have no one left to carry forward your name, and your blood line will be destroyed. Hence, I tell you and your men, there are only two choices: surrender or death. Choose what seems more desirable. It is a moment of choice. Victory to Maharana Bhupsinh!'

Everyone was stunned by this unexpected turn of events. As soon as Shankar Maharaj finished his speech, his men and Maniraj's soldiers encircled the outlaws, their rifles ready to fire. Ratnanagari's forces were emboldened by Shankar Maharaj's revelation of his loyalties. The outlaws lost their nerve. They were starving, weary and in tatters. Sursinh and Bhimji had egged them on with a promise that Kumud Sundari was about to fall into their hands. When they discovered that morning that their enemies had out-manoeuvred them, they turned despondent. The disappearance of Bhimji and Chandandas further depressed their morale. Vaghji and Pratap brought them the news that all the surrounding villages had been alerted to their presence. They had briefly found new vigour and hope when Shankar Maharaj joined them with his forces. Sursinh's ultimate call to their valour had prepared them for a fight to death. But Shankar's treachery completely devastated their morale. His long speech further dampened their spirits. They saw that by remaining with Sursinh, they would serve neither his nor their own interest. To challenge a well-fed, well-armed force with their blunt and broken weapons was like jumping blindly into raging fire. One man came forward, folded his hands in respect and addressed Sursinh: 'Bapu! There is nothing now left of this battle. The Karbhari's daughter has escaped from your hands like Devaki's infant girl who flew out of Kansa's hands. Only the living can obtain riches. Shankar is right. Our thirst will not be quenched by jumping into a dry well; we will only jump to our deaths. Each one of us has a wife and children back home. Hitherto, we pledged our lives to you because we believed we could be of some use to you. But now, surrender is the only option. We will gain nothing in death. Bapu, hitherto, we have always obeyed you. Today, we plead that you follow us. Shankar Maharaj, our life and death is now in your hands. I surrender my sword to you.' Some outlaws immediately followed him. Others stood in a quandary, debating their choice. To Pratapsinh it was clear that he would not be able to lay even a finger on Kumud Sundari; seeing his opportunity, he quietly slunk away. All eyes were on the small heap of arms at the feet of Shankar's horse. Hesitant, full of fear and misgiving, gradually the other outlaws came forward one by one and added their arms to the growing heap. Those who had surrendered stood aside, trying to avoid Sursinh's wrathful gaze, shrinking in their skins with shame and mortification. Two of Shankar's men picked up the surrendered arms.

All eyes were on Sursinh. Sursinh felt bleak, despondent and full of helpless rage. His fate had turned against him. His men had deserted him; he looked at them with disdain. His legs restlessly grazed the sides of his horse. He looked for Pratap, and finding him gone, silently addressed his son: If you live my son, take revenge. There was only one man left by his side—his son Vaghji. This gave him some solace; he felt proud of Vaghji. Sursinh saw death in the face. He was merciful that even at this moment of death, his Rajput valour had not deserted him. As he sat up erect, squaring his shoulders and arching his back, his horse, too, reared up on its hind legs, neighing loudly as if to encourage his master. Sursinh touched Vaghji lightly on the shoulder, gave Shankar a scathing look and turned his horse around. He found Harbhamji blocking his way. Harbhamji's strike of the previous day was still fresh in his mind. He turned his horse away from Harbhamji, and quite suddenly, without warning, Sursinh charged full speed into the circle formed by Shankar's men with his sword raised high. His visage was fearful, his eyes burned like the very fires of hell. His adversaries looked on petrified, breaking ranks to let him pass. Sursinh's men felt ashamed and sorely repented their surrender. Vaghji became his father's bard and cried: 'Bapa, you are fearless! Bapa, there is none as brave as you! Your enemies tremble! The earth trembles! Victory be yours, Bapa! May your Rajput blood prevail!' Sursinh felt a rush of blood in his head and heart. He saw Shankar Maharaj before him. 'Traitor!' he roared, kicking his horse's flanks—the horse jumped over Shankar and his mount like lightning as Sursinh's sword pointed straight at Shankar's chest. Everyone watching was stunned by the Rajput's valour and dazzled by his swordsmanship. Sursinh astride his leaping horse looked like a lion that had caught an elephant by its neck. His long, double-edged sword seemed to have pierced Shankar's body. Everyone took Shankar for dead. But when Sursinh charged upon him like death itself, the brahmin, familiar with Sursinh's techniques, moved his body ever so slightly and raised his left hand, allowing the sword to pass through harmlessly without touching him. He swiftly caught Sursinh's sword-wielding arm and, in a flash, cut it off with a powerful blow of his sword. Sursinh's right hand fell to the ground like a cut branch, drenching him and his horse with warm blood. At that very moment, Vaghji brought down his sword to cut Shankar into pieces. But Harbhamji, ever alert, rushed in to thwart Vaghji's blow in mid-air and there was a loud clanking noise as the two swords struck each other and sparks flew. Vaghji's sword slipped from his hand and flew up in the air. Everyone moved away to save their head. The sword fell harmlessly to the ground and was picked up by someone. Vaghji was without his sword, but true to his name, like a leaping tiger he jumped his horse over everyone's heads. Mount and rider flew like Hanuman crossing the sea. The horse regained its balance as it landed and galloped away to safety with its rider.

The others could only watch in awe. Weakened by the sudden loss of blood, Sursinh had fallen from his horse; he was alive but unconscious. Shankar Maharaj's men quickly bandaged his arm to contain the bleeding, made a stretcher with the long cloth of their turbans and carried him off towards Suvarnapur. Calls of 'Victory to Maharaja Bhupsinh!' rang through the surrounding villages. Vidya Chatura's soldiers were all praise for Shankar Maharaj, Sursinh and Vaghji. Together they moved towards Kumud Sundari's carriage, proclaiming victory.

11 Smouldering Embers

Abdullah, Fatehsinh and their men went ahead to stop the charge of Sursinh and his men while Manchatura stayed back with a chosen few to protect Kumud Sundari. He was alert to the slightest danger, his eyes were focused on the battle and yet he observed all four directions. His body felt reinvigorated, his mind sharp, his forehead was furrowed as his eyes scanned the scene like a telescope, his white moustache twitched in anticipation—he looked like a lion ready to leap upon his prey. He held the reins of his horse in one hand and fidgeted with his sword with the other. As brave old Manchatura prepared himself for battle, his legs impatiently awaited the signal to nudge his horse into action.

Kumud Sundari raised the curtain of her carriage time and again. She closely watched her grandfather's changing expressions and from them tried to gauge the fate of the battle. Manchatura was so engrossed that he did not relate any news of the battle to Kumud. The soldiers guarding her tensely also did not talk among themselves. The driver of the carriage sat alert, holding the reins firmly, ready to move at a word. His bullocks, which could run as fast as horses, sensed the tension and were ready to gallop. But right now it was futile to move the carriage forward or backward, so they watched and waited. The men, whose energies were completely focussed on the outlaws, could think of nothing else. At that moment, weary, alone, aggrieved by Pramaddhan, Kumud's heart, too, turned an outlaw—it wandered restlessly in search of solace; it accompanied Chandrakant in search of Sarasvatichandra through this dangerous terrain; it trembled at the thought of the ignominy that evil Kalika would have heaped on her at her in-laws' house. It was as if Kumud were in a double bind: caught by the outlaws and defeated by the machinations of Pramaddhan and Krishna Kalika, her heart sought a way out. Time and again, she would impatiently lift the curtains to look outside and lower them again to withdraw inside and weep. She stared blankly at the canopy of her carriage, read Vanleela's note again and again, gazed at the trees, listened to the waters of the Subhadra rushing past. She imagined the cool depths of the river, looked vacantly at the pillars of the stone bridge and sighed, and yet, she regained her composure from time to time.

Sarasvatichandra! Where are you in this perilous terrain? Why must you suffer so? Have you, like Dhruv, felt slighted? What faith moves you to this penance? Are you enthused by the aspirations of a Robinson Crusoe? Or are you like Emperor Babar who sang poems in the forest when he lost his empire? You once wrote:

My path is as unbridled as kites that fly
Like them, I too shall soar

A kite is attached to a string, and thus grounded, but you do not want even that.

Neither above nor below
Is there succour to be found
Destitute and forlorn am I

For whose sake do you suffer so? It is I, the wretched, I am the cause of your suffering.

I shall be like the forest breeze, invisible, but
Carrying aloft the fragrance called Kumud
My forehead is inscribed with the wealth of the world
And its renunciation
I am the people, and I the king
But in my heart, only you reside.

That wretched Kumud! Why wasn't she born a stone! Oh jewel among men, what did you see in this lustreless Kumud? Why do you offer penance for her ill fortunes?

O' Jehangir, your Noorjahan is lustreless
Why do you long for her?
Even Pramaddhan does not care for her
Why do you love her so?
Jehangir becomes an ascetic
He walks with animals in the wild
He longs for worthless Kumud even as
He forsakes the palace for the forest

As Kumud wept, she fell into an uneasy sleep. She woke up, startled by a sound. She thought of Pramaddhan: Oh my husband and master, I would have been fortunate if you had put your sword to my neck. I cannot be with the one who pines for me. I crush my desires and cling to you, but even you are not mine. I deserve this punishment. If you had killed me, my punishment would have been complete. But why should one as wretched as I receive such good fortune? Dear Vanleela, why do you feel sorry for me? Outlaws, why have you become so heartless? Why do you let me live? Have you lost your art so completely that your bullets cannot find their mark and bring this futile existence to an end?

Kumud raised the curtain and, gazing at the distant trees, murmured: Oh Lord, who will change my destiny? Who will right the wrong? But it is true—my fate is sealed on either side; even God cannot change it. She looked at the trees again and thought: Is it not possible that Chandra is hiding amid those dense trees? Who knows what all he has suffered in this forest infested with wild animals and outlaws? Whatever he endures is for my sake. He has suffered such agonies for me. And I? What have I done for him? I am ungrateful. I am cruel. I am heartless. Kumud beat her breasts in anguish, self-loathing and helpless rage. She sat up erect. Anger was unfamiliar to her heart and tongue. Her delicate features turned harsh and she wept with rage, speaking aloud: Who can be as cruel as me? I do not die to make the one who lives happy. Nor do I die for the one who longs and yearns for me. I abhor myself. Yet I don't know how to end this miserable life! I still lust for life! Dear Chandra, you preach:

Bear with what cannot be forsaken
Play the hand dealt to you ...
Forget that which cannot be forgotten and
Bear with reality.

You may be right. But what my husband desires outweighs your wise counsel. I am a thorn in his side. He desires to be freed of me, a worthless wife. He wishes I were dead. His heart silently commands me: Die, woman! Leave me be! I, too, desire death for I know the gains it would bring.

Chandra pines for me
I wonder how he is today
All he endures is for me
Why must I then live?

My death would free me from the charge of being ungrateful. The dark clouds of suspicion that hang over me will be dispelled; my parents will be freed from my abasement and ignominy. At this thought, Kumud was suddenly filled with a tranquil joy. She smiled weakly and said aloud: This life is a sea of sorrows, but death is where the sea meets land. Once I cross that path, I shall attain freedom from this wretched life. I must seek that freedom. But as this idea took root in her mind and gained strength, she heard Sarasvatichandra's voice speaking to her: 'Beloved Kumud, you are deceiving your soul. Only a good death gives us moksha, freedom from the cycle of births and deaths—suicide cannot grant you that freedom. To seek death is suicide. A wick that is snuffed out leaves behind odour, smoke and soot; it meets with an undesirable death. But a wick that burns itself out fully and naturally attains peace, it becomes one with the elements and attains freedom—that is moksha. Dear Kumud, to be weary of pain and to seek death is to undo the obligations and actions enjoined upon us—it is a rebellion against God'.

Lost to the world, Kumud had grown completely oblivious to the danger surrounding her. She was jolted out of her reverie by loud screams and shouts. Kumud thought that the outlaws were surely upon her. Face to face with imminent and real danger, all melancholy and suicidal thoughts vanished. She instantly got up, tucked her petticoat tightly between her legs and took out the dagger that was tied at her waist. She sat up tense and alert and waited. Just then Manchatura raised the curtain and said, 'Behn, there is no danger now. Our troops have returned triumphant'.

The soldiers were celebrating Sursinh's capture. The triumphant party now flew towards the carriage. Abdullah came forward and caught the reins of Shankar Maharaj's horse. He addressed Manchatura in his Hindustani: 'Bhai Sahib, this Shankar Maharaj is Buddhidhan's man. He has bravely captured the outlaws and sent them off to Suvarnapur!' Abdullah laughed uproariously. Manchatura and Shankar Maharaj were introduced to each other. Men from both sides introduced themselves, greeted each other and embraced joyously. Finally, Shankar Maharaj gave a graphic description of the morning's events. He told them how he had followed Buddhidhan's instructions and policies while dealing with the outlaws. He had been trained by Buddhidhan and he was pleased and proud that he had passed the ultimate test—Maharana Bhupsinh's last enemy had been subjugated.

All the men were in a celebratory mood. Manchatura addressed them: 'My brave soldiers! Step down from your horses and give them some rest; give them fresh water from the Subhadra. But Mukhi, I will have to exclude you from this rest. Gunasundari must be waiting anxiously; rush to Manoharpuri with the good news. Tell her that in the next three to four hours we will be there with Kumud'. But before he had completed the sentence, Mukhi Patel had already disappeared down the road to Manoharpuri. All the others got down from their horses. They patted them, gave them water, drank some themselves, lit their bidis, chewed on betel nut and chatted. But Shankar Maharaj remained astride his horse and moved about, looking into the distance. Manchatura walked up to the carriage and said to Kumud, 'The soldiers are taking rest. You too come out and take some fresh air, take a walk near the river. Fatehsinh, have this carpet spread on the river bank; Kumud will sit there and refresh herself'. As Manchatura took Kumud's hand and helped her out of the carriage, he felt a sense of accomplishment. This handsome, proud old man led his delicately beautiful granddaughter towards the carpet and made her sit on it with affection. He sat down beside her. Harbhamji also sat with them. Few others sat at some distance. Different parts of the surrounding landscape were pointed out to Kumud. Water was brought for her in a silver pitcher.

Manchatura was aware of Shankar Maharaj's uneasy movements. He got up and went to him, patted his horse and asked, 'Shankar, why don't you also relax?'

Shankar got off his horse and said, 'Bhai Sahib, there is nothing to worry about. But both sons of Sursinh are alive. I am not concerned about Vaghji; he is brave and will never commit a cowardly act. But Pratap is tricky; he is evil and debased. He has no companions but, like Ravana, he can act stealthily and commit lowly acts. Where can he be? I wonder if he is not lurking somewhere nearby. While we relax he should not come and attack suddenly. I was just being cautious.'

Manchatura smiled with disdain and asked, 'Is he so stupid as to do something so brazen?'

'We should not treat him with such contempt. Pratap has vowed to capture Kumud Sundari. His intelligence works treacherously. I know him well.'

'All right, all of us will keep an eye.' Manchatura and Shankar Maharaj walked towards the carpet where Kumud sat. He posted a man each to guard the four directions.

It was only about seven in the morning, but in the forest it looked as if it was already nine. The sun rose through the tall broad-leafed trees. Its light hurt the eye. The sky looked like an immense ground filled with sparkling sand. Sunlight spread upon the earth, the trees and the riverbank. The river flowed under the bridge, swirling playfully around its pillars. Kumud Sundari stood up and walked closer to the bank. She looked into the gurgling waters; the bottom of the river was not visible. She asked Manchatura, 'Dadaji, how deep is the river?' Harbhamji went up to her and said, 'Behn, near the bridge the water is deep, at least as high as three-four fully grown men.'

As Kumud walked along the river, she silently contemplated the deep waters and thought: Sarasvatichandra, have you been adventurous? Have you jumped into the river? She looked at the river intently, as if searching for him. Her eyes came to focus on a point on its eddies and she murmured:

My Jehangir has become a mendicant
He floats with the fishes
Pining for worthless Kumud
He abandoned his palace
Only to be washed away
A jewel has fallen into your lap,
O' Subhadra, care for it well

O' Subhadra, you are clever and generous. Don't let your waters drown him. Keep him safe. Hold him to your bosom. Why do you seem so full of joy?

He is a prince among men:
Hold him close to your bosom
You would be a fool not to rejoice
Holding this jewel against your heart
You owe your glow to this union

You need not be jealous of me, Subhadra. I have a husband who has no love for me. My beloved loves me deeply but I have no right to love him. I belong neither to my husband nor to my beloved.

Forsaking me, my husband turns to another
Having abandoned me, my beloved seeks me anew
What the lover seeks is futile: I am his.
Having given my body to my husband
How do I reclaim it now?
The husband who forsakes me
Is still the master of my body
While the lover cannot give up
The ties that bind us
If I give up this useless body
If I burn this love to ashes

O' river, help me forget
The love of my beloved
Do what you must to keep him alive
If he cries upon your shores
O' river, wipe away his warm tears
If he stands upon your shores
Chanting my name and weeping
Lonely when he remembers me,
And falls asleep upon your sands,
If he enters your waters to bathe,
And lost in thought, is swept by your currents,
O' river, remember to be kind:
Save his lonely heart.
Standing in your waters, his tears merging with them,
He will write upon your currents
The letters of my name
This is how he loves me.
Such is his state because of me.
Once wealthy, learned and wise
He has lost his body and mind over me.
Deep in the forest, he made a poem of me
But I cannot hear it, and so
He tosses his precious self away
He pours his heart out to the creatures of the wild
Writing poems of love on leaves and bark
O' river, I know this, I see this—
Yet I let his tears flow unabated.
I make myself love this ingrate body
Why does it not singe and turn to ash?
I do not seek my beloved
I do not douse that divine body's fire
Take me into your arms, O' river
Give my dead body to the fish.

Kumud's heart wept without restraint. She accepted her husband's mastery over her body. But her heart had set out like an outlaw to seek the one who ruled it. She stood perfectly calm and still as a statue on the riverbank under the bright blue skies, as her passions raged within.

She stood there delicate and fragile as a creeper. Like the moon sees its reflection in the river, she saw her bright face made lustreless by the pallor of sorrow in its waters. To Kumud it seemed as if the river's responses were coded in that reflection. The clear, petal-like nails of her feet whispered something secretly to her soft lips and her arms, as if they were the wings about to carry her body away.

By now the victory celebrations had subsided. Manchatura stood leaning upon his sword. Shankar Maharaj stood by his side, his eyes on the ravines where Kumud stood gazing into the river below. The soldiers were solemn and quiet as they awaited instructions for the onward journey.

All at once, Shankar broke the spell—he suddenly dove into the gurgling waters like an eagle. 'What happened? What happened?' everyone cried out. They saw three figures in the river: Kumud, almost drowning, followed closely by Pratapsinh, and Shankar Maharaj swimming forcefully against the current behind them. A few others immediately jumped in, but the sheer force of the river flung them back. Manchatura was also about to dive into the river, but he realised it was futile—he was certain he would not be able to reach Kumud and he would lose her forever. Instead, he leapt onto his horse and rushed in the direction in which Kumud was being carried by the flow. Manchatura planned to jump into the water and bring her out as she neared the riverbank. Others acted on their own counsel. A few furlongs further downstream the river took a sudden turn. Some rushed towards that spot. A few ran towards Manoharpuri.

The carriage remained where it was parked. The coachman was from Suvarnapur; he knew of Pramaddhan's secret life. He went to the spot where Kumud Sundari had stood just moments ago and examined it carefully. He looked down at the fiercely flowing river. Neither Kumud Sundari nor any of the others who had followed her could now be seen. He examined the spot carefully once again and wondered if she had fallen into the river because the edge broke, because she was dragged in by the outlaw, or because, weary of Pramaddhan's ways, she had attempted suicide? The coachman could not decide. He rolled up the carpet which had been laid out for her to sit on and put it back into the carriage. He picked up Kumud Sundari's belongings and a bundle of papers and gave it to a soldier from Ratnanagari, saying, 'Give these to Gunasundariba; it is useless to carry them back to Suvarnapur. I have no hope of their return given the force of the river. If God wills it, she will be saved. We will go on to Manoharpuri then. If something untoward happens, I will return to Suvarnapur. In that case, take her belongings to Manoharpuri. We will wait at the bridge for news.'

The solider was already in tears. He took the bundle and climbed up on his horse. The coachman yoked the bullocks. They stood waiting despondently on the bridge. The soldiers spoke of Kumud Sundari's kindness. One of them said, 'Today is a black day. We had vanquished the outlaws, and now this had to happen! She was so young and yet so wise. Kumud Sundari was a divine being. How could she live on this earth? Wherever she went, riches followed in her wake. Whenever she spoke, pearls fell from her mouth. She was a goddess reincarnate. Buddhidhanbhai could vanquish Shathrai because of her grace!'

The coachman replied, 'What you say is true. She certainly had traces of the divine. Even one as haughty as Alak behn walked in her steps. It was as if she cast a spell around her—anyone who saw her and spoke to her felt affectionate and respectful towards her. Buddhidhanbhai holds her in such high esteem. She was so pure one could have bathed her feet in milk and drunk it as nectar. She was so virtuous one would wish to be born of her. Oh God, You are all merciful, let no harm come to her! Do what You will but return Kumud Sundari to us unharmed! How will we ever show our face to anyone again if we don't find her?'

The ascetics carried away Sarasvatichandra. The river carried Kumud away. Their paths were different, but their destination was one. Many eyes followed after them. Many searched for them. But they could only imagine what God willed.